Pierre Bourdieu and Physical Culture

The work of French sociologist, anthropologist and philosopher Pierre Bourdieu has been influential across a set of cognate disciplines that can be classified as physical culture studies. Concepts such as *field, capital, habitus* and *symbolic violence* have been used as theoretical tools by scholars and students looking to understand the nature and purpose of sport, leisure, physical education and human movement within wider society.

Pierre Bourdieu and Physical Culture is the first book to focus on the significance of Bourdieu's work for, and in, physical culture. Bringing together the work of leading and emerging international researchers, it introduces the core concepts in Bourdieu's thought and work, and presents a series of fascinating demonstrations of the application of his theory to physical culture studies. A concluding section discusses the inherent difficulties of choosing and using theory to understand the world around us. By providing an in-depth and multi-layered example of how theory can be used across the many and varied components of sport, leisure, physical education and human movement, this book should help all serious students and researchers in physical culture to better understand the importance of social theory in their work.

lisahunter researches and teaches in movement, subjectivities, epistemology, research methods (participatory activist research, visual, narrative, sensory, (auto) ethnography), pedagogy, sex/gender/sexualities, and fields of sport/leisure, health, and education.

Wayne Smith is a Senior Lecturer in the Faculty of Education, University of Auckland, New Zealand. Wayne drew on Bourdieu's framework for his doctoral thesis and subsequent published articles.

elke emerald is a Senior Lecturer in The School of Education and Professional Studies, Griffith University, Australia. elke's current research investigates the impacts of research on the researcher.

Pierre Bourdieu and Physical Culture

Edited by
lisahunter, Wayne Smith and
elke emerald

Routledge
Taylor & Francis Group

LONDON AND NEW YORK

First published 2015 by Routledge

2 Park Square, Milton Park, Abingdon, Oxon OX14 4RN
711 Third Avenue, New York, NY 10017, USA

Routledge is an imprint of the Taylor & Francis Group, an informa business

First issued in paperback 2016

British Library Cataloguing-in-Publication Data
A catalogue record for this book is available from the British Library

Library of Congress Cataloging-in-Publication Data
Pierre Bourdieu and physical culture / edited by lisahunter, Wayne Smith
and elke emerald. -- 1st Edition.
pages cm. -- (Routledge Research in Sport, Culture and Society ; 40)
Includes bibliographical references and index.
ISBN 978-0-415-82969-4 (Hardback) -- ISBN 978-0-203-62874-4
(eBook) 1. Physical education and training--Social aspects. 2. Bourdieu,
Pierre, 1930-2002. 3. Sports--Social aspects. 4. Human body--Social
aspects. I. lisahunter, editor of compilation. II. Smith, Wayne William,
1954- editor of compilation. III. emerald, elke, editor of compilation.
GV342.27.P54 2015
613.7--dc23
2014020881

ISBN 978-0-415-82969-4 (hbk)
ISBN 978-1-138-20833-9 (pbk)

Typeset in Times
by Saxon Graphics Ltd, Derby

CONTENTS

Foreword

Michael Grenfell

Since his death in 2002, the reputation of the French social theorist Pierre Bourdieu seems to have gone from strength to strength. Known in his lifetime primarily as a sociologist of education and culture, he nevertheless published in a wide range of discipline areas: economics, politics, philosophy, arts and literature, religion, gender, etc., and it is now common to see application and extensions of his ideas in all these areas and others – architecture, geography, journalism, etc. In some ways, the study of *physical culture* is quite a late development in Bourdieuian study, which is perhaps surprising and for a number of reasons. Bourdieu's whole view of social agents is as located within social space that is both cultural–virtual *and* physical–actual. Individuals are spacially (*sic*) placed. They also exist as bodies that are both physical and embodied. For Bourdieu, generating structures of thought and action are incorporated and regenerated in physical bodies – *hexis* – and this is as true for mundane everyday actions as it is for the 'trained body' in such activities as dance and sport. Sport, as a part of physical culture, also gets extensive coverage in his writings: for example, 'How can one be a Sportsman?' from *Questions de Sociologie* (1984); 'Programme for a sociology of sport' from *Choses Dites* (1987/1994); and 'The state, economics and sport' (Bourdieu, Dauncey and Hare 1998); not to mention frequent references to sport in his study of cultural habits in France (e.g. *La Distinction* 1979). Bourdieu himself was also a keen sportsman, and had a special affinity for rugby, a particularly popular game in south-west France, from where he originated. Combat sports also fascinated him: indeed, one of his closest collaborators published a study of boxing (Wacquant 2002), and the title of the 2001 biographical cinematic documentary, following a year in the life of the sociologist, is *La Sociologie est un sport de combat*. The allusion is a telling one and conjures up the picture of sociological engagement being a kind of hand-to-hand encounter and sociology as a martial art with which one can protect oneself. Yet the 'physical' and 'physicality' do not necessarily feature explicitly in Bourdieu's work; and, where they are addressed, discussions of such topics as dance, physical health, physical education, etc., appear as subordinate to other analyses of culture and education: appearance and bodily modification, for example, or sports of distinction. It is therefore left to others, for example Shilling (1993) and the contributors to this volume, to develop this aspect of his writings and to draw links with other writers' preoccupations with physical culture and the body, for example in the work of Michel Foucault. The present volume attests to the richness and diversity of Bourdieu's work and the insights it provides into physical culture. I write in praise and reservation of the texts herein gathered, but first a personal note.

I first met Bourdieu personally in 1980, soon after the publication of *La Distinction*. At that time he was relatively unknown outside of France, although he had made an impact in the academic world with his concept of 'cultural capital' as an important factor in explaining differences in scholastic achievement with respect to social provenance. Spending various study periods at the École des Études en Sciences Sociales in Paris in the 1980s and early 90s, I was able to experience the reception of key texts at first hand – *La Noblesse d'état* (1989/1996), *Homo Academicus* (1984b/1988), *Le Sens pratique* (1980/1990), and *La Misère du monde* (1993a/1999) – and with them his evolution from marginal sociologist to 'public intellectual'. Somewhat committed to his theories, I felt a moral, as well as intellectual, imperative to speak up for these ideas in a world that did not speak French. In so doing, I translated many textual extracts, since most were not available in English. All that changed in the later 1990s: Bourdieu became an international intellectual star, known both at home and abroad and outside of the academic fraternity. He also took on a more politically active role, appearing on radio and TV and sponsoring a series of publications – *Raisons d'Agir* – aimed at a general public. Translations of his texts appeared with greater frequency and a shorter time after publication: *Les Héritiers* (1964/1979) took fifteen years to be published in English; *Pascaliennes méditations* (1997/2000) just two. The Bourdieu industry exploded at that time and has not stopped growing since.

We need some understanding of Bourdieu's own personal biography to appreciate this intellectual trajectory. He was someone born on the peasant margins of society who took the royal route to the Parisian elite schools and graduated as a *normalien* in philosophy; but it was his socio-cultural epiphany in the context of military service in an Algeria at civil war with itself that directed him to the path of anthropology and a highly philosophised version of sociology at a time when this discipline was still hardly taught in higher education. This background shaped Bourdieu, his ideas and all his subsequent works, from the early studies of Algeria and peasant farmers in the Béarn to mid-career analyses of culture and education and the later texts on social suffering and neo-liberal economics. What can be read across these publications is a parallel formative process of two Bourdieus – one empirical and one scientific – something of which he never ceased to remind me. This personal facet of his work was a surprise to many when explicitly stated in his final lecture at the Collège de France in 2001 as a kind of intellectual denouement or *raison d'être*. I make this point strongly: what we have in Bourdieu's existing texts is the attempt of one man – a Frenchman in the second half of the twentieth century – to objectify the social forces surrounding and acting on him. So what are we to make of them?

Bourdieu was always keen to insist on what he called a 'socio-genetic' reading of his work, by which he meant that it should be placed in its socio-historic context as a way of understanding what it was attempting to do *at the time* – not easy when translated texts do not follow the chronology of their French publication dates. He also drew attention to the 'international circulation of ideas': the way they get moved around from one national context to another, again without a contextual appreciation of their provenance. In the Preface to the English edition of *Homo Academicus* he also mischievously drew attention to the fact that, of the many so-called intellectual 'stars' exported from France, few of them would be eligible to supervise doctoral theses in their own country since they did not have PhDs themselves. He also referred to these ideas as 'French flu' caught by people from overseas. So are we perhaps guilty of catching a 'Bourdieuian flu' in our attachment to his writings? What do they buy us that other approaches do not?

In working with Bourdieu and his ideas for more than thirty years, and in that time also engaging with many others doing the same, I have ended up with a key list of the salient aspects of his work, many of which feature across the various chapters of this book. It is worth having these in mind when reading and using his work. There are five, and I shall address each of them briefly in turn.

Firstly, there is the *epistemological base*. Bourdieu's entire sociology is based on philosophy, and this emerged and was synthesised from different traditions: for example, the existentialism of Sartre and Heidegger; the phenomenology of Husserl, Schutz and Merleau-Ponty; and philosophers of the history of science such as Bachelard, Canguilhem and Koyré; not to mention the Catholic intellectual dissidents of the 1930s (Mounier). Who reads these now to understand Bourdieu? And yet they are all present in his writings. Bourdieu took such writers – and others – on board together with his critical reading of the philosophical aspects of the founding fathers of sociology: Marx (particularly his *Theses on Feueurbach*); Durkheim (in terms of his theory of knowledge); and Weber (on ideas in space). As noted, Bourdieu's subsequent break from philosophy arose as a result of his own epiphanic experience in Algeria, leading him to embrace anthropology, which he criticised in terms derived from the writers mentioned above and especially as represented by the principal French anthropologist of the day, Claude Lévi-Strauss. The key to Bourdieu's philosophical synthesis is *structure* – but structure in its various forms: phenomenologically intensional (*sic*) in individual cognitive relations to material and ideational surroundings (the search for psychic equilibrium in the 'control' of Self, Others and Objects); embodied dispositions (so important in the case of understanding sport); and 'objective' relations found in social organisation. For Bourdieu, *structuring* and *structured* structures – at all levels – are both co-terminus and mutually constituted/constituting. Such an approach requires dialectical thinking to grasp an epistemology that attempts to transcend usual oppositions of the subjective and objective (a dichotomy described by Bourdieu as 'fundamental and ruinous' (1980/1990: 25)). The issue is then, what is the nature and consequence of the resultant knowledge?

Secondly, there is *Theory of Practice*. Bourdieu's is an approach that has been called a 'science of existential dialectics'. In other words, it is attempting to capture something that is in flux not stasis. It is not deterministic but dispositionally dynamic and reproductive about the social phenomena it seeks to represent. Time itself has to be rethought in this case: real time (past, present and future); social time (seconds, hours, days, months, weeks and years); biographical time (people are born, they live, and die); socio-cultural time (arenas of activity come into being, exist and fade); and individuals' socio-cultural biographical time within social space (someone's presence – real or virtual – within such arenas). Social space, for Bourdieu, is multidimensional. Its complexity cannot, therefore, be captured in totality. However, *positions in social space* can be mapped according to their homologous structural relations revealed in the *space of symbolic stances*. The world is ultimately symbolic for Bourdieu and governed by systems of norms – orthodoxy. This positioning, this topography of social space, is critically important in Bourdieu's approach to the representation of social phenomena. He seeks to exercise three breaks – each of which has a particular philosophical base (empirical, phenomenological and objective knowledge) – in order to arrive at a new form of 'practical knowledge' about the world dynamic. There is, finally, an additional break from this knowledge itself in installing a 'new gaze', or metanoia, on social reality. Empirical data for analysis collected from the world is in practice at the core of his method; in fact, he never theorises for the sake of theorising and seeks at all costs to avoid replacing the 'things of logic' with the 'logic of things' (Bourdieu 1987/1990: 61). That data can be almost anything – interviews, questionnaires, and documentary and visual materials – and a whole series of ethnographic techniques are implemented to analyse them. Statistics too, although he warns researchers against efforts to 'crush one's rivals' with numerical correlations. Bourdieu himself made extensive use of *Multiple Correspondence Analysis*, a sophisticated form of visually representing multivariable correlations that literally 'map' individuals' positions in a range of social dimensions, or 'clouds'. At all times, Bourdieu is not seeking simply to explain the past, present and future through a series of causal links – a weak form of constructivism – but to capture something of the dynamic of occurrence and change, as well as their underlying generative structures. For him, the whole of social space is governed by this logic – whether at the macro or microcosmic level.

Thirdly there are his *concepts*. Bourdieu developed a sophisticated series of conceptual terms which he referred to as 'thinking tools'. These arose in the course of intense empirical involvement and were, he insists, logically necessitated by the data. Common terms are *habitus, field* and *capital*. But these are not simply, and should not be thought of as, heuristic devices to overlay data analysis, but act as intense 'epistemological matrices' which, when used, bring with them the entire theory of practice in practice to practice. Too much is often made of the throwaway comment that 'Bourdieu is good to think with' (Jenkins 2002: 11). Such a statement risks relativising concepts that have greater technical integrity as analytic instruments. It also invites imaginative flights of conceptual fantasy as authors make up their own. In fact, in Bourdieu's own analyses, he is conceptually quite ascetic; one should therefore guard against 'embroidering' terms as, for example, emotional *capital*, institutional *habitus* and the like. Physical *capital* itself needs to be understood in terms of Bourdieu's basic epistemology and the way it related to the primary forms of *capital* therein: *social, economic, cultural* and *symbolic*. It is not simply a descriptive metaphor. As analytic instruments, these terms also provide an *associative language* for those working in this paradigm, and the sharing of the *metanoia* to which his work points. It is, therefore, important that they should be based on the shared, consensual understanding of a critical community. Behind this issue lie important questions about academic principles and integrity. Too often, so-called extensions or 'limitations' of Bourdieu are based on a 'knower mode' of action, rather than a 'knowledge mode'. Here, assertions of personal standing are often passed off as 'improvements' on the original theory and method, when they are really interest-laden dispositions of the individual researcher, themselves un-objectified. For Bourdieu, these amount to little more than expressions of intellectual bad faith. Consequently, part of the formation of this new world view is that those making it disclose their own position by turning the instruments of analysis back on themselves.

Fourthly there is, therefore, *reflexivity*. As above, Bourdieu seeks to operate a final break from scholastic knowledge by the 'objectification of the objectifying subject' for the invisible assumptions occulted into a certain world view characteristic of the *doxa* of the scientific *field* itself: the individual *habitus*, the orthodoxy of the discipline and, indeed, the relation of *leisure* (skholè); and thus break from the empirical imperatives implied by the 'objectifying gaze'. The result is a kind of 'reflexive objectivity' where both an 'objective subjectivity' and a 'subjective objectivity' become one. 'The truth is that truth is at stake' for Bourdieu. Such participant objectivation, or sociology of sociology, is both a moral and intellectual necessity for him. Moreover, such cannot be operated simply by an isolated individual in the belief that 'thought can transcend thought itself'. Rather, it is part and parcel of the intellectual practice of the knowledge *field*, and the way it constitutes itself as a community. Not to do this is to ignore the self-serving interests of the *field* and the individuals who occupy and fight for position within it. Such power can only be instituted by a *field* to the degree that it acts independently; indeed, the science of a *field* is objective to the degree to which it is independent. Whilst absolute independence is unlikely in the academy, the opposite is true: science is less objective to the degree that it is interfered with by external agents who undermine its capacity to form a critical community of practice, and thus the processes of verification it can exercise.

Fifthly, and finally, there is *resistance*. For Bourdieu, the notion of 'knowledge for knowledge's sake' is as vacuous as 'art for art's sake'. For him the world is full of *symbolic violence* and suffering, an imposition from one to another. The whole point of his stance is to provide insight and, ultimately, weapons of resistance, to 'free' individuals from the social forces active on them, or at least to understand them. For him, the act of entering the world in this way is itself an intervention, a refusal to accept judgement and justification on the basis of 'interested' parties. Those armed with this knowledge therefore ultimately become 'praxeological agents', acting almost as intellectual resistance fighters on the inside, on the side of reason – both personal and group – and truth. In other words, it is a radical stance with political consequences, and at many levels. Bourdieu is not just arguing for political activism, although there are occasions where this is necessary, but for a personal stance of critical insight that carries with it moral responsibilities in terms of subsequent action. What is the substantive objective of any particular research project? If it is predicated by some form of social justice, and ultimately it should be if it is to go under a Bourdieuian banner, how is this operationalised in practice and to that end? For Bourdieu, the purpose of research is, therefore, ultimately an act of resistance – to show up *misrecognition*. The researcher needs to accept that such a position is not necessarily comfortable, and that the interests of *doxa* are substantial and their power not easily given up.

In another publication (Grenfell 2012), I have argued that these aspects can be framed methodologically by a three-phase approach: the *construction of the research object*; *field analysis*; and *participant objectivation*. Field analysis is then made up of three levels – the *field* and the relationship it holds with the *field* of power, the structure of the *field* itself, and the *habitus* of those occupying positions within the *field*.

Physical culture and sport are almost perfect examples of how to understand Bourdieu's theory of *practice*, with its related methodologies and epistemology. Besides physical culture as a series of *fields* with their relative position to various other individual activities within them and, often, the governing bodies of each (understood in terms of volume and constitution of forms of *capital*), there is the symbolic value that each both give and receive as part of the *field* of power, including politics, the commercial world and the media. At an individual level, there is the way physical and sporting activities can be related to a range of categories within social classification, as well as the entire embodiment of sport and physical activity in terms of related *practice* and rules of the game. Sport and physical culture may therefore be understood in terms of the dialectic of phenomenological and objective structures within the social world, and at multifarious levels, as the chapters in this book attest. In other words, physical culture and bodily action are both created and experienced in terms of the individual, others, and their surroundings. Dance, for example, is a personal discipline (an embodiment of rules and practices), a social phenomenon (choreographed or not, it is valued accordingly) and an entertainment (often with commercial outcomes).

I have raised the five *principles*, three *phases*, and three *levels* above in lieu of a systematic encounter with each of them in the chapters that follow, since many of the latter include partial aspects of all of them. Indeed, I have drawn attention to them in order to encourage a 'certain conformity' and greater systematicity in using Bourdieu and his method. No one is saying that Bourdieu was perfect and knew it all, or that applications of his method need policing. However, my sense is that we will get most out of him if we work with him on his own terms, rather than create a personal perspective each time any one individual takes the approach on board in the belief that he has limitations. In the spirit of participant objectivation, these limitations themselves need to be understood and objectified in terms of our own position in the *field*.

I therefore offer this Foreword to act as something that the chapters can read with and against, and in the hope that it will encourage greater convergence in how we use Bourdieu, why, and to what ends.

Preface

This book is about the theoretical work of Pierre Bourdieu applied to the field of physical culture. The term 'physical culture' was originally associated with health and fitness training or exercise systems in the nineteenth century English speaking world. However, the term itself and its definition has been revived amongst scholars and today includes various informal forms of movement associated with play, recreation and leisure, as well as the formalized systems of movement and movement education found in dance, physical education, sport and university courses in human movement. So, the term physical culture now refers to a diverse array of movement and can include such movement as Australian Aboriginals using games to pass on stories or practice valuable lifeskills, early Buddhist monks practicing tai chi, Roman soldiers involved in military training, or royalty in Hawai'ian society surfing the waves. Students and academics setting out to navigate social theory in physical culture for the first time could easily be overwhelmed by the amount of work now available. This book brings together some of the work from scholars in fields of physical culture using one social theory, not to reify Bourdieu any more than others, but to show how one author's work can generate new knowledge and a knowledge community in its own right. The fields represented here include human movement studies, kinesiology, health and physical education, sports studies, dance, movement education, and physical education teacher education.

Academic institutions involved in Sport and Leisure Studies, Human Movement Studies, Kinesiology, Sport Pedagogy, Sports Studies and Sports Sociology and the like, use the work of scholars who draw on Pierre Bourdieu's theoretical tools. These tools include *field, habitus, symbolic violence, doxa, capital,* and *misrecognition.* In this first chapter, each of these concepts is explained. The second section of the book (Chapters 2-15) contains several empirical chapters, the application of the tools is demonstrated by authors who have used these Bourdieuian concepts to advance theorising and practice. Each of the chapters demonstrate one or more of Bourdieu's 'tools' at work. In the final chapters, 16, 17 and 18, authors critique the use of Bourdieu's theory in empirical or conceptual work and discuss some of the challenges and tensions of using Bourdieu's theory. They address problems associated with choosing theory, speaking back to theory, taking on a theoretical framework only in part, and using theory for theory's sake in the academic game rather than to purposefully advance knowledge. A concluding chapter (Ch 19) then summarises the advances in the field using Bourdieu, leaving several challenges for those intending to use Bourdieu's conceptual tools and those working in the physical culture field.

Part I

An introduction to Pierre Bourdieu's concepts

1 Pierre Bourdieu and his conceptual tools

lisahunter, Wayne Smith and elke emerald

> **Keywords:** *Theoretical tools, Habitus, Field, Capital, Practice, Hexis, Doxa, Symbolic violence, Reflexivity*

Here we introduce Pierre Bourdieu and those of his theoretical tools that have offered particular insight into studies of physical culture. We briefly explain who Pierre Bourdieu was and explain his tools, including *Habitus, Field, Capital, Practice, Hexis, Doxa, Symbolic violence* and *Reflexivity*.

Pierre Bourdieu was a French social theorist who provided us with a reflexive social theory that drew from sociology, philosophy and anthropology. He was born in France to traditional rural peasant farmers in a small country town, Denguin, in 1930 (see Grenfell 2008 for more details). Knowing a little about his life situates where his ideas came from and what he was trying to do through his conceptual tools as developed within, and applied to, French society at a particular time and from his position within that society. As his work argues, he is a product of society, all the while acting with some form of agency to shape that society. He drew on the work of Émile Durkheim, Claude Lévi-Strauss, Martin Heidegger, Edmund Husserl, Marcel Mauss, Maurice Merleau-

Figure 1.1 Pierre Bourdieu
1930–2002

Ponty, Karl Marx, Max Weber, Ludwig Wittgenstein and Blaise Pascal among others. Bourdieu was a social activist, known in France through the media and, over time, beyond France, with translations of his work into many languages. His work was taken up quickly, but behind his contemporaries such as Foucault, in the USA. Working in France, he was a prolific writer up until his death in 2002.

As a means of understanding *practice*, Bourdieu provided conceptual tools that articulate the dialogue between structures that shape a society and their interaction with the individual person. Significantly, Bourdieu located the body as an important locus of social theory. His conceptual tools offer a theory of embodiment that is useful for understanding deeply entrenched forms of embodied existence and differentiated social power relations. Using these tools we can come to some understanding of how we embody culture while at the same time, through our *practices*, changing and/or replicating the status quo. The ontological and epistemological positioning of corporeality is of particular importance in the context of this book: the/our body's definition and neglect within our *practices* and research concerning physical culture.

Bourdieu also developed historical, political and sociocultural critiques of education systems in an attempt to explain how, despite a popular assumption of equity, schooling and higher education reproduce structures (such as social class) and dominant inequitable ways of knowing, acting and being (Bourdieu and Passeron 1977). His theories went beyond the formal institutions of schooling and universities to consider broader potentially educative or socialising institutions such as television (Bourdieu 1998b), art (Bourdieu and Johnson 1993) and sport (Bourdieu 1988a). Through Bourdieu, we can recognise that movement and the body are constituted in physical cultures both in formal institutional experiences (school and university) and in non-school/university experiences in sport, leisure, dance and so on. These physical cultures, their structures and social orders of legitimation and domination become naturalised as 'common sense' or 'taken-for-granteds' by means of systems of classification instituted through our bodily social *practices*. Chapters 2–15 explore many different *fields* and *sub-fields* of physical culture: dance, teacher education, surfing, school physical education, rugby coaching, boxing, sport and snowboarding.

Below we provide an explanation of some of Bourdieu's tools. Our explanations are designed as an introduction for you to then explore the chapters that employ these tools. The concepts are by no means simple or uncontestable, so our explanations are not without this caution. Further, we advise that you read other sources that have endeavoured to 'define' Bourdieu's concepts, and indeed, read Bourdieu's own explanations. Bourdieu's own explanations are complex, multilayered, revisited and developed over his lifetime, and situated in his context. While this might seem daunting, as his work is arguably difficult to fathom at first, it is in the practice of grappling with and playing with his concepts that scholars have been rewarded with new ways of understanding the contexts and practices within which they work.

It would be remiss of any of us not to appreciate that these concepts are situated in a particular time and place, and further, that English was not Bourdieu's writing language, so that his works in English are translations. You will note, as you read more widely, that like many sociological tools, Bourdieu's have been used well, but they have also been used poorly, inappropriately, for means other than those originally designed, and in new or misleading ways that Bourdieu himself probably never imagined possible. Even in putting this chapter together we had many discussions to clarify what we think Bourdieu's concepts mean and how to communicate this meaning to you within the constraints of this book. Meaning is a slippery thing, but Bourdieu's ideas were translated and clarified through and with others such as Richard Nice (Bourdieu and Nice 2008) and Lois Wacquant (1989) to try and make the concepts comprehendable. And thus do ideas weave their magic, inspiring new *practices*, challenging the status quo, and perhaps even reifying the status quo! Nonetheless, it is in the application in our *practices* of concepts such as those Bourdieu offered that we can form a language to constitute one way of 'knowing', albeit partially and situatedly, what *might* be going on in the physical cultures within which we operate. It also acts as a looking glass to our already held ideas and beliefs about our worlds and our ways of knowing our worlds. That is the challenge for the authors in this book. Not all will agree on how they use Bourdieu's tools, nor the exact meaning of those tools, but it is in their *use* that we remain open to their potential to help us understand ourselves and our world. It is also important to note that not all authors in this book necessarily agree with Bourdieu's concepts for one reason or another, some of which will be explicated in the book. But it is in getting to know a theorist and her/his ideas in depth and in context and then applying them to our world that we clarify our own ontologies, epistemologies, methodologies and theories. For you, this book may be just a beginning of this process. For us, this book is just one of many cycles as we continue to clarify, change and play with ongoing dialogues that include theories and *practice*.

Bourdieu: the tools

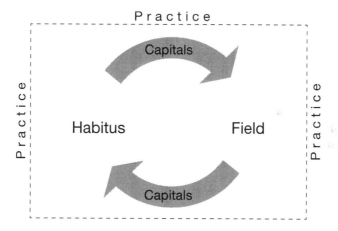

Figure 1.2 The interaction between *field*, *habitus* and *capital* through *practice*

Practice

Practice is one of Bourdieu's most widely used concepts and one that was the focus of much of his own empirical work. In this first section we explain the notion of *practice* and show how it is often used in conjunction with Bourdieu's other conceptual tools.

Bourdieu proposed (1980/1990) that it is our taken-for-granted, recursive daily *practices* that reveal the visible, objective social phenomena that determine the nature of our society. His own field-based anthropological research led him to conclude that *practice* should be the primary focus of all social analysis, because it is *practice*, derived from the subconscious, that reveals both the logic of the actions of individuals and the structuring of the *social space* in which they are embedded. In his *The Logic of Practice* (1980/1990), Bourdieu argued that objects of knowledge are constructed in our taken-for-granted *practice* and that 'the principle of this construction is the system of structured, structuring dispositions, the *habitus*, which is constituted in *practice* and is always oriented towards practical functions' (p. 52). We will explain more about *habitus* and its structured and structuring function in the next section, but for the moment we will continue to focus on the importance of our everyday, taken-for granted *practices*.

Social *practice*, what we do as individuals and social groups, is the product of processes that are neither wholly conscious nor wholly unconscious (Bourdieu 1980/1990). Rather, social *practice* is the product of a subconsciously embodied and embedded, taken-for-granted, *practical logic*. Bourdieu qualified this by stating that although *practice* is accomplished without conscious deliberation, it is not without purpose. Individuals, actors, or agents, do have goals and interests, but these are, in part, located in their own experience of reality – their *practical sense* or *logic* – rather than their conscious, rational deliberations. In this way, *practical sense* orients our choices, though not deliberately (1980/1990). Social *practice*, in all its complexity, is not determined by inflexibly-structured rules, recipes, or normative models, but rather by a sub-conscious *practical logic* (*practical sense* or *practical consciousness*) with an inherent fluidity and indeterminacy. This *practical logic* is, in part, determined by the actor's embodied understanding of how things 'are' or 'ought to be done': that is, the nature of their reality.

Bourdieu often used an analogy of how players engage in sport or games to explain the nature of *practical logic*. He suggested that it is our *practical logic* that enables us to intuitively 'read the game' and act accordingly. He argued that although games have set parameters and rules (structures), it is a shared, intuitive, *practical sense* of how the game is played that enables the players to play the game and implement strategies in particular ways. It is the players who determine the nature of the game, not necessarily in a conscious way, and if necessary change the rules when they no longer serve the needs of that/their game. With reference to Bourdieu, Harker *et al.* (1990: 7), expressed this analogy as follows:

> [Bourdieu's] analogy with games is an attempt to provide an intuitive understanding of the overall properties of fields [of practice]. First, a sphere of play is an ordered universe in which not everything can happen. Entering the game implies a conscious or unconscious acceptance of the explicit and/ or implicit rules of the game on the part of the players. These players must also possess a 'feel' for the game, which implies a practical mastery of the logic of the game.

In a cyclical or dialectical manner, it is the individuals' participation in their everyday social *practices* that establishes and reinforces social structures, and these same social structures in turn determine the nature of the individuals' *habitus*, which in turn determines their social *practice*. In this way enduring cultural values, beliefs, dispositions and actions are both embodied in the individuals and embedded in the social structures that constitute a way of being and behaving. As an example, school students who perform well at sport more often 'get' how to stay on side with the PE teacher and 'get away with' a lot more disruptive behaviour than the student who cannot perform and challenges the teacher. It is in the best interests of the student to perform well enough, while not necessarily performing to their peak. Good performance gives them legitimacy and therefore positions them more strongly with the PE teacher. This student will not necessarily consciously be manipulating the teacher, but has a feel for the school game and enough *physical capital* in the form of ability to stay 'on side' (Hunter 2004). As another example, ensuring one wears the 'right' sports clothing in 'the right way' (Thorpe Ch. 14; emerald and Barbour Ch. 2; and Paradis Ch. 8) or moves in a certain way (emerald and Barbour Ch. 2) are all *practices* that situate one within a physical culture while reinforcing such *practices*.

Practice, therefore, is 'the product of a *habitus* that is itself the product of the embodiment of the immanent regularities and tendencies of the world' (Bourdieu and Waquant 1992: 138). For example, the idiom 'That's just not cricket' is employed to indicate *practices* or behaviours which are not 'the way they should be'. 'Should' being the assumed 'correct' *practices* played out by those who want to maintain the status quo and for whom there are usually benefits in keeping it that way. *Practice* is both the result and the process by which *field* and *habitus* are evoked. This can be illustrated by the athlete, coach, PE teacher or instructor who reproduces taken-for-granted *practices* of sexism. These oppressive *practices* have been unknowingly taken up in the athlete's/coach's/teacher's/instructor's *practice* as a result of normalising and totalising *practices* of the society into which she or he was born and which she or he has learned to re-enact. Such *practices* might be the elevation of historically male-dominated and hegemonic masculinity-driven sports and the *misrecognition* that certain sports are not for girls. In this context, girls can unconsciously avoid being active, more so than boys who are expected, and might even expect themselves, to be more active as a sign of maleness.

Social Space and *Field*

Bourdieu employed the concepts of *field* and *social space* to replace the more commonly used, but diffuse, notion of 'society'. He argued (1984a) that all *social space* is made up of multiple, competing, intersecting and hierarchically positioned *fields* with their own distinctive features. *Fields* have their own objective structures, such as rules, categories, positions, conventions, rituals, interests, valued objects and ways of being, while also being represented within, and in the daily *practices* of, the individuals or groups who make up the *field*. A *field* is:

> both a field of forces, whose necessity is imposed on agents who are engaged
> in it, and as a field of struggles within which agents confront each other, with

differentiated means and ends according to their position in the structure of the field of forces, thus contributing to conserving and transforming its structure.

(Bourdieu 1998a:32)

In some of his own empirical research Bourdieu (1979, 1984a, 1988a, 1990c, 1998b and 2000) analysed the relationship between differentially positioned individuals and groups who make up a *field*. He commented on many *fields*, including those of education, media, artistry, literacy and economics, as well as science, sociology and culture. He argued that *fields* grow out of, and determine, the social positioning and actions of the individuals and collectives who identify with them. As social arenas within which individuals interact and engage in their everyday *practices*, *fields* are characterised by struggles, conflicts, and the implementation of strategies to obtain control of the available resources and capital that the *field* has to offer. As such, '*fields* have their own differentially constituted agents who are at all times defined by a system of objective relations of power between social positions' (Harker *et al.* 1990: 8).

All *fields* contain people who dominate and people who are dominated and it is these relationships of inequality that cause people and groups in the *field* to struggle for the transformation or preservation of the *field*. The boundary of a *field* is where the *logic* of the *field* stops having an effect. But these boundaries can be shifting, blurry and overlapping, they need not be thought of as being in 'implacable opposition but, in terms of multiple disjunction, overlap and conflict' (McNay 1999: 113).

Bourdieu defined a *field* as:

> a network, or a configuration, of objective relations between positions objectively defined, in their existence and in the determinations they impose upon their occupants, agents of institutions, by their present and potential situation (situs) in the structure of the distribution of species of power (or capital) whose possession commands access to the specific profits that are at stake in the field, as well as by their objective relation to other positions (domination, subordination, homology, etc.).
>
> (Bourdieu and Wacquant 1992: 97)

The *field* of sport, for example, is made up of structured systems of power relations. These relations might be between the governing bodies of individual sports at international, Olympic, national, regional and club levels; each nation's government funding body for sport; officiating and credentialing organisations for coaches and umpires/referees; the athletes themselves; those who support the athletes, whether spectators or friends and relatives; the mass media; athlete sponsors, athletic equipment and clothing manufacturers, and so on. In the specific example of PE in schools, these relations are often constituted by the educational authority and its policy workers; teacher educators; registration boards; curriculum writers and their governing bodies; individual school administrators; teachers; students; auxiliary staff; and others who have less structured and defined positions, such as parents. As constructed by the definition of position, each position has a level of power and a social position associated with it. One's position within the *social space* is framed by the *field* and defines not only the level of power but also the way in which that power may be used; those with more powerful positions being in a 'better position' to legitimise that power and the forms it can take.

We can see from the above that *field* is a particularly useful theoretical concept because it allows us to identify and differentiate between different *social spaces, practices* and positions of power, or as Bourdieu (1985) noted, objectify *social spaces*. Using Bourdieu's conception of *field* we can identify, categorise and distinguish between the many *fields* and *levels of fields* (*subfields*) of physical culture. In the empirical chapters of this book, for example, lisahunter (Ch. 4) examines the *logic of practice* at work in the *field* of surfing. She demonstrates how the inferior positioning of female surfers within the *field* affects the quality of the waves they may be offered during a competition. This limits the movements women can complete to demonstrate their skill. In competition host countries where women are sexually objectified and positioned as inferior to men, women's opportunities for the best waves are lower than in countries where they are positioned as equal. emerald and Barbour (Ch. 2) question how elke's physical appearance and her bodily *hexis* (how she moves) position her in a new dance *subfield*. Thorpe (Ch. 14) tracks the movement across contexts in the *field* of snowboarding.

By viewing the social world as multiple, overlapping and hierarchically differentiating *fields*, we are better able to understand the relational properties and power struggles between individuals and groups (Bourdieu 1987/1990). Some *fields* are treated as more important than others within a society. For example, compare the *field* of sport to the *field* of arts in a country like the USA as compared with Sweden. And within a *field* there are *subfields*; for example, consider the relative power and value assigned to the *subfields* of scientific sports medicine and traditional Chinese medicine in the *field* of medicine in Europe. In the course of a week you may participate in many *fields*: family, sport, education, medicine, art, media. You and your ways of knowing will be positioned differently in each.

We can see in Bourdieu's concept of *field* that individuals and groups occupy relative positions of difference within the different *social spaces* of society, and although they are often invisible, it is these relational positions that are revealed through the *practices* embedded in the *field*. This concept of *field* provides an enabling framework for examining the uneven and non-systematic ways in which subordination and domination are realised in people's lives. It is the relational positions within *fields* where the real principles of domination and subordination are embodied. However, it is not the *field* alone that determines an individual's or group's actions but the relationship between a *field* and an individual's or group's *habitus*. So it is to Bourdieu's understanding of *habitus* that we now turn.

Habitus

The notion of '*habitus*' is perhaps Bourdieu's most useful tool for examining the generative basis of social *practice*. It is also one of the most used tools amongst scholars working in the *field* of physical culture. Bourdieu made the body central, explicit and whole, drawing attention to problems caused by Descarte's influence in theoretically separating mind and body and hierarchising the mind over the body. Bourdieu referred to *habitus* as if it existed, embodied within an individual like part of their physical anatomy and constituted by the *field* in which that individual *practices*. In doing so, he offered a theoretical construct to better understand the tacit and often misrecognised dialectical relationship between objective social structures and subjective human agency. For example, the way one walks is often gendered, and for those who walk in a feminine way, but are not female, there can be negative consequences. The movie *Billy Elliot* is effective because the narrative of a boy dancing ballet is one that does not fit the cultural norm of the place and time of the movie. Billy's movement is applauded in the *field* of ballet but such movements are shunned by those who embody the tough physical labour of breadwinning miners in a late twentieth-century British mining town. In another example, lisahunter's undergraduate classes predictably and audibly cringe on seeing an image of a heavily pumped, muscular body builder who is female, but are quite comfortable with a similar image of a male. What constitutes male and female in dance, sport, and even the act of walking or throwing a ball (Young 1980), is heavily inscribed in bodily habits and *practices* that are regarded as either normal and therefore justified, or deviant and shunned. Together with Bourdieu's use of the notion of *practical logic* or *practical sense*, *habitus* helps explain how individuals and groups engage in social *practices* at the implicit taken-for-granted level. These examples illustrate the tacit and often unrecognised dialectical relationship between objective social structures and subjective human agency.

Bourdieu (1980/1990, 1984a) asserted that *habitus* is the generative basis of *practices*. At various times he described the *habitus* as being: a set of principles; socially-constituted dispositions; subconscious schemes of perception; or strategies that produce particular *practices*. In *The Logic of Practice* (1980/1990), Bourdieu described *habitus* as:

> systems of durable, transposable dispositions … which generate and organize practices and representations that can be objectively adapted to their outcomes without presupposing a conscious aiming at the ends or express mastery of the operations necessary in order to attain them. Objectively regulated and regular without being in any way the product of obedience to rules, they can be collectively orchestrated without being the product of the organizing action of a conductor.
>
> (1990b: 53)

Through our engagement in social *practices*, we internalise social structures and develop particularised perceptions of the world. It is these subconscious schemes of perception that give meaning to, and produce particular ways of, doing things. This predisposition gives rise to a *practical sense* or a *practical logic* that is inscribed in the body as a device upon which and in which the very basics of culture, the *practical logic* of our social *practices*, are imprinted and encoded.

In this way the *habitus* is inculcated as much, if not more, by experience as by explicit teaching; it exists in our flesh as the way we walk, stand, gesture, think and feel. It is no accident or gene that makes for the valorisation, appreciation and success of elite ballet dancers or rugby union players in some countries and not others. The power of *habitus* derives from habit, often taken on without realisation through the primary socialising fields of the family and schooling, rather than consciously learned rules and principles. Being embodied in this way, the *habitus* may be beyond being made explicit or beyond conscious reflection and voluntary change. emerald and Barbour wonder about this in Chapter 2.

We can see, then, that the point of intersection between *habitus* – an embodied set of dispositions, guiding principles, or strategies – and a socially-structured *field* gives rise and meaning to our social *practices*. '*Habitus* reveals itself ... only in reference to a definite situation. It is only in the relation to certain structures that *habitus* produces given discourses or *practices*' (Bourdieu and Wacquant 1992: 135). Drawing on our *habitus*, we subconsciously interact with the social structures of a *field,* and in this way produce *practice* that is not mechanically determined but rather the intuitive product of knowing – what Bourdieu referred to as the rules or strategies of the game.

We should recognise, also, the important part that history and cultural precedents play in developing one's *habitus*. 'The *habitus* – embodied history, internalized as a second nature and so forgotten as history – is the active presence of the whole past of which it is the product' (Bourdieu 1980/1990: 56). A history of social relations is inscribed into the flesh of individuals, that is, into the mental and corporeal schemata of perceptions, appreciations and actions, and passed from individual to individual through a history of social interaction and cultural *practices*. The subjective positioning of individuals is embodied through an incorporation of the social into the body. As such, although located within the individual the *habitus* embodies social and cultural messages that pass between individuals and through *fields* as discourses. Bourdieu explains this as follows:

> First and foremost, *habitus* has the function of overcoming the alternative between consciousness and unconsciousness. ... Social reality exists, so to speak, twice, in things and in minds, in *fields* and in *habitus*, outside and inside agents. And when *habitus* encounters a social world of which it is the product, it finds itself 'as a fish in water', it does not feel the weight of the water and takes the world about itself for granted.
>
> (Bourdieu in Wacquant 1989a: 43)

The 'fish in water' analogy can be applied to the physical education teacher who embodies the *fields* of sport, health and fitness as dominant *fields* influencing physical education. The teacher's personal investment in the subject area is a reflection of their *habitus*, so much so that they cannot recognise the oppressions that are part of the 'water'. *Misrecognising* sport as always good, for example, is a taken-for-granted, which may be worked through the embodied *practices* of the teacher who promotes sport as good. It is at this site or moment of *practice* that discourses from within the *field* not only operate but become re-inscribed by those practising.

We can now better understand the dialectical relationship that exists between a *field* and a corresponding *habitus*, in that, on the one hand, *fields* are the objective structures that are the enduring products and producers of the actions of human agents; and on the other, the *habitus* is the embodiment of the generative and transformative schemes of social structures (Bourdieu 1989a). Bourdieu described this interdependence thus:

> the objective structures ... form the basis for the representations of the agents and constitute the structural constraints that bear upon interactions; but, on the other hand, these representations must also be taken into consideration particularly if one wants to account for the daily struggles, individual and collective, which purport to transform or to preserve these structures. This means that the two moments, the objectivist and the subjectivist, stand in a dialectical relationship.
>
> (1989a: 15)

Bourdieu's theoretical framework also offers a way to analyse the enduring behaviours, characteristics and cultural *practices* of social groups or classes. Bourdieu (1984a) suggested that a collective or '*group-habitus*' is possible after a long period of shared or similar social experiences leading to a parameterising and exclusivity of *practice*. A *group-habitus* is evident when only those individuals who embody a shared history of involvement in a particular *field* possess the code, knowledge of the rules, or the classificatory schemes necessary to understand their *social space*. Thus inclusion within a collective *habitus* presupposes mastery of a common code. It 'implies a sense of one's place, but also a sense of the place of others' (Bourdieu 1989a: 19). This is because the *habitus* tends to interpret social events and generate common-sense responses within the limits of the objective structures that produced it. The actions of individuals are likely to be positively sanctioned by those who share a *group-habitus* only if they conform to the *logic of practice* of the particular *field* in which the *habitus* was produced. Again to quote Bourdieu (1980/1990: 55-6):

> being the product of a particular class [or group] of objective regularities, the *habitus* tends to generate all the 'reasonable', 'common-sense', behaviours (and only these) which are possible within the limits of these regularities, and which are likely to be positively sanctioned because they are objectively adjusted to the logic characteristic of a particular field, whose objective future they anticipate. At the same time, 'without violence, art or argument', it tends to exclude all 'extravagances' ('not for the likes of us'), that is, all the behaviours that would be negatively sanctioned because they are incompatible with the objective conditions.

As an illustration, in this volume Chapters 11 (Knez and lisahunter), 8 (Paradis) and 2 (emerald and Barbour) dwell on particular forms of clothing worn by females. Knez and lisahunter and Paradis are about extremes: the hijab worn by Qatari females within Qatar (Knez and lisahunter, Ch. 11) and the controversy over short skirts worn by female boxers (Paradis, Ch. 8). In emerald and Barbour's chapter, elke finds she wears the 'wrong' sorts of dancewear. In these chapters, common sense *practices* around clothing are brought into the limelight, for different reasons. In a sense, the *group habitus* is questioned. In Chapter 3 Smith's contention is that the Bachelor of Physical Education (BPE) staff shared a particular group-*habitus* relating to the nature and *practices* associated with Health and Physical Education Teacher Education, and it was this that was the generative of the collective actions of the group and the individual actions of those who identified with the group. The BPE group's shared history and routinised ways of doing things created (and was created by) a *logic of practice* and a cultural *field* that, if we accept Bourdieu's theorising, was the result of the members' embodiment of a group-*habitus* in the same way that particular classes develop and act according to their class *habitus* (Bourdieu 1984a). Their group-*habitus* gave them a distinctive social identity and explained some of their common dispositions and actions.

Habitus, whether situated between a *field* and an individual or a *field* and a class/collective, is positioned within a *field* through the mechanism of *capitals*, another widely used Bourdieuian concept to which we now turn.

Capitals

Bourdieu's conceptualisation of *capital* goes beyond that of the economic form championed by Karl Marx. His other forms of *capital* include social, cultural, and symbolic. *Symbolic capital* is the form that the other types of *capital* assume when they are recognised and valued within a given *field* (Bourdieu 1986).

As we know, *economic capital* refers to wealth and is arguably an ontological foundation to capitalist societies. But what is less well recognised is how the other forms of value, or what Bourdieu referred to as *capital,* can be translated into *economic capital* and vice versa through a means of exchange. *Social capital* is defined by a network of lasting relations, a belongingness or connectedness with others in the *field.* The lasting relations of family or schooling, such as that associated with old boys 'school tie' networks in private schools, continues well beyond the original structure and affords ways of being well located in *fields* such as law, medicine and business in elite circles. *Cultural capital* pertains to the culturally valued possessions and attributes as well as the socially valued *practices* of a *field.* This might be manifested in the books one reads, the qualifications one attains, the type of school or university one attends, the possessions one has that may reflect one's social class, a distinction more clearly embodied in some cultures than others. A symbolic valuing of *social* and/or *cultural capital* can lead to economic gain and therefore the accumulation of *economic capital. Symbolic capital* refers to the authoritive power attributed to *economic, social* and/or *cultural capital*, with the holder of such *capital* having the agency to influence, and in extreme cases determine, the nature of a *field.* The accumulation of *symbolic capital* through other forms of *capital* determines one's location in a particular *field*, which, in turn, determines the possibility for accumulation of more symbolically-valued *capital* and the ability to redefine/legitimate the form that the *capital* might take.

One of the strengths of Bourdieu's framework is that it provides a lens for us to better see how individuals are distributed in the overall *social space* of *fields* according to their *field*-specific *capital*. In Bourdieu and Wacquant (1989) he argued that these specific *capitals* are defined by the forces that are active in the *field*:

> A *capital* does not exist and function but in relation to a *field*: it confers a power over the *field*, over the materialized or embodied instruments of production or reproduction whose distribution constitutes the very structure of the *field*, and over the regularities and the rules which define the ordinary functioning of the *field*, and thereby over the profits engendered in this *field*.
>
> (Bourdieu and Wacquant 1989: 39)

You may note that *physical capital* is not mentioned above. Despite the emphasis on embodiment through the concept of *habitus*, Bourdieu saw *physical capital* as being just another form of *cultural capital*. However, Shilling (1993) argues that, 'the corporeal is too important to be seen merely as a subdivision of another form of capital' (p. 58). Shilling, consequently, developed the concept more broadly through his sociology of the body, in which he suggested that *physical capital* encompasses the symbolic value of the exterior surface of the body in the form of shape, weight, physique and looks. The physical body is the external manifestation of the *habitus* as well as constituting the *habitus* and therefore the notion of *physical capital* can make a useful contribution to our understanding of physical culture. As such, it warrants inclusion in the definitions and practices where the body is central. You may notice that some authors of subsequent chapters in this book make reference to work that has gone beyond that of Bourdieu, Shilling being but one example. The relative power of each *capital* is dependent on how it is symbolically valued and functions in relation to the *field*, as it is the *field* that defines and legitimates the *capital*.

The accumulation of appropriate *field*-related *social, cultural,* and *physical capital* is important within all *fields*. Ultimately, *cultural capital* becomes particularly influential, as it is that form of *capital* that one acquires when a relationship of homogeny, being at one with the world, is established between an individual's *habitus* and the *cultural field* of its production. In the institutionalised *fields* of dance or sport, cultural competence can be acquired through one's physicality (*physical capital*) and/or one's sporting prowess or other means of social preference such as who one knows within the *field* (*social capital*), and in this way is recognised and constituted as symbolically significant *cultural capital. Cultural capital* becomes particularly powerful when it is officially sanctioned and valued by those who recognise and legitimise the *field*, such as the media (lisahunter, Ch. 4); judges and officials such as the International Olympic Committee (Thorpe, Ch. 14); the International Boxing Association (Paradis, Ch. 8); or teachers of PE (Brown and Aldous, Ch. 7; Christensen and Rossi, Ch. 9). So it follows that these taken-for-granted, culturally accepted social *practices* take on the form of *symbolic capital* and thereby enable those people who possess the necessary *capital* to impose a cultural arbitrary on others due to their positions of knowledge and dominance within the *field*. In this way these people have a form of power which makes it possible for them to privilege their own social practices and positions within the *field*.

Bourdieu (1989a) explained the importance of acquiring *symbolic capital* and, by association, power, stating that in the first instance it is accrued through the successful use of the other kinds of *capital*. He argued that:

> the transformation of any given kind of *capital* into *symbolic capital* ... is the fundamental operation of social alchemy ... owing to the fact that *symbolic capital* is nothing other than *economic capital* or *cultural capital* when it is known and recognized, when it is known through the categories of perception that it imposes, symbolic relations of power tend to reproduce and to reinforce the power relations that constitute the structure of *social space*.
>
> (Bourdieu 1989a: 21)

At this point we have visited the main conceptual tools that you are likely to encounter throughout this book and certainly in most of the scholarly work in physical culture that draws on Bourdieu. However, there are many more concepts that he developed in suggesting how we might make sense of our world/s. While it is beyond this book to even touch on all of them, we want to mention several others both to whet your appetite a little more but also to prepare you for the chapters to come. Although less commonly used in the scholarly literature, *doxa, misrecognition, symbolic violence* and *reflexivity* have been useful tools to deconstruct many of our taken-for-granted assumptions about *practice* – in our instance, in relation to physical culture.

Doxa

Bourdieu (1987/1990) recognised that all groups or social classes have theories about the world and their place in it, with individuals and groups generating an on-going reality in, through, and as a part of, everyday life. This reality for each individual may be conscious but the real power, according to Bourdieu, is beyond consciousness. It is a *practical sense* or *practical logic* – a 'feel for the game'. It is

> the practical mastery of the logic or of the imminent necessity of a game – a mastery acquired by experience of the game, and one which works outside conscious control and discourse (in the way that, for instance, techniques of the body do).
>
> (Bourdieu 1987/1990: 61)

Due to one's position within *social space*, individuals become familiar with certain traditions and come to accept them at a taken-for-granted level of consciousness. 'The mental structures through which they apprehend the social world, are essentially the product of the internalisation of the structures of that world' (Bourdieu 1989a: 18). As a collective, members of a group subconsciously re-establish or reinforce modes of *practice* and theories about appropriate ways of doing things within their social world. Over a period of time, the cultural traditions and the individual's or group's familiarity with these traditions provide a sense of security and belonging. This familiar, unquestioning sense of knowing and belonging within a particular social world creates what Bourdieu called a '*doxic modality*' or state of *doxa*.

Doxa is 'the relationship of immediate adherence that is established in *practice* between a *habitus* and the *field* to which it is attuned' (Bourdieu 1987/1990: 68). Elsewhere in this same book (p. 20) he describes *doxa* as:

> the coincidence of the objective structures and the internalized structures which provides the illusion of immediate understanding, characteristic of practical experience of the familiar universe, and which at the same time excludes from that experience any inquiry as to its own conditions of possibility.

A *doxic modality* arises from and reinforces the *practical logic* of a particular *field*. Because the *practical logic* is produced by experience in the *field*, it gives one a tactic, taken-for-granted feel for the *field* and at the same time gives meaning – a *raison d'être* – for the logic underpinning the *practices* of the *field*. Practical mastery of the *practices* of a *field* provides a sense of rationality for the actions of every individual who identifies with the *field*.

Bourdieu (1987/1990) further proposed that a state of *doxa* imposes a 'practical faith' in the internal logic of the *field*, which is not a conscious adherence to a set of instituted dogmas or doctrines but rather a state of the body (1990a). *Doxic* conditions treat the body as a living memory pad that leads the mind subconsciously along with it. It is a state that gives one a practical sense of not only knowing how to act, but also a tacit belief that those actions are most appropriate. In this way, the body becomes a repository of precious values that are 'the form *par excellence* of blind symbolic thought' (1987/1990: 68). Practical faith is an inherent part of identifying with and belonging to a *field*. As Bourdieu stated (1987/1990: 68):

> Practical faith is the condition of entry that every *field* tacitly imposes, not only by sanctioning and debarring those who would destroy the game [*field*], but by so arranging things, in *practice*, that the operations of selecting and shaping new entrants ... are such as to obtain from them that undisputed, pre-reflexive, naïve, native compliance with the fundamental presuppositions of the *field* which is the very definition of *doxa*.

Just as practical faith provides a sense of belonging, it also provides a basis for excluding from the *field* those who do not share the same history and, by association, the same practical beliefs. This is why

> one cannot enter this magic circle [of a field] by an instantaneous decision of will, but only by birth or by a slow process of co-option and initiation ... One

cannot really live the belief associated with profoundly different conditions of existence, that is, with other games and other stakes.

(Bourdieu 1987/1990: 68)

This is also why Bourdieu argued that social research is most meaningful when it is undertaken within one's own *field*; that is, within a *field* in which the researcher is able to truly feel, understand and interpret the internal logic and practical beliefs of the inhabitants.

Misrecognition **and** symbolic violence

Bourdieu also acknowledged that all *fields* of practice are arbitrary in nature and therefore the inherent *doxic* modality of a *field* is really no more than a cultural arbitrary. Even though those who identify with a particular *field* have an unquestionable faith in its logic, there are no absolute conditions of existence that are beyond social determination and therefore beyond change. The unquestioned faith in the logic of a *field* is a form of what Bourdieu refers to as *misrecognition*, a process that evolves from collective *practice* and is 'sustained by a collective *self-deception*, a veritable collective *misrecognition* inscribed in the objective structures...and the mental structures' (1998a: 95). Collective *misrecognition* excludes the possibility of thinking or acting otherwise:

> the countless acts of recognition which are the small change of the compliance inseparable from belonging to the *field*, and in which collective *misrecognition* is ceaselessly generated, are both the precondition and the product of the *field*. They thus constitute investments in the collective enterprise of creating *symbolic capital*, which can only be performed on condition that the logic of the functioning of the *field* remains *misrecognised*.
>
> (Bourdieu 1990a: 68)

Culture is arbitrary in its content and how it is imposed. The imposition of cultural meaning, so that it is accepted, experienced and taken for granted as legitimate, can be a form of *symbolic violence* where one becomes complicit in creating conditions of one's own domination. It is 'a form of cultural violence that is exercised upon a social agent with his or her complicity' (Bourdieu and Wacquant 1992: 167). It is the outcome of people taking the world for granted, accepting the world as it is, and finding it natural because 'their mind is constructed according to the cognitive structures that are issued out of the very structures of the world' (Bourdieu and Wacquant 1992: 168). In this way *symbolic violence* is not purposefully manufactured by the dominating group but rather an insidious, hidden persuasion of all agents who naturally accept the way things are in the world, that is, a *doxic* acceptance of the world.

Symbolic violence is in the very logic of our everyday *practices* because the mechanisms that produce it are *misrecognised* (Bourdieu 1977a). Bourdieu argued that the education system is an example of institutional *symbolic violence* in that it privileges the powerful and marginalises others. Hidden within its very social structures are forms of *symbolic violence* that help to perpetuate the social advantages of dominant groups through the ideological and practical justifications of the established ways of schooling. For example, the privileging of academic versus practical subjects and the direct linking of qualifications to employment are examples of our taken-for-granted *practices* that allow some to dominate and others to become marginalised in society. We are sure you can think of similar examples in physical culture/s such as those discussed in Chapters 4, 11 and 14. In *Reproduction in Education, Society and Culture* (Bourdieu and Passeron 1977), perhaps his best known work apart from *Distinction* (1984a), Bourdieu provided a sociology of education that suggested a theory of *symbolic violence*, reproduction of privilege inherent in the pedagogic action of institutions such as schools:

> The legitimatory authority of the school system can multiply social inequalities because the most disadvantaged classes, too conscious of their destiny and too unconscious of the ways in which it is brought about, thereby help to bring it upon themselves.
>
> (1977: 20)

As you will see, in this book we have included a number of chapters that take on the importance of schools in relation to physical culture, in particular through physical education. This was a deliberate move both to recognise where some significant Bourdieuian work has been done in the *field* of physical culture, but also as recognition of the importance of the secondary site of socialisation (family being the first) that Bourdieu positioned as greatly influential in the inculcation of *habitus*.

Like many of Bourdieu's concepts, *symbolic violence* and his thinking around the work of institutions such as schools has created great debate and disagreement, some of which will become apparent in your reading of chapters such as those by Fitzpatrick (Ch. 16), Pringle (Ch. 18) and McDonald and McCuaig (Ch. 17). We will address some of the debates beyond Bourdieu in the final chapter of the book (Ch. 19), but before concluding this chapter there is one other concept that we believe is pivotal to understanding if one is to engage with Bourdieu, and that is *reflexivity*.

Reflexivity

Bourdieu's epistemological reflections and critiques are heralded as one of his greatest strengths (see, for example, an introduction to and critique of Bourdieu by Richard Jenkins, 2002). Central to Bourdieu's work is an insistence on *reflexivity* as a vital part of the research process. He asks us to critique and position his work, and our own, in the processes of theory, method and epistemology. He attempts to model how empirical research, theory, epistemology and reflection go hand in hand by using an invitation to see if it works for you in your own circumstance and understandings of the world, and go from there! *Reflexivity* is now common practice in critical paradigms such as feminism, race theory and postcolonial theory. In his works *An Invitation to Reflexive Sociology* with Loic Wacquant (1992), *In Other*

Words: Essays Towards a Reflexive Sociology (1987/1990), *Homo Academis* (1984b/1988), *Sketch for a Self Analysis* (2008) and *Science of Science and Reflexivity* (2004a), Bourdieu subjected himself and his social origins to his own theories and posited the practice of *reflexivity* as a basic necessity of research. He encouraged calling the intellectual world into question through critical *reflexivity*, 'the objectivation of the subject of objectivation' (2004a: 93). He suggested that as researchers we characteristically enter our work loaded with preconceptions. A way to address these is to explicate and expose them as part of the research process. This explication is a process espoused in research associated with critical theory. Our 'scholastic point of view' (1998a: 127–40) affects how we see the world and perhaps imposes structures or logics, mistaking 'the things of logic for the logic of things' (Bourdieu 1987/1990: 61). Taking such a position is not without its problems, not the least of which is whether Bourdieu or any of us could ever deliver (see, for example, the work of Lisa Adkins 2003, 2004). However, as you will recognise in some chapters, *reflexivity*, or the explicit positioning of the researcher and their beliefs and values within the research, is presented to suggest that there is no 'view from nowhere'. There is no inherent truth to the world, but, instead, truths from somewhere that are located in time and space, objective science being but one of a multitude of realities rooted in epistemological and ontological perspectives shaped by the cultures and perceptions we embody.

Having reviewed several of Bourdieu's focal concepts, we now turn to the question of how Bourdieuian sociology contributes to the *field* of physical culture.

A note about the field of physical culture and Bourdieu

As you will see, both in this book and other publication sites for academic work associated with physical culture/s, Bourdieu's concepts have been taken up, employed, critiqued, remodelled, rejected and reviewed. Chris Shilling's 1991 development of Bourdieu's 1978 concept of *physical capital* is one well-known example. Bourdieu's frequently referenced game and sporting analogies to explain *field*, his attention to the holistic body or *habitus*, his attention to *physical capital*, his 'Program for a sociology of sport' (1988a) have been explicit connections to physical culture. Within sport there was the early work of Bourdieu's colleague Loic Wacquant focusing on pugilism (1995a, b).

In the recent special issue of *Sociology of Sport Journal* (2011), where physical culture studies (PCS) were being marked out as an 'emerging and alternative intellectual project' to sport sociology, Michael Silk and David Andrews (2011) pointed to Bourdieu's contribution. In the same issue Atkinson took the opportunity to define PCS as 'an inter- and trans-disciplinary approach to the analysis of human movement, embodiment and corporeal representation within and across social institutions and cultural groups' (Atkinson 2011: 139), so it is easy to see the potential efficacy of Bourdieu's work to PCS. But the relationship is not without caution, as Richard Pringle demonstrates (Ch. 18). We have also seen the use of Bourdieu at the intersection of sport and education *fields*, such as physical education, with early proponents including David Kirk (1998, 1999a, 1999b),

Richard Light (2000), and John Evans (2004). Mary Lynn Stewart's less dominant take on physical culture as comprising the 'personal hygiene, deportment, exercise, and beauty regimens' taught to French girls in the 1880s to1930s (2001) also invites Bourdieuian frameworks associated with bodily appearance. Such an invitation is taken up in several chapters of this book.

Bourdieu in this book

In the empirical section of this book we have collected a range of scholars who have used, extended, adapted, stretched, reinterpreted or interpreted Bourdieu's concepts to enlighten the *field* of physical culture. You will see that not all the authors entirely agree with Bourdieu nor with each other. That is the nature of scholarly work as we grapple and play with ways to understand our world.

elke and Karen (emerald and Barbour, Ch. 2) explore elke's re-entry into the *field* of dance, more specifically the *subfield* of contemporary dance, after a 25 year absence. They unpack her journaled experiences in terms of the ways her *habitus* and *hexis* do and do not afford *symbolic capitals* in what is, for elke, in some ways a familiar, and in some ways a new, context. They then ponder *reflexivity* in three ways: as applied to the self-reflexive act; as defined by Bourdieu and then developed by others; and as habituated for some contemporary individuals or groups, including themselves, as social researchers, always analysing and researching 'on the fly'.

In Chapter 3 Wayne (Smith) uses Bourdieu's thinking tools of *field, habitus* and *capital* but also his potentially more critical concepts of *doxa, illusio, misrecognition* and *symbolic violence* to reflect on the nature of his *practices* during a period of structural change at his university. Using Bourdieu's thinking tools, he interprets the competing views of academics and members of the Faculty leadership during the restructuring process.

lisahunter deliberately sets out to recognise low capital surfing whilst investigating the research object – surfing. In Chapter 4 she reports on an incident she witnessed while gathering field texts as an ethnographer at a surf festival, when a female spectator resisted the intrusion of the wandering media photographer on the beach. lisahunter uses Bourdieu's thinking tools of *symbolic violence, capital* and *field* to explore the scene that unfolded in front of her.

In Chapter 5, Toni, Rachel and David (O'Donovan, Sandford and Kirk) venture into the school physical education changing room. They draw upon the work of Bourdieu, in particular his concepts of *field, capital* and *habitus*, to identify the ostensibly unremarkable changing room as a site of juncture between a number of core *fields* (principally schooling, physical education and physical culture). We hear the voices of girls aged 11 to 14 years and their teachers and see excerpts from their researcher field diaries as Toni, Rachel and David argue that as a 'changing place' (both literally and metaphorically), changing rooms are in fact highly charged transitional spaces.

In Chapter 6 Richard and John (Light and Evans) work to take seriously Bourdieu's encouragement to use his concepts as methodological tools, rather than only as explanatory lenses. They provide an example of how *habitus* can be operationalised by reporting on a study on coach development that endeavours to understand the precedence that experience has in the formation of coaches' beliefs, dispositions and *practice*, and the inability of formal coach education programmes to compete with it. They use *habitus* as a methodological tool in the generation and analysis of data.

David and David (Brown and Aldous, Ch. 7) use Bourdieu's work to address the practical problem of challenging the gendered cultural economy in physical culture and, within this, school sport and Physical Education (PE). In his teaching career before he became a sociologist, David Brown became aware that PE teachers' embodied identity and biography are a significant source for the construction of their professional identities as teachers. He experienced first-hand, what Bourdieu (2005: 47) referred to as the 'dialectical confrontation' of these gendered embodied biographies (*habitus*) coming together with the gendered context (*field*) of teaching physical education. David and David demonstrate how Bourdieu's ideas move beyond a conventional theory and start to resemble a theory-practice method.

Elise (Paradis, Ch. 8) examines media coverage of the declaration that Olympic women boxers should wear skirts in the ring. She uses Bourdieu's theory of *doxa, crisis* and *hysteresis* and the concept of *liminality* to discuss what has been perceived as a major setback for women boxers after their inclusion on the 2012 Olympics programme. She exposes the different coexisting *logics of the field*, which range from 'women shouldn't box at all' to 'warriors shouldn't wear skirts'. These differences illustrate the *crisis* that is currently occurring in the *field* of boxing and Elise uses the concept of *hysteresis* to articulate this *crisis*. As we did not review *crisis* and *hysteresis* in this first chapter, Elise's chapter will be an excellent introduction to the use of these as analytics.

Erin and Tony (Christensen and Rossi, Ch. 9) use the concepts of *capital, habitus* and *field* to examine the context that confronts first-year teachers as they transition from teacher education programmes into school. Their concern is with the work that first-year teachers do to negotiate the schools' organisational landscape. The staffroom is a pivotal micropolitical context for beginning teachers to navigate: here they learn customary and desirable behaviours and perspectives of the teaching profession and navigate their own position in the *field* of the school. In Chapter 9, Erin and Tony look in detail at Larry's' story as he begins his career as a PE teacher.

Symeon and Thomas (Dagkas and Quarmby, Ch. 10) explore the way in which *social, economic,* and *cultural capitals* shape young people's physical activity dispositions and *practice*. They draw from empirical work conducted in the past with young people from economically deprived social groupings in diverse *fields.* They interrogate notions of social class and family as *fields* where young people, through their various interactions, develop *habitus* and engage in *practice*. Bourdieu's concepts are therefore used to highlight social inequalities across various *fields* and help us understand how the multifaceted influences that operate in and through combinations of family and social class influence young people's engagement with physical activity.

Chapter 11 focuses on two issues: the paradox of physical activity for Qatari women and researcher *hysteresis* and *reflexivity*. Physical activity and physical appearance are the subject of a narrative that accompanies the chapter. Kelly (Knez) and lisahunter draw on a dialogue between Qatari culture, a Qatari woman and the two researchers, employing tools of *habitus*, *capital*, and *field* to try to understand what is going on in terms of Qatari women and physical activity. They also invite you, as a reader and potential researcher, to use Bourdieu's concepts alongside their analysis to consider your own *reflexivity* in ethnographic projects, whether as 'insiders' or 'outsiders' who might experience *hysteresis*, the feeling of being a fish out of water.

In Chapter 12, Hayley and Peter (Fitzgerald and Hay) explore dis/ability in the context of the PE classroom. Ability is a term that is widely employed within the education community, in a manner that appears to assume its enduring and inherent constitution. The performative culture of contemporary neoliberal education systems has been particularly influential in positioning ability as a measurable entity with definable and discriminating properties. As a key site of physical culture, PE is not immune to the performative imperatives of the broader education system and consequently the notion of ability is similarly characterised by discourses of measurement, standards and the valuing of performing bodies in reference to defined appearances and capacities. This chapter uses Bourdieuian tools to better understand how ability is imposed, pursued, and acquired in a PE context, but also note that we need to pursue this exploration in broader sites of physical culture.

Karin, Birgitta and Håkan (Redelius, Fagrell and Larsson, Chapter 13) are interested in the structures that sustain heteronormativity in PE in schools. They examine how the taken-for-granted norms, or *doxa*, condition the participation of all students, regardless of gender or sexual identity. They use the tools of *doxa*, *symbolic violence*, *field* and *symbolic capital* to analyse and understand gender, sexuality and normality in this school subject characterised by physical exercise and bodily movement.

Holly Thorpe has employed an array of compatible theoretical and methodological approaches to deepen and enrich her understanding of snowboarding's cultural complexities. In Chapter 14 she discusses the value of Bourdieu's conceptual schema for explaining the snowboarding body as a cultural and social phenomenon. She illustrates how Bourdieu's relational concepts of *habitus, capital,* and *field* facilitates insights into snowboarding bodies as possessors of power, and alludes to some of the struggles (between and within groups) over legitimate use and meaning of *physical capital*.

In the final of the empirical chapters (Chapter 15), Qiang Gao makes a somewhat philosophical exploration of *habitus*. He explores Bourdieu's theory of the body and embodiment with interpretations of the body from other theorists and other theoretical perspectives, particularly those that draw on modern epistemological thinking. Qiang Goa makes two interpretative readings of *habitus*. The first emphasises the embodiment of knowledge and the second recognises the body as being a form of knowledge in itself.

Chapters 16, 17 and 18 make a turn from analytic to reflective and critical engagement with Bourdieu. In Chapter 16, Katie (Fitzpatrick) reflects on the limits and possibilities of Bourdieu's tools in her study of young people. Informed by critique of Bourdieu's method and theory that suggested Bourdieu would provide an overly deterministic explanation of class-located actions and school achievement of the young people in the study, Katie at first resisted Bourdieu and looked more to the postcolonial theorists such as Homi Bhabha and Edward Said and to the poststructuralist ideas of Foucault and the feminist ideas of Judith Butler. However, she found in the end that Bourdieu's theoretical tools did offer a way into the young people's stories, while simultaneously highlighting the importance of the wider social and political contexts. In this chapter Katie explores the limits and possibilities by way of comparison with the theoretical lens of Homi Bhabha's notion of hybridity in her examination of the intractable underachievement and social marginality to which the young people in her study were both subject and complicit.

Doune and Louise (Macdonald and McCuaig, Chapter 17) take a reflexive position and ask two questions of several of the authors of the empirical chapters in the book: 'What is the researchers' thinking behind the adoption of Bourdieu's concepts?'; and, playfully borrowing from Bourdieu's interest in taste and consumption, they ask their colleagues to reflect on the question: 'Does my research look good in Bourdieu?' or 'Should I be trying on someone else's theory?'. They were interested to explore what attracts us to Bourdieu's work to make sense of research questions and data and enhance our analyses. They also explore what other theories have been used or considered alongside Bourdieu's. Doune and Louise unpack four of the themes that emerged as they talked with some of the authors: personal resonance; clearly articulated tools for analytic work; micro-analysis; and potential theoretical partnerships.

In Chapter 18 Richard (Pringle) explores the questions 'Why the popularity of Bourdieu?' and 'Why now?' to make a reflexive analysis of the circulation of ideas within the sociology of sport *field*. Noting that Bourdieu's theoretical tools remained somewhat marginal in the (intersecting) *fields* of the sociology of sport and sport pedagogy throughout the 1980s and 90s, Richard ponders the influence of Bourdieu in shaping a *field's* epistemological and methodological practices since the dramatic increase in the use of these tools, especially since 2003.

We title the final chapter 'Working with, against and beyond Bourdieu'. In this chapter we suggest there is much utility in the engagement of physical culture research with Bourdieu's work as methodological, epistemological and theoretical frameworks to understand what is going on. Like Bourdieu, we also encourage working beyond and against such frameworks in the dialogue and scholarship of our work, a dialogue into which you are invited. We argue for the importance of such dialogue in order to ensure that 'fast scholarship' and disregard for social science by neoliberal *doxa* do not undermine the production of ideas. We hope to generate new debates, challenges to *doxa* and challenges to various forms of *symbolic violence* inherent in our projects and our own *practices* in our contemporary academy and public scholarship within the *field* of physical culture.

Part II

Bourdieu in practice

Using theory to understand physical cultures

2 'I'll go back next week – it's complicated'

Returning to dance with the help of Bourdieu

elke emerald and Karen Barbour

Keywords: *Dance, contemporary dance, field and subfield, habitus, capitals, reflexivity*

Prologue

I have just been to dance class. It was truly awful. I rolled about on the floor like a beached whale (others were rolling too, not just me you understand). I am bruised all over as my shorts have an excessive and ostentatious number of zippers. I may not be able to walk tomorrow. The rest of the class are bendy stretchy, turn themselves inside out 18 year olds. I'll go back next week – it's complicated.

(Email from elke to her daughter: Diary Week One)

To put one's body out on display, as in dancing, presupposes that one consents to externalising oneself and that one has a contented awareness of the image of oneself that projects towards others. The fear of ridicule and shyness are, on the contrary, linked to an acute awareness of oneself and of one's body, to a consciousness fascinated by its corporeality.

(Bourdieu 2004b: 585)

Introduction

The context of contemporary dance, as expressed in our lived experiences as a student returning to dance after 25 years (elke) and a dance practitioner (Karen), provides an opportunity to explore and apply Bourdieu's related concepts of *field*, *habitus* and *capital* and then to extend our exploration to a consideration of *reflexivity*. Being based in embodied experience, these concepts seem particularly relevant to apply to dance. elke's journal of her lived experiences in returning to dance offers valuable insights and epiphanies (Bochner 2002) into her *reflexivity* and her engagement with key processes in the (re)development of a dance *habitus* within the newly experienced context of contemporary dance (Wainwright and

Turner 2003; Wilcox 2005). Such epiphanies offer dancers and researchers the opportunity to 'reflect on something they are not usually consciously aware of, namely, their "*bodily habitus*"' (Wainwright and Turner 2003: 6). They offer us, as social analysts of the *field* of physical culture, an insight into the *subfield* of dance and the constraints and enablers of physical activity.

elke kept a journal of her experiences in attending weekly open contemporary dance classes taught by Karen at the Academy of Performing Arts in Kirikiriroa/ Hamilton, Aotearoa/New Zealand in 2011. Both women are academics, seniors lecturers in the broader *field* of education, with elke working in education research and ethnography and Karen focussed on dance and creative practice as research.

Remembering that Bourdieu asked social researchers to use his framework as a method to understand *practice* and 'trace out operant social mechanisms' (Wacquant 2011: 82), in the first section of this chapter we discuss excerpts from elke's journal using Bourdieu's concepts of *field/subfield*, *habitus* and *capitals* as tools to understand elke's dance experience. In the second section we explore our own processes of analysis by engaging with the concept of *reflexivity* as Bourdieu outlined and then as others have developed. Finally, we transport the concept of *reflexivity* into the context of dance to make some preliminary observations on Karen's understanding of the *reflexivity* embodied within the *habitus* of contemporary dance.

Field and subfield

Extract A

> Ballet, jazz, tap and modern – I did them all. But this class, today, is 'contemporary'. I am so out of the swim now that I am not even sure where this fits in the taxonomy of dance. Is it like modern – or something completely different?
>
> (elke's journal, Week One)

Extract B

> Floor work – oh no – my least favourite thing. Rolling about on the floor has never quite taken with me. And to make matters worse I am wearing shorts with many superfluous zippers. By the end of the floor session I am a Monet of bruises. As I quip to Karen in a brief interval later, 'the floor hadn't been invented when I last danced'. Of course it had, but we didn't spend much time down there, and I didn't like it then either.
>
> (elke's journal, Week One)

At the beginning of the contemporary dance classes (Extract A&B), elke identifies that she was participating in a *field* of dance, or more accurately, the *subfield* of contemporary dance, that was not the same as the dance forms she recalled from her dancing 25 years ago in Australia. While sharing many of the general logics and characteristics of the *field* of dance, the *subfield* of contemporary dance appeared to elke to have internal protocols, rules and *practices* that she was unfamiliar with

(Thompson 2008). Contemporary dance uses the floor in very specific and deliberate ways, quite unlike the modern dance, tap, ballet and jazz that elke danced previously. To move from the larger *field* of dance to the *subfield* of contemporary dance, a 'genuine qualitative leap' was called for (Thompson 2008: 73), both as a participant in dance and as a social analyst seeking to understand it. Later in the journal (Extract E) we find another qualitative leap that elke must make to enter this *subfield*; to understand the purpose of movement in contemporary dance and the relationship between movement and music. There is, then, a dissonance between elke's memories of the *field* and her new experiences in the *subfield* of contemporary dance. In this space of rupture, moments of epiphany and some painful realisations occurred.

Habitus

Dissonance notwithstanding, elke recognised and began to participate again in the core *practice* of attending regular dance classes, appreciating this *practice* as an ongoing way of engaging in the community and practising dance. 'Open' contemporary dance classes are offered in most contemporary dance communities and are intended to allow dancers with a range of levels of engagement in dance to participate. Thus dancers like elke are welcome, and there is typically a generosity towards, and acceptance of, the multitude of purposes that classes serve for dancers. However, these values are not necessarily apparent to all dancers initially and elke immediately felt different from the other dancers in the class:

Extract C

The only other dancer who is not a young, bendy stretchy 18 year old still, clearly to me, knows what she is doing. The arms are always a giveaway. Hers are in perfect place, although under no instruction. The feet are the topic of instruction, but she knows what to do with her arms. Aha! Dancer! My heart sinks. I surmise I truly am, quite simply, out of my league...

(elke's journal, Week One)

Extract D

My old dance gear is 1990's aerobics gear, suitable for a dress up, but not what these dancers wear at all. They are all in black long pants and some form of sporty singlet. I'll just stick to my shorts for now. I think I'll look even more conspicuous and wannabe if I show up in conspicuously new dance rig.

(elke's journal, Week One)

Extract E

I realise I will have to learn how to move to the music in this way – to my uneducated 'contemporary dance' ear, the movement does not seem to follow the melody necessarily, or the beat – if there is one. The relationship between movement and music is different to me, different to what I experienced so many years ago. So much contemporary dance seems to be set to contemporary music which, again, I am not educated to listen to.

(elke's journal, Week One)

We can understand elke's difference, as articulated in her journal, as related to *habitus*. In understanding *habitus* generally, there is a recognition that there is a corporeal body that is socially shaped but this 'body is socially moderated, not simply invented by society' (Wainwright and Turner 2003: 7). In Extract C, elke identifies elements of the social shaping of another's body. *Habitus* can be understood as the embodiment of socio-cultural norms, in this case, norms of contemporary dance, that are then expressed through a dancer's embodied ways of moving, speaking, feeling, knowing, walking and dancing in the world. Importantly in this dance context, Reay (2004) emphasises that *habitus* is embodied, 'not composed solely of mental attitudes and perceptions' (432). In the extracts above, elke recognises the *habitus* of another dancer (Extract C) and recognises the clothing that aligns to the contemporary dance *habitus* (Extract D). She recognises too that the structures of the *habitus* are not set. *Habitus* 'captures how we carry within us our history, how we bring this history into our present circumstances, and we then make a choice to act in certain ways and not others' (Maton 2008: 52). So the structures of the *habitus* are 'durable and transposable but not immutable' (Maton 2008: 53), in that elke can *learn* to appreciate the contemporary dance relationship between music and movement and can be *educated* to understand contemporary music itself (Extract E).

Embodiment is usefully articulated holistically, recognising difference in race, gender, sexuality, ability, biology and environment, while simultaneously incorporating socio-cultural aspects including cultural context, history, spirituality, intellectual and emotional actions (Barbour 2011). This normalised, habitual embodiment is not always consciously apparent to individuals. However, as we saw in the extracts above, elke observed differences between the *habitus* of the other contemporary dancers in the class and her own.

Just three classes later, elke notices something deeply embodied and subtle:

Extract F

I feel 'up' after class. This is interesting, especially given the sheer effort and my apparent lack of competence (still) – is it purely physiological (endorphins), I think not, there is something deeply psychological and emotional in my response to the experience of dancing.

(elke's journal, Week Four)

Bourdieu wrote that 'There is a way of understanding which is altogether particular, and often forgotten in theories of intelligence; that which consists of understanding within one's body' (1990a: 166). In Week Four of attending classes elke notices that she is experiencing a deep response to moving (Extract F). In discussing this extract with elke, Karen recognises that this kind of embodied sensitivity, an awareness of self on many levels, is a potential aspect of the contemporary dance *habitus*. As Janna Parviainen (2002) states, 'Epistemic openness requires not only bodily sensitivity and responsiveness, but also the living body's awareness of itself' (16).

elke's journal reveals further insight into the habitus of the contemporary dancer.

Extract G

> They still all look a little the same to me, they are all young and beautiful, with open lovely faces and supple confident dancing bodies. They are not thin and ethereal, there is a mix, some large, small, thin, solid. But their sameness to me is in their dancing confidence and their joy of dance.
>
> (elke's journal, Week Four)

Extract H

> [D]ance class is not a one day fling, it is a commitment. At least a semester of commitment to a space. A commitment to a creative space. Something is made in a space like this and everyone must be present in their awareness to make it work.
>
> (elke's journal, Week One)

Here elke identifies joy and confidence in the dancers around her. She cites creativity, commitment, presence and awareness as integral to the dance experience. These observations refer to Reay's (2004) mental attitudes and perceptions rather than only corporeal (bodily) bearing. In reflecting on this extract, Karen noted that dance is something beyond learned movement, but is a way of being that embodies a particular presence (Lepecki 2004a), awareness, receptivity and expression. Karen identifies these as key processes in the *habitus* of contemporary dance that can lead to a state of wellbeing from sensation and expression. In her ruminations, elke identified these subtler layers of *habitus*.

Capitals

In her diary entry (Extract D), elke also ponders the delicacies of negotiating belonging in terms of the symbolic value of clothing, in this case dancewear, concluding that the negative symbolic value of shorts is less than the negative symbolic value of appearing 'wannabe' by attending class in 'conspicuously new dance rig' (Extract D).

By week two, the diary documents explicit consideration of the *capitals* at play:

Extract I

> I am aware I don't have enough of any sort of *capital*. For example, I am aware that my shorts mark me as outsider. All the others have the appropriate clothing

– cultural capital perhaps. I have a little of the necessary *cultural capital* in my history of dance. Just a smattering of corporeal *capital* in the sense that I can pull off appropriate arm positions. And some *linguistic capital*, in that I can respond confidently to some of the dance terms. But in the main, high value *capitals* are lacking: so the *symbolic capitals* are low here.

(elke's journal, Week Two)

Experienced dancers bring corporeal *capital* in the form of a familiarity with general movements such as floor exercises, warm up patterns and various swings, turns, falls, rolls, leaps and more specific steps relating to a range of styles/forms of dance. As Wainwright and Turner (2003) note, experienced ballet dancers 'often speak of "muscle memory" – the ability of their bodies to remember particular sequences of dance steps perhaps years after they last danced them' (p. 7). This can be as specific as anticipating a preparation or transition or the tempo of an exercise. Principles of functional alignment will likely be embodied by experienced dancers (Extract C above) and can be evident to other experienced dancers and teachers as *hexis* (Bourdieu 2004b: 582), or 'bearing' (Bourdieu 2004b: 584), that is, that part of our *habitus* that includes deportment, stance, gait, quality of movement (clumsy, graceful, sensual, awkward), the way people 'carry themselves' (Thorpe, Barbour and Bruce 2011: 117). Corporeal *capital* may be evident in the ability to apply common movement principles of contemporary dance such as release, suspend, contract and spiral. Corporeal *capital* in this sense is integral to being a dancer and something dancers will invest in heavily. Leena Rouhiainen (2003) argues that the accumulation of *capital* helps to explain why contemporary dancers will continue to attend open classes to enhance their skills and to remain participants in the ever-shifting processes within the contemporary dance community.

As a result of cultural, corporeal and linguistic *capital*, dancers with some experience are able to join open classes and participate in this key activity with some confidence, drawing on both their individual histories and understanding of collective norms. That is, they embody a contemporary dance *habitus* that enables them to participate with confidence, or in Bourdieu's terms, with 'contented awareness' (Bourdieu 2004b: 585, see this chapter's opening quote) in the *subfield* of contemporary dance. In her journal, elke reveals that she does not experience 'contented awareness'!

Reflexivity

While necessarily brief, we see here how the tools of *field*, *habitus* and *capital* can be used to gain some insight into a field of physical culture. However, as social analysts working together on such a project, further questions arose for us. The business of being a social analyst of one's own life raises all the usual questions of qualitative social research: questions of what counts as data, validity, truth, accuracy and questions of representation. These questions have fascinated many social researchers and have been extensively interrogated in the fields of ethnography, anthropology and autoethnography (see for example Ellis 2004).

We will venture some way into this terrain by exploring, firstly, the facility of Bourdieu's concept of *reflexivity* as applied to the self-reflexive act, then *reflexivity* as defined by Bourdieu and then developed by others, and also *reflexivity* as an habitual element of contemporary dancer *habitus*.

In Bourdieu's terms, the aim of *reflexivity* in research is to construct a research account that is not unknowingly reflecting the researcher's own relation to the research participants/subjects, topic or site. That is, 'the unthought categories of thought that predetermine and delimit what is thinkable' (Deer 2008: 204) are made explicit. These categories of thought may encompass many things: theoretical trajectory, analytic methods, life story, personal biases, prejudices and political commitments. In Cecile Deer's (2008) words, 'For Bourdieu, *reflexivity* means that all knowledge producers should strive to recognise their own objective position within the intellectual and academic field' (p. 201). Deer cites Bourdieu's description, discussion and theorising of his own personal trajectory as an illustration of how the social scientist can objectify her own position and *practice*.

The practice of *reflexivity* has become fairly commonplace in the social sciences, understood to be something of an essential element of work to make sense of the social world. It is often characterised as something akin to 'researcher know thyself' (Pillow 2003: 181) and actualised as a researcher's account of their own theoretical and methodological practices of analysis. *Reflexivity* is, however, a widely used term and appears in many different guises (Burr 1995). Reflexive practices ask us to 'confront our own processes of interpretation', that is, 'how we think we know' (Visweswaran 1994: 79).

Bourdieu described *reflexivity* as a privilege of those who are 'disposed to study the world' (Grenfell 2008: 225). He also recognised, however, that a crisis, dissonance, disruption or disjunction between *habitus* and *field* can force anyone into *reflexivity* (for example Thorpe 2009). The tension and misalignment between *habitus* and *field* may seem quite subtle in this dance context. After all, elke is not completely new to dance. However, it may provide some insight into the *reflexivity* at work here as she deliberatively identifies the elements of her *habitus* that are out of alignment with the contemporary dance *field* and thereby are either benignly useless or actively working against her. For example, in these classes the modern and balletic *hexis* of particular hand positions was benignly useless in that it did not impede movement or draw correction from other dancers or Karen as instructor; but the habit of turn out (the turned position of legs and feet) actively disabled some movement and elke had to consciously undo that element of *hexis*. This sort of *reflexivity* is ad hoc and discontinuous (McNay 1999; Thorpe 2009), in that it is responsive to dissonance and disjuncture. In Karen's terms, elke experiences an epiphany (Bochner 2002) as the *habitus/field* disjuncture leads her to reassess the *capitals* she has available to trade here (Extract I above).

Something more is happening here also. Because we are both social researchers and deliberately enter this site as participants and researchers, we have particular tools at our disposal, including some knowledge of Bourdieu's tools, and are hence able to analyse our ongoing actions and analysis. This is a less ad hoc, more continuous, *reflexivity*; it is the *reflexivity* of the reflexive analyst *in situ*.

Extract J

And then we have to change partner and I meet Lucy. As we stretch we fall into a conversation about her sport training. She tells me all about it. I notice that I overlay a theory of lifespan development as an explanation for her telling; young people like to talk. I imagine that she would tell this detail of her sport training to a friend too. I notice too that I draw instantly on a 'lifespan development' analysis, but not a 'generation' analysis (although these would not be mutually exclusive).

It interests me that I:

1) do the analysis in the moment
2) choose a particular sort of analysis and
3) then do the meta analysis – an analysis of my analysis – at the same time.

I appreciate my ethnomethodological background. The 'state-of-mind' that seeks to understand how participants make sense of a scene is very good training in qualitative analysis. I make a note-to-self too – think about this experience in terms of *field* and *capitals* – I am light on privileged *capitals* here – what are they – think this through.

(elke's journal, Week Two)

In elke's diary extract above (Extract J) she is already analysing 'on the wing', as it is happening. In actual fact, of course, the journal is written *after* the class, so we rely on accuracy in elke's reporting that she indeed *did* begin theorising *during* the stretching rather than half an hour later as she sat over the journal. Either way, elke, as participant, is also analyst, and, further, reflexive analyst in that she names the theories she uses to understand her world – all while participating in a stretching exercise.

Karen brings her expertise in dance and social analysis to bear in her reflections on elke's journal. Of course this is not unexpected from an academic in dance – in a sense, Karen's dance classes are always participant research as she engages in embodied knowing and teaching while teaching about embodied knowing and teaching. Ultimately, Karen sees even attending open classes for enjoyment as an opportunity to develop embodied ways of knowing and to make use of, apply and integrate embodied knowledge throughout our lives. In Extract J we see an explicit theorising of dance class and engaging in dance that is beyond the matter of getting the steps 'right'.

And this is just our point. As Lisa Adkins (2003) and Paul Sweetman (2003) have both noted, albeit in different contexts, reflexive practices may be *habituated* for some contemporary individuals or groups. Rather than the product of some crisis of *field* and *habitus*, Sweetman and Adkins both argue that the 'flexible or reflexive habitus' (Sweetman 2003) is an element of contemporary times. As researchers, we are both positioned in 'contemporary' times – as one must always be – but further, as social analysts, we are additionally privileged to have certain lenses or tools (potentially) always at play, and the 'schole', that is, 'the 'leisure time', the 'pure gaze' of the intellectual researcher (Grenfell 2008: 225).

Bourdieu's reflexivity, as nuanced and extended here by Adkins and Sweetman in the idea of the *reflexive habitus*, may then be a tool that helps us understand the (critical) reflexivity of the participant social researcher as itself habituated, that is, an element of the researcher *habitus*; part of the practical knowledge of the field of academe in which the 'rules, procedures and *capitals* are (at least theoretically) oriented towards reflexivity' (Shirato and Webb 2003: 545). Not only might we engage in the reflexive practice of 'objectivation of the knowing subject' (Deer 2008: 201) – naming and examining our own philosophical or theoretical standpoint as part of our researcher practice – but as habitually reflexive participant researchers, reflexivity becomes a way of understanding the ongoing world and living our lives. As noted in elke's journal,

Extract K

Ongoing, contemporaneous analysis is part of the very rhythm of my routine thinking – I find this very useful as a life skill.

(elke's journal, Week Four)

There is a further reflexivity at play here also – perhaps one that transports Bourdieu's reflexivity beyond his intended definition. Karen notes, in reading elke's journal, that reflexivity is crucial within embodied ways of knowing and, as such, there is a reflexivity inherent in the *habitus* of the contemporary dancer. Karen articulates embodied ways of knowing as a dancer's experience of recognising knowledge as constructed, contextually specific and embodied (Barbour 2011): as a way of being and living. Participating in contemporary dance classes, she encourages dancers to recognise the existing knowledge they already embody from their dancing and their lives in general, and to appreciate that there is potential for them to construct and re-construct this embodied knowledge through investigations undertaken in class and in further reflection of their movement experiences. When dancers are engaged in exercises designed to enhance kinaesthetic sensitivity, such as attending to the expansion of the lungs and ribcage in breathing, or observing the shift of their shoulder blades as they lower their arms to their sides with palms facing upwards, they are awakening and enhancing awareness of and through their embodiment. Sometimes further investigation and reflection occurs through discussion within classes or following class but, significantly, in the moment of dancing small epiphanies can turn repeated movements into embodied insights that can be transferrable and liveable (Barbour 2011). For example, an experience of counter balance and suspension of weight in falling to the floor may be connected to prior knowledge of physics or to observations of movement by children or athletes, and become a transferable movement principle to be employed in subsequent activities involving falling; whether choreographed or improvised or in wider life experiences in which we may need to suspend as we fall, release expectations and give into an experience in order to recover and find firm footing again. This 'embodied knowledge arises in the lived experience of combining different ideas through experimentation', as we transform, as we 'creatively search for and judge potential new combinations and juxtapositions of familiar and perhaps seemingly unrelated knowledge and experiences' (Barbour 2011: 95). In the moment of dancing, we actually 'live out' the possibilities, and when we stumble or fall, we learn, reflecting in the moment to discard the unhelpful actions and ideas, and adopt the useful actions and apply relevant principles.

So, as we noted above, it is not only possible for learned movement to become normalised within the process of dance training as *habitus*, but also for a way of being that embodies sensitivity, awareness, receptivity and expression resulting in alternative embodied ways of knowing to become a key process in the *habitus* of contemporary dance. This requires presence (Lepecki 2004b), and can be understood as living in the moment of dancing, 'using techniques of awareness to move from within' (Wilcox 2005: 13). Thus, as a consequence, the *habitus* of the contemporary dancer offers a *reflexivity* about self in relation to the world through training sensory awareness, embodied expression and presence – ultimately embodied ways of knowing.

In returning to dance, it could be asked 'Why would a person, bruised all over and unable to walk, go back to dance class?' As elke initially recorded in her journal – 'Well, it's complicated.' Bourdieu helped us understand some of the processes at play in elke's return to dance, and gave some insight into the complexities of putting 'one's body out on display', While elke did not perhaps 'fear ridicule', she certainly had, to paraphrase Bourdieu in the opening quote, an acute awareness of herself and of her body – and she remains 'a consciousness fascinated by its corporeality'(Bourdieu 2004b: 585).

3 Bourdieu, physical culture and universities

Wayne Smith

Keywords: *Logic of practice, HPE teacher education, sport science*

Introduction

In this chapter I aim to show how I used Bourdieu's theorising, and in particular the primacy he gave to '*the logic of practice*', to examine and interpret the nature of the *field* of physical culture in my own university. In 2002-6 I undertook a research project that drew not only on Bourdieu's well known concepts of *field, habitus* and *capital* but also his potentially more critical concepts of *doxa, illusio, misrecognition* and *symbolic violence* to reflect on the nature of my *practices* during a period of structural change. Armed with these concepts, I was able to gain a deeper appreciation of the sedimentation, domination and contestation of the *field* of physical culture in my institution. Initially, I was fluctuating between Giddens' (1979) theory of structuration and Bourdieu's (1977, 1980/1990, 1997/2000, 1998a) *logic of practice*, but it was Bourdieu who won the day because his 'conceptual tools of analysis' offered a language for my analysis. I used Bourdieu's (1986) theoretical concepts not only because they offered a theory of social *practice* but also, in the way that Jenkins (2002) described them, as 'thinking tools' that enabled me to examine and reflect on the social dynamics of my everyday *practices* within my cultural *field*.

The context of my research was this: In 2002 the New Zealand government announced that it intended to reform the country's higher education sector. One of their decisions was to merge the country's remaining colleges of education, which specialised in teacher education, into their neighbouring university. At the time I was a physical education teacher educator in the country's largest college of education, so these reforms were clearly going to impact on me. As expected, in 2004 my college of education was merged into New Zealand's largest university and the college became the greater part of what is now a Faculty of Education. It was a particularly difficult time for many of us who were teacher educators, as we found ourselves in a completely different professional space with a significant loss of *cultural* and *symbolic capital*. The merging of the college's ways of doing things with the university's ways of doing things resulted in two different *logics of practice* competing for the same social space.

Pre- and post-merger I held a head of programme responsibility for a Bachelor of Physical Education (BPE), which was a long established, four-year undergraduate professional teacher education programme. At the same time, the university had, within its Faculty of Science, a Department of Sport and Exercise Science with a major specialising in the related but different field of sport and exercise science. From the beginning the university leadership team had proposed that the sport and exercise science major and BPE teacher education programme should merge, with the BPE and associated staff moving over to the Department of Sport and Exercise Science. For me, and many of my colleagues, who identified as socially-critical physical educators, this was an untenable move. We identified as educators not scientists, so naturally this proposal signalled a head-wind of contestation over what would become the nature of our social space and with it the way the *field* of physical culture would be framed in our university. It was also the catalyst for the research project which ran parallel to the restructuring from late 2002 until mid-2006.

Although my reflections draw on my personal experiences, they also highlight an underpinning *logic of practice* that has become institutionalised in both the objective structures of higher education and embodied by, and made evident in the work of, academics more broadly. It is intended that this 'reading' will help exemplify how our *field* of physical culture in universities is underpinned by a taken-for-granted *logic of practice* that has become increasingly dependent on scientific ways of knowing. As a social *field*, the *field* of physical culture is subjected to the characteristics that Bourdieu ascribes to all *fields*. That is, it is arbitrary and contestable in nature, inclusive of some practices and individuals and exclusive of others; it contains different forms of *capital* and differentiated positions of power. Perhaps most importantly, it subjects the individuals who identify with the *field* to the conditions of *doxa*, *illusio*, and at times *symbolic violence* through *misrecognition*.

As used in this chapter, *doxa* refers to a concurrence between one's habitus and a social *field*. *Doxa* is 'an adherence to the relations of order which, because they structure inseparably both the real world and the thought world, are accepted as self-evident' (Bourdieu 1986: 471). It is the unquestioned belief one has in their *field of practice* (Bourdieu and Wacquant 1992). *Illusio* refers to '*an investment in the game*' (Bourdieu and Wacquant 1992: 98 [italics in original]), that is, the level of personal investment one has in the *practices* and valued *capital* of a *field*. *Misrecognition* is perhaps a more powerful concept because it focuses on a form of *symbolic violence*; that is, a form of social violation "which is wielded precisely inasmuch as one does not perceive it as such" (Bourdieu and Wacquant 1992: 168). All three concepts make reference to our fundamentally different, pre-reflexive assumptions about the world in which we live. We all engage in the world as it is, finding it natural, because our minds are constructed according to the very structures of the world (Bourdieu and Wacquant 1992).

As the above would suggest, the way we are conditioned to think and act, in all walks of life, is tailored by our subjective-positioning within our social world. Higher education in Western societies is no different. It is an arbitrary world of valued knowledge and *practices* that condition us to think in certain ways and privilege some forms of knowledge over others. I contend that it is this conditioning that led to the reforms of New Zealand's higher education sector during 2002-6. These reforms were heavily influenced by global initiatives and neo-liberal socio-economic policies influencing higher education across the Western world at this time. It was a time when accountability discourses dominated the policy-makers' thinking. In human movement studies these accountability policies supported reductionist scientific discourses, and by association the way we have come to frame the study of physical culture in our universities. Today, within the world of *sport science* and physical education, the study of human anatomy, biomechanics, motor control/learning, and exercise-physiology form the building blocks of most university studies and our ways of thinking about human function and behaviour.

The privileging of scientific discourses gains strength when this biophysical knowledge of human form, function and behaviour is assumed to serve society by addressing health-related issues, daily functional needs and elite sporting interests. Because it is assumed to have consumer value, scientific knowledge about the body, health and exercise is valued by a market-driven higher education sector. It is knowledge that can be transformed into *economic capital* in the form of grants or industry-funded services. As such it has established and maintains a privileged position in our university faculties. It is now a form of *cultural capital*, which is symbolically valued for its marketability. But how informative is this reductionist biophysical knowledge for a broad understanding of physical culture?

Following a general reflection about the place of physical culture in universities, I draw on my research project to exemplify how the *field* of physical culture was represented and contested in my own university during the time of our institutional restructuring. I reflect on how physical culture has come to be represented in higher education and how and why it has been 'captured' by scientific ways of knowing due to the *logic of practice* of many university departments and academics.

The *logic of practice* underpinning physical culture in universities

I take a philosophical position that the *field* of sport and exercise science and that of health and physical education are different and therefore should occupy different *social spaces* within the broader *social space* of higher education. The *logics of practice* underpinning the *fields* of health and physical education as an educational practice and sport and exercise science as a sub-discipline *field* of the natural sciences represent different ways of viewing and examining physical culture in university contexts. In a Bourdieuian sense, the close relationship between the two is due to the blurring of the boundaries between their different *logics of practice*, but if we are to retain the *social space* to study and practise both forms of physical culture then the differences between them must be understood by those who hold the power to constitute university *fields*.

Universities consist of multiple overlapping *fields* that are most often defined by the traditional discipline *fields* of the arts, science, medicine, education, engineering and law, etc. Within these discipline *fields*, it is possible to identify many of the sub-discipline *fields* of physical culture, such as sport science, human movement, physical education and dance, for example. Each of these has their own defining *logic of practice*. The boundaries between these and other sub-discipline *fields* of physical culture, like all social *fields*, are determined by the points at which their underpinning *logics of practice* cease to influence the daily work of the participants who inhabit them. The boundaries between these *fields* are not fixed but always in a state of flux as social forces from within and outside the *field* contest their very logic. As well as the numerous institutional and social forces from beyond the boundaries that impact on the *field*, the academics, through their daily *practice*, are engaged in implementing strategies to gain control of the underpinning logic. All of these academics have their own ways of representing themselves, as they strive to strengthen their self-interests and differentiate their *social space* from that of others.

Bourdieu argued that over time the *logic of practice* of a *field*, such as a *field* of physical culture, becomes so deeply embodied in individuals that it operates at a subconscious taken-for-granted level. Once deeply embedded in both the institutional structures and the individuals who associate with the *field*, its power to influence and impose a form of cultural dominance within the *social space* of the *field* is often misrecognised due to its familiarity. In such cases a state of homogeny is established between the *field* and the individuals. This state of homogeny creates a form of cohesion or, as Bourdieu termed it, a state of '*doxa*', that is the conditions of unquestioned adherence between the *field* and its inhabitants. A *doxic* state can, in turn, lead to the condition of '*illusio*', which is the condition that exists when someone, such as an academic, has so much investment and belief in the logic of their own *practice* (through their qualifications, status, and research history) that this logic establishes a powerful stranglehold on the individual. This logic is then most often left unquestioned and, indeed, deemed by those under its hold to be unquestionable. It is a logic that is passed from individual to individual through their everyday interaction and cultural *practices*. In this way, academics can acquire a sense of ownership of and a professional identity with 'their *field*'. Their whole professional status, life investment and personal identity become attached to it, so much so that a threat to the social dynamics of the *field* is viewed as a threat to them personally.

The status attributed to the different *subfields* of physical culture within the *social space* of higher education plays an important role in determining how universities frame the knowledge production about physical culture. In recent decades, universities have adopted the logic of increased accountability, via research and publication outputs, which in turn reflect a market-driven *logic of practice*. Within this accountability environment, the research outputs of academics provide the means and grounds for state funding bodies to assess and allocate funds to universities. It follows that the closer the *field*'s research practice is linked to the broader economic goals of governments, the more government funding support it can expect. In Bourdieuian language, the more a university's *cultural capital* is able to be transformed into *economic capital*, the more government funding it is likely to attract. Given this direct linking of *cultural* with *economic capital*, it is not difficult to understand why the more industry-related scientific discourses have been privileged in our universities. Scientific knowledge has more *symbolic value,* enabling it to gain better access to funding than the research and knowledge of the less directly connected *subfields* of the humanities. Ultimately, scientific research as a form of *cultural capital* enables those academics who possess it to impose cultural arbitrary on the *field* of physical culture in higher education. In this way these academics have a form of power that enables them to further privilege their own scientific research practices in universities.

The way in which the natural sciences dominate most university practice exemplifies how we have come to accept the way that the higher education game is played. It is, as Bourdieu argues, a form of *symbolic violence,* that is, a form of domination that is exercised upon social agents with the help of their own blind complicity (Bourdieu and Wacquant 1992). It is made possible in university faculties because many university academics accept the world as it is, finding scientific method natural because in most cases it is derived from the very structures of the scientific world in which they had their grounding (Bourdieu and Wacquant 1992). The fact is that today, in our market-driven universities, scientific-research outputs are the valued currency.

The research context – exemplifying different *logics of practice*

I now draw on my research findings to exemplify how I used Bourdieu's theorising to interpret the competing views of the HPE academics and two members of the faculty leadership during the restructuring process.

When the College of Education was merged into the university in September 2004 we, the teacher educators, found ourselves in a completely different *social space.* Much of our *cultural* and *symbolic capital* had been devalued, and with it our sense of professional identity and status. As an established group of physical education teacher educators we shared a common *habitus* that had been embodied over a long period of time, and this was now being threatened. Bourdieu argued that embodying a *logic of practice* is a significant investment in the *cultural practices* of a *field* and a threat to this from outsiders is often greeted with resistance and a sense of loss.

On the surface, a move of physical education teacher education (PETE) to a faculty of science could be viewed merely as an institutional restructuring, but such a view does not capture the tensions involved in merging the different *logics of practice* of different *fields.* The *logic of* our *practice* was very different from that of sport and exercise science. In short, our PETE *logic of practice* was underpinned by expert practitioner knowledge, the practice of quality teaching, and our service to the teaching profession. We were physical educators, not sports scientists. Our *symbolic capital* was derived from our position as teacher educators in higher education and our highly valued position within the teaching profession more generally. On the other hand, the sport scientists embodied a *logic of practice* that was underpinned by a science-based research culture. Their *symbolic capital* was deeply connected to their academic status acquired through their research history and titled position within the academic *field* of sport and exercise science.

Using ethnomethodology, I monitored the actions of key players in this merger over a three and a half year period. This was made possible because of my everyday onsite contact within the natural settings over a long period of time, an approach advocated by Alverson and Skoldberg (2000). I constantly drew on Bourdieu's theory of *practice* throughout the process.

Early on in the research, I found that the sport and exercise scientists and we, the teacher educators, were able to see clearly the different *logics of practice* underpinning our respective *fields*. Both groups were able to draw definite boundaries between the two *fields* and both were determined to retain the *logic of practice* of their own *field*. A merger was not desired by either party. However, the university and faculty leaders, as outsiders to both *fields*, could not see the problem. They believed that the similarities outnumbered the differences. Both philosophically and economically it made sense to them to merge the two. Consequently, while we argued to retain our professional practice in the *social space* of the Faculty of Education, the faculty leaders found it difficult to support our view, seeing some form of collaboration as more desirable.

I use the following examples to exemplify some of the ensuing power struggles between the two parties. The first example is the view of two HPE academics and is used here to capture the essence of the HPE group's stance. The second shows the different stance taken by the faculty leadership team.

When it was announced that the BPE programme and staff were to move to the Department of Sport and Exercise Science, we presented the faculty leadership team with this statement:

> Physical education is not sports science. It is concerned with the pedagogy and practice of educating young people about body use, body care, and the fostering of physical competence that underpins all human learning. Therefore, physical education must be based clearly within the Faculty of Education, not the Faculty of Science.
>
> (Centre for Health and Physical Education Submission
> to Joint Task Force 2003)

Later in the process Brian, one of the HPE academics, wrote to the faculty leadership, stating that when sport science and physical education are combined:

> most often [they have] morphed into sports science or human movement studies or kinesiology … and staff have shifted from being physical educationalists to seeing themselves as scientists or sociologists or historians etc. So that, with time, the heart that centres on teaching and learning that takes place in schools disappears…
>
> (Brian's letter to Dean 1/4/05)

He continued this in a later statement during an interview with me, adding:

> I suspect that it's [the reason they want to shift us to sport science] a deep prejudice against physical education by the academics in the School of Education which has fed that prejudice, which is prevalent in the managers [here], so they can say, 'Well we can dismiss physical education.' I mean, I think it comes right from the Deputy Vice-Chancellor who said 'Oh no. Phys Ed can go straight to sports science.' They immediately just see it as being sport and, you know, they see it as something that's quite peripheral to the main function of education.
>
> (Personal Interview, 4/05)

I also interviewed David, another of the HPE academics, seeking his view of the two *fields*, and he responded:

> I make the distinction between the scientific basis of PE and sports science because one of the comments is that we may shift some of our science-based, if you like our bio-physical foundations of PE, to a sports science area of the university. Now to me, that's completely incompatible and shows a lack of understanding of what PE is. We are firmly grounded in education. It's inherent in everything we do and implicit in everything we do. It's education of the physical through the physical. It's not about sports science; it's not about some clinical-medical model of anatomy, physiology, or ruminations of how the body works. It's about the body in physical activity and human movement. It's quite a specialised field that we ground our teachers in, in order to make them aware of the role of the bio-physical foundations of their subject in a teaching construct. It's not about sports, it's not about medicine; it's a model which is enshrined in education; it's TE, it's PE and TE.
>
> (Personal Interview, 6/03)

It is clear that both Brian and David identify with the *field* of PETE. They embody the *logic of practice* of the *field* and present a sense of pride and ownership of it. Brian's argument to retain PETE in a faculty of education serves to demonstrate how his embodied history of experience, his *habitus*, strengthens his feeling and emotional ties to the *field* and perhaps at the same time pressures him to dismiss other ways of viewing it. This is what Bourdieu (1977, 1980/1990) referred to as a state of *doxa*, a state of unquestioned attachment to and respect for a *field*. Brian also presents the conditions of *illusio*: a history of investment and acquired status within the *field*. He wrote to the 'management' in an effort to retain the status quo not just of the *field* but also his place within it. However, in Brian's argument we read more than mere self-interest and the conditions of *illusio*. As an insider to the *field*, he was able to offer an otherwise unforeseen 'illumination' when he argued 'when the two fields are merged they often morph into sport science … and the teaching and learning that takes place in schools disappears'. It is a vision that perhaps only an insider with a history of knowledge and the *habitus* of the *field* can see.

As a point of difference, consider now the view of the faculty leadership team at the time; firstly, the view of the Dean of Faculty. I asked the Dean if he had discussed a possible merging of PETE with sport and exercise science at higher levels during the negotiation process and he replied:

> Yes, we were certainly aware of the link between physical education and sports science. In terms of the extent of it and how it would develop, there were no details discussed around that…
>
> (Personal Interview, 6/06)

I also asked him if he was concerned that the essence of the BPE programme may be lost if it was merged into the sport and exercise science programme. He replied:

> I don't know that we really thought too much about that. I don't think anybody got quite as sort of specific as that … That said, I suppose if you asked most people who were not necessarily Phys Ed specialists … I suspect that the answer would come back in that area of science more than any other.
>
> (Personal Interview, 6/06)

When I responded by saying that the sport and exercise science discipline and the health and physical education discipline were totally different, the Dean replied:

> Now it's natural once you merge with another institution, you tend to view things in terms of, well these people are not going to come and take anything we've got and I can understand that kind of thing, but I think you've got to build a bridge and get over it. At the end of the day, we're now part of this big institution that probably can contribute a great deal to what we do here…
>
> (Personal Interview, 6/06)

I then interviewed the Associate Dean of Faculty. I asked him for his stance on the HPE academics' argument that sport and exercise science and health and physical education are totally different. His response was very similar to the Dean's:

> To me, that's your constraint. I think that it's a psychological barrier. I have a sense that the barrier is one where people do feel, as you're describing it, as a real difference. I think it's a psychological difference. It does worry me that we're not going to make the best of the opportunity to pull those two things together because we're sitting in, it seems to me, opposing camps to some extent and making demands of each other or not, as the case may be.
>
> (Personal interview, 3/05)

We read here that the Dean and Associate Dean presented an argument for some form of collaboration between the two discipline areas. In their argument they dismissed the 'insiders', viewed as being self-centred and a psychological barrier to the greater opportunities the merger offered. Naturally they were viewing the *field* of physical culture in our university from their positions of responsibility to the university, but what they could not see was how a merging of the two *fields* had the potential to redefine the *logic of practice* of PETE within the university. They were not able to see the *field* of PETE with the same subtlety as Brian and David had when they said physical education is not about sports science, it is an educational process.

Discussion: how has Bourdieu helped my understanding of the situation?

I turn now to explain how Bourdieu helped my understanding of this situation. He did this in two important ways.

In the first instance Bourdieu helped with his relational concepts of *field, habitus* and *capital. Field* and *habitus* explain the inextricable link between the constraints imposed on all individuals by the structured world in which we live and the agency afforded them by the structuring process of their daily *practices*. The third element, *capital*, recognises the stakes involved and the reasons one acts to contest the nature of a *field. Field, habitus* and *capital* are thinking tools that provide a conceptual language that enables us to engage in a form of reflexive consciousness about our social world. When we understand the relationship between the three we are better able to recognise and interpret the significance of our everyday *logic of practice*. In this research project it allowed me to recognise that the sport scientists, the university leaders and we, the physical educators, were differently positioned and, more importantly, how we were all, in different ways, coloured by our own *habitus*. Our differently structured external and internal worlds positioned us to interpret the process of change with different interests at heart. The different *logics of practice* that underpinned sport and exercise science versus health and physical education were deeply embodied in the individuals and collectives who practised in these very different *fields of practice*. This *logic of practice* is, as Bourdieu explains, much deeper than can be explained by any rational discourse.

Bourdieu also argued that our social world is made up of a multitude of hierarchically or comparably positioned, overlapping *fields*. The power to influence and determine the *logic of practice* of one's own *field* is often dependent on this *field*'s relationship with others. As I learnt during this restructuring process, this was certainly the case with my own *field* of PETE. The politico-economic forces driving the world of higher education and the hierarchically positioned rationalising agenda of the university and faculty leaders enabled them to determine the way that PETE was viewed during the restructuring process.

A second level of analysis was made possible using Bourdieu's more critical tools of analysis, *doxa, illusio, misrecognition* and *symbolic violence*. These conceptual tools provided a language for understanding our different levels of frustration and anxiety during the change process. During the process of negotiating change, these tools empowered us to engage more productively in the restructuring struggles by bringing our state of being, our *habitus*, i.e. our subconscious, to a level of consciousness. Our state of *doxa* and *illusio* within our *field* explained why we held so tightly to our different points of view and why we fought so hard to retain our ways of practising, but just as importantly they also explained why the faculty leaders could not see what we could see.

Fields of physical culture, in universities and elsewhere are, like all social *fields*, constituted by contestable physical and social constraints and the conditioning of our *habitus*. In this research project, I set out to interpret and purposefully engage in the restructuring process. Bourdieu's social theory provided me with the conceptual tools I needed to achieve these goals. I am pleased to conclude that today, in our institution, PETE remains and is thriving in the Faculty of Education, albeit with some restructuring, and it is still focused on the teaching and learning that occurs in schools, as Brian, David and I, along with my fellow teacher educators, would have it.

4 'Stop': 'No'.

Exploring social suffering in practices of surfing as opportunities for change

lisahunter

Keywords: *Surfing, ethnography, photography, logics of practice, symbolic violence*

Why study cultures, subcultures, physical cultures or *practices* within *social space*? There will be many different answers, even amongst those in this book, but for me it has been about understanding human *practices*, why humans do what they do, particularly in terms of access to participation in a better life. As academic work, for me it is also about how I might contribute to a better life. This evokes words such as human rights, recognition, equity and liberty; concepts steeped in social hierarchies and their mechanisms. I came to Bourdieu's work quite by accident while researching the (problematic) mechanisms of schooling for students transitioning from primary to secondary school (Hunter 2002). Richard Light suggested that bodily *hexis* and *habitus* were concepts that might have explanatory power to help me understand what might be going on in the transition project. Now, for me, Bourdieu's work is a heuristic framework made up of a set of conceptual utensils that have methodological and theoretical bite for my work. This framework can provide initial readings of the world and also a way to plan for change through my research. I say 'initial readings' because his utensils have helped me to 'think' with him, but also beyond and against him, as was his invitation (Bourdieu and Wacquant 1992: xiv). Others' ontologies, epistemologies, theories and methodologies also thread through my perceptions, affects and communications, sometimes in parallel and sometimes in sharp contrast to Bourdieu, depending on the research question at hand. Michael Grenfell notes that 'Bourdieu's concepts have no value if they are not used in practice' (2008: 5). My academic work, and very possibly my everyday lived experiences, work with, beyond and against Bourdieu, as I illustrate below.

In the research project that I draw on for this chapter, I had deliberately set out, as a research (and therefore political) act, to 'recognise' low capital[1] surfing whilst investigating the research object – surfing. At the same time I was trying to unpack the way surfing was constructed using Bourdieu's methodological approach to studying the *field* (Bourdieu and Wacquant 1992: 104-5). I accept research as political: what we research, the questions we ask, the findings that are recorded or memor(ial)ised, the paradigms and authors' work we choose to embody in our research practice, is political. Previous research and literature that has highlighted the *fields* of power that operate in surfing have focused on male views, participation and histories, particularly dominant/dominating Caucasian, Western and, more recently, the shortboard form. Much less is known of 'others'. By 'known' I mean available, recognised, documented, and by 'others' I mean explored by and of 'others', in the general perception of society and in research. This 'less' is in terms of *capital* accrual and *field* positioning by 'others', less in terms of quantity of what is known about 'others', and less in terms of their access to participation. An individual's enjoyment of an activity and their mental or physical access to participation can be influenced by such factors as an absence from the received history of 'people like them' (e.g. female or indigenous), inequity and physical and *symbolic violence* towards particular social classes (e.g. female or indigenous). Surfing ultimately acts as another '*field*' that perpetuates sets of violences to particular social groups. The challenge for my boarding projects was to enhance recognition and participation for those lower in the social hierarchies – in the case of this chapter, for females in surfing. While the project is still ongoing, this paper presents aspects of one event where the *logics of practice* from the *field* of surfing converged with two mediating *fields*: *business* in the form of the surf industry, and *media*. The event took place in what I consider to be a conglomerate *subfield* (Bourdieu 1987/1994: 144) of surfing – the surfing festival.

Surfing has many forms including windsurfing, tandem, kiteboarding, skurfing, wakeboarding and skysurfing. Another form rapidly growing in popularity, Stand Up Paddling or SUP, uses a paddle that enables the board to be ridden on waves but also on flat water. Body womping, body bashing or body surfing is claimed, at least by those who do it, as the 'purest' form. However, the orthodox form that has been naturalised as 'surfing' is the activity using a standing position on a board, without the aid of other technologies, to ride water (usually sea) waves. Early forms are located in ancient and pre-European Polynesian cultures such as fa'ase'e or se'egalu in Samoa and he'e nalu or wave sliding in Hawai'i. This involved craft such as single hulled canoes, or wooden planks such as the alaia (Clark 2011) now in renaissance (*Surfer Magazine* 2010).

Waves were ridden by females and males, as ritual, courting and performance of skill, those in the ruling classes having access to the best beaches and waves. Modern surfing, a heterogeneous *field* that has developed into a recognisable *field* globally, as a form of physical culture has been influenced heavily by Hawai'ian, Californian and Australian developments over the last century. It is practised as a leisure activity, a tourism theme, a sport and a lifestyle. One of the many sites of (re)production of surfing, alongside magazines and film and websites, is the event as competition or festival. I distinguish between competition and festival by the activities that converge and constitute the event: competition being largely characterised by competition only, whereas the festival includes many other activities such as concerts, displays, athlete signings, merchandising, and often significant publicity, sponsorship and media coverage. Festivals range from relatively small-scale local events to ones that attract international competitors and spectators. One such event is the focus of this chapter, the Association of Surfing Professional's (ASP) 'Quiksilver/Roxy Pro'. This was a men's competition (which represented and was sponsored by Quiksilver) and a women's competition (which represented and was sponsored by Roxy, part of Quiksilver) joined as one. It was the first leg of the World Championship Tour for 2011 and was held on the Gold Coast, Australia.

Inspired by Pierre Bourdieu's commitment to public political scholarship and as part of a long-term project across several sites of *field* production, I was photographing the female competitors in action with a mind to identifying and positively influencing their positioning within the *field*, that is, creating more visibility as competent athletes in both the public media *field* (e.g. lisahunter 2006a; lisahunter 2011a, 2011b) and the research *field* (e.g. lisahunter and Austin 2008b; lisahunter 2013). I was working from earlier findings (Booth 2001; Comer 2004; Henderson 2001; lisahunter 2006b; Stedman 1997) and more recent findings (Franklin 2013; lisahunter and emerald 2013; Olive, McCuaig and Phillips 2013) that concurred about female positioning – females in surfing have either been absent as competent athletes or sexually objectified. I considered females/women as one simplified, and powerfully contained, form of *social class*, 'sets of agents who occupy similar positions and who, being placed in similar conditions and subjected to similar conditionings, have every likelihood of having similar dispositions and interests and therefore of producing similar practices and adopting similar stances' (Bourdieu 1985: 725). In this way females are people with a signifier that creates group classification and positioning within a social *field,* normalised by a Western Eurocolonised patriarchy. My practice was attempting to counter what I understood to be a form of *symbolic violence*. For example, as an indicator of the positioning of women, previous festival visits had revealed that many of the media cameras were often put down during the female rounds of competition.

In the lead up to the event, during and after the festival I collected a wide array of field texts (Clandinin and Connelly 2000). In this chapter, the research text (Clandinin and Connelly 2000) draws on two of these field texts, a condensed diary entry and a photograph. These provide an illustration of *practice* from the *field* and for further discussion, drawing on Bourdieu's utensils.

'Stop'. 'No': Logics actualised in practice (from a condensed visual diary entry)

I'm settled again, as the workers take away the black shelter they've just packed up, having replaced it with the pink one that signals we will be moving from the men's heats to the women's. Sheltered spots are hard to find and harder to create alone when parking was so far away and I was lugging camera gear, lenses, chairs, clothing for all weathers and laptop to the beach. Not all this gear is mine though, and what is has cost me a bomb. My lens envy grows. The 600mm beside me, owned by the bloke from the big surfing mag, sits idle and I wish I could be bold enough to ask for a go. Through my lens I sight several more 600's sitting idle as the women's heats get under way. My more distant shots will have to do. Nothing is happening in the surf yet, not a good point in the tide. Click. I'll look at what the media are doing around the beach. The big screen shows a high camera angle of two women walking along the beach in their bikinis. Click. The wind is getting up and the surf isn't providing many good rides for the competitors to show their skill at all. Click. I continue plotting how I can get a 600mm lens. My fantasy breaks.

The cells in every part of my body are on edge with a rush of adrenalin. I keep my finger on the shutter release of my camera for several shots and then rip my hand but not my eyes away. I freeze. I want to yell out 'stop' but I'm fixed to my gear and the loose sand that seems to shackle me under the pink tent. Motionless I consider leaving my gear to get the version of events by those who are in my lens. The spectator telling the cameraman to stop filming her has resisted the position 'victim' and been agentic, but with little impact. The perpetrator keeps his lens on her, despite her hand indicating that he should stop. He and his camera is only about a metre away from her hand. He smiles.

'Bastard' I catch myself saying. My discomfort has me questioning my lack of action in following up the incident and my anger and disappointment at witnessing what has just happened. No one seemed to support the woman who resisted having her image sent around the world. No one had intervened to stop the filming, other than the female indicating he should stop. The female interviewer continued to scan beachgoers for possible interview candidates. She did not reprimand the cameraman who had not asked permission for what he did. Perhaps she did not even notice. Perhaps she was just lucky to have the job so chose not to ruffle feathers. The three sitting nearby watched on in the same way they watched the competitors. It was all entertainment. We were all complicit. Why did no one act to support her? I remember the story of the woman raped outside a set of apartments where lots of residents heard her cries for help, but no one acted.

Making sense of practice

Returning to 'Bourdieu's concepts have no value if they are not used in practice' (Grenfell 2008: 5), what follows is a discussion of the *practice* that I refer to as 'Stop': 'No'. In the festival *social space* my *practices*, and the *practices* of others within it or contributing to it, revealed a *doxa* and an orthodoxy. No-one defended the woman's right not to be filmed, a choice explained by the relationship between media and the public in a public place, and perhaps by the 'healthy heterosexual male gaze'. The mutual reinforcement between the *subfield* of the festival and *habitus* was captured in the malaise of the situation and the tacit approval by all agents other than, and despite, the woman resisting. Our perceptions and *practices* reinforced the *symbolic power* of the media-business-surfing relationship in this space, so that the cameraman's *practice* appeared acceptable. I say 'appeared' as there was no action by anyone to disrupt the incident, but also note that doing nothing is doing something. The 'natural' legitimacy gave the cameraman permission, firstly to select and film anyone on the beach for international broadcast[2] without their consent, and secondly to continue, despite implied tacit consent being withdrawn, as per this example. The broadcast images were routinely of particular bodies, bikinied women that might attract the normal label of 'sexy', and routinely as pieces of women, that is, breasts, faces, and bottoms. His photographic roving and the choice of what was broadcast was illustrative of what might be legitimated as a form of *symbolic capital* (Bourdieu), as *physical capital* (Shilling 1993, 2004), in terms of appearance, through the powerfully positioned media.

Could anyone have done what he did? Could he have demonstrated such *practices* without having the authority of 'official media'? What are the social circumstances within which this *practice* was embedded that made the outcome a possibility? I reflected upon this for some time afterwards, as well as reflecting on the ethics of me making an image of her resisting an image being taken and why I did not act, hence contributing another layer to the violence enacted upon the spectator.

Symbolic power was embedded in the cameraman as a recognized embodiment of an institution, the media, whose relationship with the public at an event such as this was one that brought acceptance by competitors, organisers and sponsors and by most beachgoers/spectators. There was a further presence of *symbolic power* in the other 'officials', underwritten by the council that had given the permission for the event to take place in that space. Although oblivious to the contract, most of us attending the event 'bought in' to this power structure, or at least were expected to.

The symbolic form of power, the *doxa*, at work in this site is a mix of an unconditional allegiance of patriarchy and capitalism. *Doxa* is 'an orthodoxy, a right, correct, dominant vision which has more often than not been imposed through struggles against competing visions' (Bourdieu 1998a: 56). The assumed permission to film/photograph women illustrated in 'Stop': 'No' is thereby dismissed as healthy heteronormativity rather than other explanations such as *symbolic violence* in the form of sexual objectification, visual rape, exploitation of a *social class*, commodification, or aggressive space taking. I hear a cacophony of 'Wouldn't any red blooded man want to film a good looking woman?'. Apart from the woman's gesture that destabilized this assumption, we also have to unpack 'What sort of man?' 'Why would he need to look at her rather than the man next to her?', 'What is it about her that means he wants to look?', 'Why her and not other people who are distinctive by their height, age, towel colour or any other arbitrary marker of difference?'. The list could go on to reveal the 'lateral possibles' (Bourdieu 1998a: 57) that have been eliminated as arbitrarily nonsensical or unlikely. What is constituted as acceptable, normal or common sense *practice* no longer has to explain itself or its *violences*, an ultimate display of *doxa* and its *symbolic power*. Looking beyond the immediacy of 'Stop': 'No', there were other relational clues outside the frame of the picture to help make sense of 'What is going on here?'. It is these to which I now turn, to then consider implications for action.

Relational practice

By recognising the cameraman as having the right to film people, putting aside for now the specifics of who and how, we at the scene were all endorsing an objective structural relationship between media and the public through our individual *subjectivities*. No doubt some people avoided media attention, for example those that may have taken a 'sickie'[3] to attend the event on a workday. Others were working to attract the attention of the media for wider recognition of their products, such as the strategic placement of advertisements at points where cameras would often be focussing. Others were even more direct at getting noticed, such as the peripheral spectators who 'photobombed' celebrity interviews, that is, placed themselves in the camera's gaze. To refuse that relationship transgressed the *practices* naturalised through the media *field*, in this case supported by a big player in the surfing industry, Quiksilver, in partnership with the city council. How can a beachgoer/spectator place themselves in opposition to that powerful allegiance? Who has what power?

Practices of this cameraman and several others, in collusion with the editor, were such that female breasts and bottoms or particularly sexualised representations of females were common portrayals of spectators on the public screen and the webcast. This is not to write out other camera targets: children playing in the water, spectators mobbing around superstar-status surfers, wide angled shots of the whole beach, 'people of interest' such as competitors' families or celebrities. There was, however, a theme of the sexual objectification of women. Some women seemed to accept and take pleasure in the attention, embodying the 'if you've got it you gotta use it' and 'sex sells' attitudes of self-objectification (Harrison and Fredrickson 2003: 217). The corporate sexualisation employed by Quiksilver and its subsidiaries Roxy and

Quiksilver for Women has been increasingly explicit, with certain female surfers receiving greater attention from sponsors and media. While not all can stay on the professional circuit due to a lack of sponsorship, others trade their sexualized appearance for media attention and therefore sponsorship, or become bound in their sponsorship to provide a certain image (Franklin 2013). *Physical capital* in terms of sexualized appearance (PCs) is what models for female surf fashion trade. *Physical capital* in terms of competition performance results (PCp) is what world champions and those competing for 'the title' trade. *Physical capital* from both sources (PCsp) proves to be substantial for surfers such as Stephanie Gilmore, one of the faces, and bodies, for Roxy. Some would encourage this orthodoxy as a form of third wave or stealth feminism (Heywood 2008) where athletes can be sexy *and* athletic. An alternative reading could be that the *habitus* of women who are able to access PCs to trade for *economic capital* (models, some surfers, sexy females), in an economy of sex and a *doxa* of patriarchy where sexual appearance is valued as *physical capital*, are embodying a complementary illusion about their influence on the *field* and 'for women'. This illusion is in terms of asymmetrical relations in sex/gender/ sexuality, as part of the *doxa* of the *field*. Recognizing the *field* of social relations and exploiting those relations for individual gain may seem strategic, but plays into *doxa* that makes 'Stop': 'No' possible as an unusual act of resistance or an erased incident. I would argue it is the same illusion that results in less access to sponsorship and prize money for female surfers relative to males, and for some female surfers over others based on their 'fit' to the idealised female surfer *habitus*/look (lisahunter 2006;, Franklin 2013), in the verbal and physical violences of sexism in the water when going for waves[4] (lisahunter in press) or in the peripheral spaces such as beach car parks (Olive, McCuaig and Phillips 2013), in relegating the female heats of mixed competitions to the poorer waves (lisahunter 2013; Franklin 2013), and in continuing to represent females as body parts for sexual pleasure.

The cultural valuation of female appearance/beauty/sex over athletic achievement reflects a 'superficiality and marketing impulse behind most mass cultural visual images of women and surfing' (Comer 2004: 246). Perhaps we are seeing a reversal of the third wave suggested by Anita Harris (2008), amongst others. Such a 'wave' noticed greater opportunities for girls and women from the increasingly available fractured subjectivities and fluid identities where essentialist identities no longer operated as discrete binaries, such as femininity and masculinity. Leslie Heywood's notion of stealth feminism (2008: 71) 'draws attention to key feminist issues and goals without provoking the knee-jerk social stigmas attached to the word "feminist".' While she suggested that 'sports like women's surfing and their practitioners' negotiations with their attendant representations articulate a decidedly "third-wave" or "stealth feminist" perspective … a more blended strategy' (2008: 71), quoting the strategy described by Comer (2004: 241). 'embracing and valuing "girl-ness" at the same time as one aims to achieve at the highest level'. If 'girlness' can only be valued as PCs, a strategy not required by males and a strategy not available to all females, the question remains whether sexual appearance and socially constructed beauty are at all a worthy *capital* to legitimate and pursue in the *field* of surfing, for the benefit of the *field* and an increasing access to participation regardless of *habitus*.

Reflections: The efficacy of Bourdieu's work

Pierre Bourdieu has clearly had a salient influence on my *practice*. He has provided me with not just a language to think with (Grenfell 2008), but also a language of epistemological and methodological *practice*. This works through the sorts of questions I ask and research of my world, to methods of constructing and analysing field texts, and to dissemination and action from research. His *reflexive* method has also contributed to me questioning my own *habitus* and research practices, including embodying to some extent 'dead Eurocentric white male' practices. I say this without disrespect to Pierre Bourdieu, but rather to acknowledge that he was a product of his timespace, as am I, and both as agents in our worlds. I use the phrase 'dead Eurocentric white male' only to call attention to the ongoing dis-ease I have in continuing the aspect of his legacy I do not want to legitimize or endow *capital* upon, namely, masculine domination.

It behoves me to keep abreast of the criticisms of Bordieu's work, and my use of his work; to continuously critique my constitution by, and constitution of, the water within which I swim, my own illusion in the academic *field*. The work of this dis-ease, though, is perhaps the very challenge he threw out to those who might use his work: to also think beyond and against him. His demonstration of working praxically with empirical evidence, his work to provide epistemologies outside Cartesian dualism, his focus on *bodily hexis*, his acts of resistance, his thinking utensils, his focus on social phenomena or *practice* and its resultant suffering, his theoretical framework that recognizes complexity and also our limits of recognition, and his challenges to our academic work all offer me starting points to elucidate social processes, suppose one's own participation in them, and consider future *agency*. Work from other scholars and my ongoing research/life experiences act as ongoing heuristics to Bourdieu's.

I imagine a world where being physical and participating in physical culture is not limited by social positioning, exploitation of and by others, legitimation of only certain identities, or the lack of socially deemed volume and type of *capitals*. Perhaps somewhat idealistically, I would argue that my imagined sociophysical space is better than where we are currently. Social suffering need not be the result of physical (sub)cultures, especially in highly privileged societies where abundant resources could be more equitably redistributed to enhance participation. Claims of gains in *capitals* often attributed to surfing, through positive lifestyle, good health, enjoying nature, enhanced spirituality or even a motivation to compete for financial profit, need not be with the negative outcomes of exploitation, marginalization or unimaginable *habitus* for some. Ongoing recognition, investigations and interventions into how surfing might practice equity and liberty for enhanced participation seem to herald a brighter future for the physical culture than the perpetuated violences currently taken for granted. Bringing Bourdieu's work into the mix provides a useful heuristic for participation.

The very nature of the concept of *field* suggests orthodoxy of *practices*, but only in so far as *habitus*, individual or group, resists change or reproduces the status quo. Investment in status quo by the winners wishing to remain winners, at the expense of the losers, is not an easy thing to change. Choosing change, for the redistribution of access to participation in surfing, free from physical and *symbolic violence*, that is to 'do otherwise'. Exploring ways to reveal *doxa* in order to then plan for the mutual (*habitus* and *field*) constitution of 'otherwise' is what I think is the point of Bourdieu's work. The conglomerate *subfield* of surfing festivals may have orthodox *practices*, but understanding these and their mechanisms reveals ruptures for exploitation or structures to break.

Inspired by the woman embodying 'Stop', we need to keep exploring ways to liberate individuals and groups from dominant imposing forces that create social suffering and *symbolic violence*. Re-viewing *physical capital* for females as holistic performance or athletic participation as opposed to the body-parts object of the sexual gaze of heterosexual males may create an alternate *doxa* that entails less suffering. My only role this time has been to expose the *symbolic violence* to you, publicly applaud 'her' actions and, after reflection upon my paralysis at the time, consider what a more direct challenge might be in future encounters. My academic and gendered conflict avoidance and physically small stature *habitus* may well temper all my *practice*: I tend to assume I can have minimal impact on the reduction of violence in surfing. 'What could I have done or what could I do?' is the topic for a whole other paper about participant *objectivation*, the *reflexivity* central to Bourdieu's work (1990; Bourdieu and Wacquant 1992). Playfully, I imagine I could investigate the intent and rights of, and with, the individuals involved. I could attract attention to the *symbolic violence* by racing down the beach, kicking sand in the cameraman's face and hitting him with my camera, but for all sorts of reasons I 'know' that exposing *symbolic violence* with physical violence might not go so well for any of us! I could distribute huge posters of the 'Stop': 'No' image around the next Quiksilver/Roxy Pro festival (would anyone like to help fund this project or act as my lawyer?). Or I could… Time to get out and *practice*!

Acknowledgements

Thanks to elke emerald, Wayne Smith, and Ros Franklin for feedback on this chapter.

Notes

1 I acknowledge that there are other classes with low capital and positioning in surfing, for example indigenous, queer, black, poor, etc and that intersectionality is an important aspect in understanding the mechanisms and outcomes of domination. However, for the purpose of this chapter I am only focusing on sex/gender as a starting point for what needs to be a more substantial exploration in another timespace.

2 Footage from this roving camera and fixed cameras situated around the beach and competition area was relayed via the web and a live television coverage of the event. It was also shown on a giant screen several stories high on the beach.

3 A colloquial term for taking an illegitimate sick day from work in order to attend to what is often a leisure or pleasurable activity.

4 Female surfers, no matter their skill level, routinely report being 'dropped in on' by male surfers. This is a form of bullying whereby one surfer takes the wave that, by rights of the etiquette of the surf line-up, belongs to another surfer.

5 Bourdieu in the changing room

Toni O'Donovan, Rachel Sandford and David Kirk

> **Keywords:** *Changing room, locker room, body, physical education*

Introduction

Getting changed for physical education is a ubiquitous feature of secondary school experience for many young people. Fusco (2004) argues that the 'common sense' understanding of changing rooms might suggest that they are relatively unremarkable spaces and that they are used and managed in seemingly insignificant ways. However, in this chapter we draw upon the work of Bourdieu, in particular his concepts of *field*, *capital* and *habitus*, to identify the changing room as a site of juncture between a number of core *fields* (principally schooling, physical education and physical culture) and thus we argue that as a 'changing place' (both literally and metaphorically) changing rooms are in fact highly charged transitional spaces. Moreover, we argue that the changing room can be perceived as a value-laden site in which the proximity to other bodies facilitates (perhaps even necessitates) a process of comparison, surveillance and self-regulation. Fusco (2006) asks in these moments of undress, what is experienced?

In this chapter, we present a narrative account of the functioning of the changing room at the fictional Highcliffe School and the social processes that take place within it, representing both pupil and teacher views about changing rooms. In constructing this narrative we draw upon the voices of girls aged 11 to 14 years, their respective teachers and excerpts from researcher field diaries generated as part of three distinct research projects in six secondary schools across the Midlands and North of England.[1] Although subtle differences in the functioning of the changing rooms were evident across the six sites in which the data for this narrative was generated, we highlight here the striking commonalities that also existed. These descriptions weave together the researchers' field notes and the voices of students and teachers.

> Highcliffe School has redeveloped itself over the past year, but the changing facilities remain rather unpleasant. They 'aren't nice places to be', there are

no windows and pupils often complain that 'they stink'. The changing room is also quite small, which 'puts some people off doing PE because they don't like being squashed and having to get changed with lots of people there'. Interestingly, the Head of PE is somewhat dismissive of these concerns, arguing that the changing rooms 'aren't the nicest of places' but don't really need to be as they 'are just somewhere to get ready from one lesson to another'. She also comments that 'for all that the pupils say they don't like them, some girls spend a hell of a lot of time in them, especially when they are getting ready to go back to lessons'. For the girls, however, the small, enclosed nature of the changing rooms is a real issue and the requirement to change into 'exposing' PE uniforms in this context is unwelcome ('We don't want to go parading around in our pants!'). One pupil confesses that in the changing rooms, 'You look around the class and compare yourself... You're just really self-conscious, you think people are going to judge you on the way that you look... When you're getting changed everybody's looking around and going "Oh my god I've not shaved my legs!"'. A friend adds, 'We're growing up you don't need people looking at you in the changing room and going "God, she's got fat legs" or "Oh she's so thin"'.

When it's time for the lesson, a familiar routine begins. The pupils queue up outside the changing room; the bell rings and the teacher unlocks the door. The pupils gradually enter the changing room. There are clearly identifiable groups (the 'girly' girls, 'sporty' girls, 'popular' girls, 'smart' girls and 'weirdoes') and pupils can be heard using these labels, often in a dismissive way, as they make their way into the space. Each pupil knows where they will go to change: the sporty girls go to the front rows where they engage in banter with their teacher; the popular and girly girls go to the back of the changing room, where they chat as they slowly get changed or until it is time to come forward and present their excuses as to why they can't take part before they then return to their social group and discuss the interaction or other pressing issues; the girls in the middle rows, meanwhile, come in, get changed quickly and try not to draw attention to themselves. The changing room routine is well established and the teacher is ready for the usual conflict. 'The school has decided to have a physical education uniform' and the teacher backs it. The pupils cannot have logos on their white t-shirts and have to wear black shorts. Some pupils ask the teacher if they can wear tracksuit bottoms because they are more comfortable, but they are told they 'have to wear your gym stuff'. The teacher is 'trying to keep up standards'. The pupils are only supposed to wear one ring and a watch. Earrings must be removed and hair must be tied up. 'It is a safety issue. These are basic PE things' and the teacher feels she has to 'hammer the rules'. If the pupils are wearing make-up, the teacher believes she should 'make them take it off'. The pupils 'push the rules' but the teacher doesn't want to let the standards slip because if she 'let it slip here it might slip at everything'. However, if the girls present notes, the teacher has few options. She questions the pupils but doesn't believe the stories she is told. Her 'hands are tied' as on presentation of a note the young people are automatically excused from the lesson and many parents are willing to write notes for their children. A sprained ankle is a favourite excuse. Once non-participation has been dealt with the teacher begins the process of negotiation about clothing, make up and jewellery. The teacher seems to have given up by the time she starts these secondary negotiations and yet they go through the familiar routine of excuse, question, secondary excuse, exasperation. She is somewhat resigned to the routine. After 11 long minutes both pupils and teacher make their way from the changing room into the gym for the lesson to finally begin.

A taken-for-granted space between fields

Despite the pupils' negative comments on the changing room as a physical space in this narrative, the teacher is somewhat dismissive of the girls' views. It would seem, therefore, that while changing rooms may function as a taken-for-granted space of physical education for teachers, possibly viewed as a somewhat sterile environment, this is not the case for pupils. We contend that attempts to acknowledge and appreciate the social and cultural spaces that constitute young people's day to day lives and, moreover, the ways in which these spaces intersect and interact, are essential if we are to gain authentic insight into their social experiences and the processes by which they come to generate understandings of both self and others (Holroyd 2003; Wright *et al.* 2003). Within this context, the sociological theory of Bourdieu, in particular his notion that the social world comprises a number of intersecting social *fields*, each with a specific structure that is based upon the differentiation and distribution of various forms of *capital* (Bourdieu 1986), has come to be viewed, particularly within the field of physical education, as a valuable means of articulating, exploring and interpreting complex social *practice* (e.g. Hunter 2004; Light 2011).

For Bourdieu, *capital* represents the 'stakes at stake' within any given *field* and, as such, is imbued with value and has the capacity to empower the holder. This is instrumental in establishing the hierarchical structure of *fields*, as individuals are positioned on the basis of both their volume and composition of these properties (Bourdieu 1985). The great value of the concept of *capital*, however, lies in its capacity for transformation or conversion, that is, the (re)investment of resources in an attempt to create *capital* with 'exchange value' (Shilling 1993). Individuals seek to maximise the quantity and quality of *capital* available to them and, through this, strive to improve or consolidate their position within a *field*. It is this that engages individuals in social struggles, both in terms of accumulation and maintenance of convertibility potential. The changing room is an interesting context to consider as it represents a transitional space both in terms of the power dynamic between the pupil-dominated informal spaces within the school (such as the playground or corridors) and the teacher-dominated spaces of the classroom, and the exchange rate of *capital* which begins to shift in the changing room as it is situated at the boundaries between the *fields*.

As such, the changing room can be viewed as a site of resistance and negotiation both between pupils who are striving to maintain or improve their position vis-à-vis others in the field, and between teachers and pupils as they each seek to pursue their own projects. Within this context, the body represents a significant resource for young people, thanks both to its visibility and relevance within this particular space and the capacity it offers to accumulate and consolidate physical *capital*. The potential for the body to become a project in this way (Shilling 1993) is explored more in the following section. Bourdieu (1993a) has suggested that the limits (boundaries) of *fields* could be thought of as being demarcated where their effects end and, when viewed in this way, the changing room can be seen to represent a complex transitional space where young people negotiate competing influences on social *practice*. Certainly, a number of *fields* can be seen to intersect within this context, for example schooling, physical culture, peer culture and the pervasive *field* of media (Holroyd 2003), each with their own structure, system of positions, valued *capital* and related *habitus*. Moreover, it is evident that, at times, the conflicting nature of social *practice* in different *fields* results in more of a collision than an intersection between fields for young people. Holroyd (2003), for example, highlights a perceived clash between the *fields* of religion and school, when she describes the anger some young women in her study felt at being banned from wearing religious jewellery in physical education lessons.

The indifference to the changing room displayed by the teacher in Highcliffe School ignores the fact that pupils remove their clothing in this space and thus – as noted by pupils in the opening narrative – expose their bodies to the gaze of others (Fisette 2011). In overlooking the importance of the changing room as a physical education space, we perhaps need to ask what informs and defines teachers' opinions about, and *practices* in, the changing room. For example, how is the body produced, transmitted and received through the changing room (for both teachers and pupils) and in what way are the teachers at Highcliffe regulating or schooling young people's bodies through the *practices* of the changing room – whether intentionally or not?

The body in the changing room

Several authors have recognised the body and its appearance as inherently linked to 'the reflexive project of the self' (Giddens 1991: 9) and have suggested that individuals are constantly engaged in the conscious management, maintenance and appearance of their 'incomplete' bodies in order to shape them in relation to their lifestyle choices and *practices* (e.g. Bourdieu 1984a; Shilling 1993). As such processes take place in very public contexts (saturated with social discourses), however, this 'body work' can perhaps more accurately be understood as being both an individual and collaborative process. As a *field* in which the development and display of bodies can be recognised as a fundamental element of *practice*, physical culture is understandably upheld as a primary site for the construction of embodied identities (Shilling 1991; Kirk 1999a; Sandford and Rich 2006). Moreover, the physical education context, as a core site within the *field* of physical culture, is viewed by many as a significant space in which young people, particularly young women, navigate and negotiate embodied understandings of self (Armour 1999; Garrett 2004; Fisette 2011). Drawing upon Bourdieu, such contexts have great significance in relation to individuals' development of *habitus* as we discuss later in the chapter.

Bourdieu (1986) argues that the role of the body in the struggle for *cultural capital* is increasingly important, and we maintain that this may be played out in a particularly significant way within the physical education changing room. There has been a growth in academic interest in the body over the past three decades, with many authors highlighting the role that the body plays in producing and reproducing social *practices* (e.g. Shilling 1991; Evans *et al.* 2004; Garrett 2004). Despite this academic interest, the reasons cited by the girls for their dislike of PE remain remarkably similar to those from yesteryear, with the wearing of PE uniform remaining high on the list (Flintoff and Scraton 2001; Gorely *et al.* 2011). Certainly, the girls whose voices are represented in our narrative articulated their dissatisfaction with their PE kit, stressing the way that it left them feeling 'exposed' and their bodies open to objectification as they got changed. In this way, the changing room again becomes a site for surveillance, where individuals' levels of *physical capital* are determined by judging bodies against socially constructed ideals; a process intensified by the challenges of puberty, requiring girls to navigate physical changes in their own bodies against those seen in others (Azzarito 2009; Fisette 2011). Bearing in mind Foucault's (1979) suggestion that power relations are apparent when bodies are on public display, it is easy to appreciate how such a process of surveillance, and the 'imaginative understandings' of how individuals *think* they are seen by others (Fisette 2011: 191), can result in the positioning of individuals in relation to their perceived levels of *physical capital* within the *field* of physical culture and, by a process of transfer, to *social capital* within the *field* of peer culture.

Our changing room narrative highlights the perceived need to manipulate bodies in line with socially constructed ideals, but it also signifies how the demand to engage in such body work varies between *fields*. The public nature of the changing room necessitates increased action in relation to constructing an appropriate embodied identity. The *field* of peers is a powerful influence seen in the physical spaces occupied by each group in the Highcliffe changing room. The need to maximise appropriate *physical capital* (through the presentation of an acceptable feminine body) and hence secure a position in relation to others (through the process of transfer to *social capital*), leads students to engage in significant negotiation about the presentation of their bodies for physical education. Authors such as Shilling (1991) and Garrett (2004) argue that the body can come to be viewed as a bearer of symbolic value and, therefore, an object both of *practice* and of power. Pervasive, influential discourses regarding 'appropriate' or 'acceptable' bodies can reproduce cultural norms or ideals and increase the pressure on individuals to engage in various types of 'body work' in order to manage the presentations of their bodies to suit a particular context (e.g. Garrett 2004). Moreover, such norms can be heavily gendered, reinforcing notions of acceptable masculine or feminine embodied identities (Paechter 2003; Azzarito 2009; Fisette 2011). The centrality of the body to the construction of identities in this way has significant implications for young people's experiences and their behaviour in different contexts. In this context, it could be argued that physical education and, specifically, the changing room as a site that exposes the body to the gaze of others, can be seen to remove some of the resources, such as make-up, jewellery and hair style, that the young people sought to use when managing the appearance of their bodies. This, subsequently, increases the level of social discomfort by reducing individuals' perceived *physical capital* and capacity to present a preferred embodied identity.

Moreover, given the overlapping and contemporaneous nature of *social fields*, it is evident that young people often have to engage in a complex process of managing the demands of competing structural influences, power dynamics and valued forms of capital when navigating the spaces located at the intersections of these sites. This is outlined in more detail in the following section.

Schooling the body for physical education

Bourdieu's focus on *habitus*, as a means by which the social world is 'written into the body', is particularly pertinent given the centrality of the body to the changing room experience. Shilling (1991) explored the links between the social construction of the body and educational practices, emphasising how such practice is inherently embodied through the *habitus*. The teacher in Highcliffe School had an established orderly and conventional routine for the changing rooms in an attempt to encourage the development of what could be understood as an appropriate physical education *habitus*. Curtner-Smith *et al.* (1999) outline how teachers in their study employed similar routines, such as getting pupils to walk in single file, thus facilitating orderly movement from the changing room to the physical education facility. In Highcliffe School many of the interactions that schooled the body revolved around the physical education uniform and ensuring that the body was presented for physical education in an appropriate way. Evidence suggests that material possessions are perceived by young people as important resources for the construction of embodied identities (e.g. Oliver and Lalik 2000). Not only is appropriate clothing deemed to signify young people's tastes and interests, but it is also a means by which they can gain significant physical (and social) *capital* among their peers. Thus changing rooms emerge as a key site for negotiation and contestation between teachers and pupils in relation to the pupils' physical presentation for PE lessons, because the image that a school uniform affords young people is often far from the 'ideal' image that counts for *physical capital* within the peer group (Holroyd 2003) and, arguably, the physical education uniform in some schools is often even further from the mark. While teachers may hold particular beliefs about how the body should be schooled for physical education, it is apparent that the young people in Highcliffe School are navigating and negotiating their own embodied identities in physical education. It could be argued, indeed, that they entered the changing room with particular projects that actively pursue the prizes or resources (*physical/social capital*) that are offered by the space. It must be questioned, however, whether the conventions of changing room practice can be perceived as worthwhile or empowering to students; particularly if, as Evans and Davies (2002) argue, young people perceive the actions of the teacher as neither necessary nor immutable. Thus we should consider the extent to which such justifications for institutional schooling in the changing room are in the pupils' interests, or even in the interests of physical education. It could be argued that the values supported by the teacher in Highcliffe School are disconnected from the values espoused by pupils and that this disconnect may be instrumental in the tensions and struggles of the physical education changing room. Evans and Davies (1986) claimed that physical education makes friends and enemies of pupils. We might reasonably ask, therefore, what damage is being done to young people's attitudes towards physical education and sport during these initial interactions in the changing room.

Closing discussion

Within this chapter, we have drawn upon Bourdieu's theory in an attempt to outline the complex social landscape of the physical education changing room, arguing that the location of this site at the intersection of various *social fields* subjects young people to a range of competing and conflicting influences on their social *practice*. In particular, we have suggested that the publicising of the body in this context heightens the perceived need for young people to manage their appearance (in line with socially constructed ideals) in order to present an appropriate and acceptable embodied identity that will allow them to consolidate or improve their social position through the generation of physical and social *capital*. We have shown, however, that this is not a straightforward process and that many young women find it difficult to engage in such 'body work' and, by extension, to negotiate a constructive physical identity within this context. Moreover, the contemporaneous nature of *fields* has been identified as representing a significant challenge for young people, requiring them to engage in a complex process of self-management as they strive to cope with the competing, and often conflicting, demands associated with appropriate *practice* in each *field*. We have argued that the relative instability of the transitional space between teacher and pupil-dominated spaces, and the highly charged nature of the changing room itself, results in inherent tensions and struggles as young people seek to mobilise various forms of *capital* to their social advantage.

We believe that it is important, therefore, that the changing room enters into the view of both physical education researchers and teachers as more than a purely physical space. Fusco (2006) has suggested that people shape, and are shaped by, the changing room and its discursive and material *practices*. Elsewhere we have argued that the negotiations in the changing room set up the tone of interactions for the entire lesson and, thus, that physical education is shaped in the discourses of the changing room (O'Donovan and Kirk 2008). Given, as illustrated within this discussion, that this space is often negatively experienced, we perhaps need to carefully consider how the pedagogical *practices* of the changing room may be having a detrimental impact on young people's involvement in physical education and what can be done to address the issue. Moreover we propose that in defamiliarising the present *practices* of the changing room, we hope to open up the changing room as a space for research on the social construction of bodies and to consider the implications of how bodies are being schooled for physical education in the changing room.

Note

1 Details of each project can be found in discussions by O'Donovan and Kirk (2008), Gorely *et al.* (2011) and Holroyd (2003).

6 Putting *habitus* to work in research on how coaches learn through experience

Identifying a coaching *habitus*

Richard L. Light and John R. Evans

Keywords: *habitus, Bourdieu, coaching, experience, rugby*

Introduction

The use of *habitus* in the coaching literature has been helpful for understanding how experience shapes coaching *practice* but the use of it to generate and analyze data in empirical research is very limited (Hassanin and Light 2013) where it is used as 'an explanation of data rather than as a way of working with it' (Reay 2004: 440). With one exception (Light and Evans 2010) the use of *habitus* in the coaching literature has been limited to an explanatory role or layered over analysis rather than being operationalized (see, for example, Taylor and Garratt 2010).

While the vagueness of *habitus* makes it difficult to identify (Jenkins 2002) and 'specify empirically' (Swartz 1997) it is, at the same time, one of its strengths because it 'follows a practical logic, that of the fuzzy, or of the more or less, which defines the ordinary relation to the world' (Bourdieu, cited Bourdieu and Wacquant 1992: 22). As Reay (1995: 357) suggests is the case in the education literature, 'paradoxically the conceptual looseness of *habitus* also constitutes a potential strength. It makes possible adaptation rather than the more constricting straightforward adoption of the concept within empirical work.' In reference to educational research she further suggests that *habitus* 'is assumed or appropriated rather than "put into practice" in research accounts, and that it is "the gravitas of *habitus*" that is desired rather than its operationalization' (Reay 1995: 440).

In this chapter we provide an example of how *habitus* can be operationalized by reporting on a study on coach development that used *habitus* as a methodological tool in the generation and analysis of data. In an inquiry into elite level rugby coaches' interpretation and use of Game Sense it sought to identify their beliefs about, and dispositions toward, learning and coaching and how this was shaped by experience in particular socio-cultural settings (Evans 2011). It identified characteristics of a 'coaching *habitus*' and sought to capture how specific experiences as players who move into coaching shape their coaching *practice*. To tighten the focus on *practice* (agency) it adopted Mutch's (2003) suggestion for examining the role that communities of practice (Lave and Wenger 1991; Wenger 1998) play in the construction of *habitus*.

Coach development and experience

Research conducted over the past decade in sport coaching confirms the dominant role that experience plays in the formation of coaches' beliefs, dispositions and *practice*, and the inability of formal coach education programs to compete with it (see for example, Cushion *et al.* 2003; Stephenson and Jowett 2009).

Understanding how this occurs has, however, proved challenging for researchers in sport coaching and has been exacerbated by common sense views of good coaches being born and not made (Cushion *et al.*, 2003). Likewise, the challenges of coaching decision-making in team sports is often circumvented by coaches who see decision-making abiity as being un-coachable because it is something that is 'God-given' (Light and Evans 2010). However, viewed through the lens of Bourdieu's analytic concept of *habitus*, decision-making ability can be seen as more of a 'practical mastery' of the game, operating as *le sens pratique* (Bourdieu 1984a), learnt over time through long-term immersion in the game (Light and Evans 2010; Light *et al.* 2014). From the same perspective, the development of beliefs about coaching and dispositions toward it can be seen to be developed over time, through experience within particular *fields, subfields* or even communities of practice (Mutch 2003).

Any interventions aimed at improving coaching *practice* must have an understanding of how experience shapes the knowledge that coaches develop, how they coach, and their dispositions toward coaching. This is important because of the ways in which the corporeal knowledge developed through these experiences and sets of dispositions toward coaching and learning structure coaches' interpretation of formal education and professional development interventions. This 'learning' has a profound influence on how agents act, speak and think because it occurs and operates at a level below the conscious scrutiny of the mind (Bourdieu 1980/1990).

The construction of a coaching *habitus*

In the coaching literature a distinction is commonly made between informal and formal coach learning or development. Informal learning typically refers to implicit or tacit learning that emerges from participation in the *practices* within particular *fields, subfields* or communities of practice (see for example, Culver and Trudel 2006; Nash and Collins 2006). Tacit knowledge operates at a non-conscious level as 'knowledge not consciously possessed by the agent or able to be articulated by her in propositional form but which nevertheless regulates her activities' (Gerrans 2005: 54).

The distinction made between formal and informal learning highlights the different modes of learning involved in coach development. Both modes of learning contribute toward the construction of the *habitus* but, in a challenge to a cognitive bias in the social sciences, Bourdieu's intellectual project emphasizes the development of the embodied nature of the *habitus* and corporeal knowledge (Wacquant 1998b). Informal learning develops embodied, corporeal knowledge over extended periods of time, expressed as knowledge-in-action and which agents cannot articulate (Kontos 2004). This makes it well suited to inquire how and what coaches learn through accumulated experiences that are so often explicitly physical. Bourdieu does not reject the importance of conscious thinking, discourse, or verbal interaction but does emphasize the importance of the body and experience in learning (Light 2011). Indeed, he has been criticized for his emphasis on corporeal knowledge and his stress on the non-conscious nature of the *habitus*, because it is seen to neglect the conscious (see for example, Noble and Watkins 2003).

The construction of habitus *within communities of practice*

Inquiry into how a coaching *habitus* is constructed requires identifying coaches' pathways of development and consideration of the nature of experience and the socio-cultural contexts that shaped it. There have been many proposals made for identifying the stages that coaches move through, as they follow a pathway from beginning sport to taking up coaching as a profession, that are useful for considering the types of experiences and the specific nature of the social and cultural contexts within which they occur (see, for example, Bell 1997; Jones *et al.* 2004). Cushion, Armour and Jones (2003) suggest that learning to coach through experience operates as a form of apprenticeship in which there are two distinct phases. In phase one, future coaches observe and experience coaching from the perspective of a player/athlete. Phase two involves movement from player/athlete to neophyte coach or assistant coach working with experienced coaches in an informal apprenticeship (Cushion 2001).

A similar progression with rugby coaches was evident in the study we draw on in this chapter but this included moving into leadership positions such as being captain or a member of a senior leadership group while players as a transitional phase, before moving into assistant coaching positions and then progressing to high level coaching positions. This typically occurred at a stage of the future coaches' careers as players, where they could see the end of their careers as players and had begun to contemplate what they would do after retiring.

This study followed Mutch's (2003) suggestion for examining how the *habitus* is constructed within communities of practice due to identification of the significance of extended periods of time that the participants spent in rugby clubs for the development of their beliefs about coaching and the associated development of coaching *practice*. It also offered a means of highlighting the individual agency that *habitus* allows for, while still predisposing the individual toward particular ways of acting (Reay 2004). While it focused on the construction of the *habitus* within rugby clubs, it attempted to locate them within the larger contexts of the *subfield*s of rugby in Australia and New Zealand and recognise how membership in other communities of practice interacted with experiences of membership in rugby clubs.

Methodology

This chapter focuses on part of a study that identified the characteristics of the 'coaching *habitus*' of four Australian elite rugby coaches as a means of understanding how it might shape their interpretation of Game Sense (Light 2004). One of the coaches was coaching the national team, The Wallabies, with the three others head coaches of provincial (state) teams competing in the 2007 Super 14 competition contested between provincial teams from Australia, New Zealand and South Africa. *Allen* was in his late forties, had a long history as a player prior to coaching and had worked as a teacher. *Lance* was also in his late forties and had spent most of his life in a large country centre where he had worked as a teacher. *Evan* was also in his early forties and had played for Australia. *Joe* was in his late fifties and had held a management position in the freight forwarding industry.

Data was generated through three semi-structured one-on-one interviews of 40 to 60 minutes duration conducted over a twelve-month period, and observations made at training sessions as a means of triangulating data. This was specifically aimed at identifying any inconsistencies between what the coaches said they did and what they actually did. The second author, who is a former coach of a national youth rugby team, conducted three sets of interviews and recorded observations.

Lau (2004: 377) suggests that *habitus* can be illustrated in the three interconnected categories of (1) fundamental beliefs, un-thought premises or taken-for-granted assumptions; (2) perception and appreciation or understanding; and (3) a descriptive and prescriptive practical sense of objective possibilities ('that's not for the likes of us' and 'that's the only thing to do', respectively). The data in this chapter was primarily generated through the second round of interviews, with questions exploring Lau's (2004) three categories.

Content analysis was used to analyze the data inductively, with data reduced by close reading and re-reading of the interview transcripts to identify and code chunks of the transcripts that could be related, or linked, to one of Lau's (2004) three categories. We then read through the data to identify and code sub-themes. This resulted in the emergence of themes that were strong across all four participants as *first order* themes, and *second order* themes that were strong with two or even three participants but not with all four (Miles and Huberman 1994). Here we only present first order themes.

Results: fundamental beliefs, un-thought premises and taken-for-granted assumptions: views on good coaching

The coaches were asked to suggest what they thought were the characteristics of a good rugby coach and we took their answers to reflect their beliefs about coaching. Analysis of their responses produced the one first order theme of 'the importance of a coach being respected by his/her players'. Their responses suggest some tension between the dispositions of the coaches toward coaching and the position the coach assumes in Game Sense.

Earning respect from players

The participants most consistently saw the capacity to engender respect from players as the strongest indicator of a good coach. This, in turn, shaped the importance they placed on good coaches having knowledge that was superior to that of their players, a good work ethic, commitment and enthusiasm. They all felt that a good coach leads through example and leads by example, as Joe suggests when asked what he thought was the most important characteristic of a good coach:

> I think just respect. I guess the players have to respect the coach. And as I said before, I said working with the players to get a result. The coach has to be the one leading the show and the players have to go down the path that he wants them to go down. But the players also have to be sitting beside him in the driving seat to get there, if that makes sense. (Joe)

They nominated the need to have superior levels of knowledge about rugby, have a good work ethic, commitment and enthusiasm but the importance they placed on these qualities was underpinned by their belief in how the display of them generated respect from players. For example, Allen suggested that 'I think you have to have knowledge. I think players want to come to a coach and be sure that they know what they're talking about in most parts of the game.' They all also valued being enthusiastic, working hard and having a passion for rugby and felt that these traits were essential for success, not only in elite level rugby coaching but also in life in general, as Lance suggests: 'I reckon you know, in anything you do in life, if you're really passionate about that, particularly about being successful, doesn't matter if it's rugby or something else, then you're half way there' (Lance).

Perceptions, appreciation or understanding: views on what makes good players

To inquire into their perceptions and appreciation, the participants were asked for their views on what made great rugby players. They very consistently suggested the following: (a) born with natural ability; (b) tough and resilient; and (c) having a strong work ethic and passion. Their views reflect a belief in the importance of capacities that separate good players from the rest. This included physical capacities such as speed and strength as well as having a highly developed 'sense of the game'. While they felt that physical capacities could be improved through coaching, they did not feel that a 'sense of the game' could be developed through coaching. This has implications for their interpretation of Game Sense with its emphasis on developing this 'sense of the game'. They valued toughness, resilience, having a strong work ethic and passion as qualities they felt could not be significantly developed by coaching.

Having natural ability

The four coaches believed that what distinguishes great players most is capacities and abilities that players were born with and which were difficult to change significantly through coaching:

> Well I think there's a sort of innate skill, like athleticism I guess, and capacity to, it doesn't have to be just in rugby, but just in sport generally, that they've just got balance, yeah, those sorts of things, I reckon it's balance. ... But I think you've got to have a basis of god-given or inherited athleticism, balance: those sorts of things. (Lance)

They felt that outstanding players had a deep understanding of the game that they saw as being an 'inherited' quality. The more specific qualities that the four coaches identified as distinguishing great players from the rest included having vision, creating time and space for themselves in attack and the ability to read the game. They varied in their views how much these capacities could be coached, with Joe being the least convinced and Allen the most inclined to believe that this capacity could be coached. He believed that they are learnt through playing games at a young age and playing with good players, suggesting that it could be developed through coaching that provides a context resembling match conditions through the use of games:

> if you have to rank it from A to E, some players can become A level, but I think it's possible to develop an E level player into a D or C level player. By manipulating the environment and putting them in situations where they start responding to patterns or start responding to cues. (Allan)

Mental toughness

The four coaches emphasized the need for players to have mental 'toughness'. They all felt that players needed this attribute to stay on top and dominate. Joe was most convinced of the need for mental toughness, saying that great players had to be 'so mentally strong and tough to stay at the other guy's throat'. He valued mental toughness enough for him to use it as a core criterion for recruiting new players.

Good work ethic and passion

All four coaches felt that hard work was essential for making the most of ability and talent: 'they have to be prepared to do the extra three per cent. So they always have to be able to do extra training, whether that be physical fitness or skill' (Allen). Lance said that 'I think [rugby] it's like succeeding in any other *field* of endeavour then; it's about hard work.'

Descriptive and practical sense of objective possibilities and the forthcoming: attitudes to innovations

To gain an idea of their practical sense of possibilities in coaching, the coaches were asked their opinions on innovation in rugby coaching. With the exception of Allen there was ambivalence toward, and cynicism about, innovation in coaching and the possibilities for coaching innovation.

Allen was the most inclined to experiment with his coaching and to use games in training. The other three participants felt that no coaching innovation could offer any significant and lasting advantage to a team. As Evan suggested: 'I don't think there's anything dramatically new. I mean you do spot things. I think everyone's got fundamentally the same broad structures but the devil's in the detail.' Finding an edge in coaching was seen to be 'enormously difficult' due to rugby's professionalization and the speed at which opponents would pick up any successful innovation.

Physical preparation

All the coaches saw a need for advances in the physical preparation of players but felt that the major advances in this area had already been implemented by all elite level teams. For example, Lance felt that his players lacked power and speed compared to other teams in the Super 14 competition and saw this as an important area for improvement:

> We need to look at different ways of improving ourselves physically so we're looking at specific power, lower limb power generation in locks, back rowers and our backs and looking at upper body power generation for our props, so getting, trying to get more specificity in our athletic development. (Lance)

Decision-making and flexible playing style.

Allan and Lance suggested a need for advances in coaching that could develop player decision-making, with Lance looking at rugby league for new ideas on how to improve the decision-making ability of his players in attack and Allen suggesting that 'If someone was able to develop a coaching system that improved decision making remarkably, then that would be a massive innovation.' Interested in developing new approaches to enhancing player decision-making and flexible playing style, his views on innovation in coaching suggest an affinity with the Game Sense approach. This was evident in his belief that successful coaching involves 'how you transfer what you do on the field, the training field, to the game'.

Discussion

In agreement with others in the field, we suggest that *habitus* offers a powerful concept for understanding how embodied knowledge and sets of dispositions are constructed through experience in particular *fields*, *subfield*s and communities of practice and how they structure *practice* (Cushion 2007; Harvey *et al.* 2010). The common characteristics of the *habitus* identified among the four coaches were those that they respected in teachers and coaches over their lives and which were valued in the communities of practice of their rugby clubs and in the larger rugby community, within the *subfield* of rugby that they entered into as they developed as players.

Habitus is produced through the interaction of structure and agency and, despite the strong influence of structure, we were also able to identify some individual variation between the coaches and tensions within their *habitus* arising from the interaction of agency and structure. This attention to agency, and our phenomenological slant in the application of Bourdieu's ideas, are shaped by his early work (see for example, Bourdieu 1977). Our inquiry was particularly useful for providing insights into the coaches' dispositions toward Game Sense as a coaching innovation and the variation between them. The lack of consideration of pedagogy, possibilities for developing tactical knowledge and decision-making and cynicism toward innovation suggested dispositions that would be at odds with a Game Sense approach but there was variation that was particularly significant with Allen.

Game Sense has a particular capacity to develop decision-making (see for example, Kidman 2001; Light 2004, 2013; Light *et al.* 2012), which is an area of coaching that typically presents a challenge for directive coaching. This was evident in Allen's suggestion for the use of games as a vehicle for its development. He also made reference to the relationship between coaching and learning and the ways in which decision-making could be enhanced through manipulation of the game environment, which is a feature of Game Sense.

Allen and Lance's experiences as teachers prior to moving into coaching may have predisposed them toward seeing, or having a sense of, player development as a process of learning, and toward the use of games to develop decision-making. Their teaching background seems to have made them both more amenable to the idea that decision-making could be coached. Allen believed in the capacity to develop and enhance decision-making within game environments but could not let go of direct learning enough to 'step back'. Instead of questioning when using training games, he provided direct feedback.

Conclusion

Bourdieu is quite clear in articulating his view that the value of his concepts lies in their use in empirical research. For example, he describes them as 'open concepts designed to guide empirical work' (1987/1994: 107) because, 'one cannot grasp the most profound logic of the social world unless one becomes immersed in the specificity of an empirical reality' (Bourdieu 1993b: 271). The study we have outlined in this chapter provides an example of how *habitus*, and the other key concepts of *field* and *practice*, can be 'put to work' as methodological tools. This case study investigated the influence of experience on coach development with a focus on how this shaped their interpretation of Game Sense pedagogy. This is a topic well suited to the use of *habitus*. However, the study's use of *habitus* as a methodological tool distinguishes it from others in sport coaching. As is the case in education research (including physical education), this typically involves overlaying research analyses with *habitus*, 'rather than making the concepts work in the context of the data and the research settings' (Reay 2004: 433). As Nash (cited Reay 2004: 440) suggests, realizing the full value of Bourdieu's method must involve 'the close investigation of definite *habitus*, as states of mind or effective dispositions'. There is thus a need for the use of *habitus* in research on sport coaching and physical education by 'putting it to work' as a methodological tool.

7 Challenging the economy of gendered practices in PE using Bourdieu's embodied reflexive sociology

David H.K. Brown and David C.R. Aldous

Keywords: *Habitus, delimited fields, practice, gender, change*

Introduction

This chapter reflects on using Pierre Bourdieu's embodied reflexive sociology, particularly the constructs of *practice, habitus, capital* and *field,* in one published article entitled 'An economy of gendered practices? Learning to teach physical education from the perspective of Pierre Bourdieu's embodied sociology' (Brown 2005). Bourdieu's sociology includes established ideas of vigilance towards *reflexivity* in terms of agency[1] (including the researcher), social science (impact of knowledge produced and production methods) and the societal (reflective social development as historicity). We argue that engaging with Bourdieu's sociology also involves adopting a 'highly vigilant' reflexivity towards the idea of an intellectualist theoretical *practice* which 'entices us to construe the world as a *spectacle,* as a set of significations to be interpreted rather than as concrete problems to be solved practically. In other words we risk collapsing practical logic into theoretical logic' (Wacquant 1992: 39-40). This is important because the problem of gender inequity in physical culture and, within this, school sport and Physical Education (PE) is, for all its rich significations, a practical one. The first part of the chapter reflects on the development and conclusions of the article. The second part of the chapter draws on Bourdieu's work to address the practical problem, identified in the article, of challenging the gendered *cultural economy* in PE.

Study background

The research project the article reported on was instigated initially as the first author's (David B's) PhD thesis. Prior to becoming a social scientist, in the mid 1990s David B worked as a Physical Education (PE) teacher in the UK. During this time, through his teaching *practice* and observing others in a diverse range of socio-economically located scholastic environments, David B became aware that the PE teacher's embodied identity and biography were a significant source for the construction of their professional identities as teachers. Many of these PE teacher identities, including his own, were forged through sustained *practice* in a number of heavily male dominated arenas within sport. Moreover, David B experienced first-hand what Bourdieu (2005: 47) referred to as the 'dialectical confrontation' of these gendered embodied biographies (*habitus*) coming together with the gendered context (*field*) of teaching physical education. As Bourdieu (2002: 56) contends: 'it is through training of the body that the most fundamental dispositions are imposed, those which make a person both *inclined and able* to enter into the social games most favorable to the development of manliness'. Therefore the long-term formation of this *habitus*, and within this specific dispositions, was deemed an important yet under-explored antecedent for better understanding how someone becomes not just a PE teacher but a *male* PE teacher (while we focus on gender for this chapter, we recognise that there are many other identity markers that may be salient in this context).

The study tracked a cohort of male student PE teachers through their PGCE[2] PE Teacher Education (hereafter PETE) year at one UK university. This involved documentary analysis and life history analysis. Documents were analysed to contextualise the *field* of PETE in the context of England and Wales and the local context of the programme offered by the institution. Following Sparkes (1992), a life history strategy was used that, as Berger notes, is particularly helpful for showing 'how society "speaks itself" through the lives of individuals' (Berger 2008: 309). Semi-structured interviews were used to collect the life stories because of the way in which this technique helps us 'to understand the world from the subjects' point of view, to unfold the meaning of peoples' experiences, to uncover their lived world prior to scientific explanations' (Kvale 1996: 1). Initially, eight purposefully[3] selected male student teachers were interviewed in depth at the beginning of the year. Subsequently, six continued with interviews in the middle and end of their PGCE year. The focus was reflexive and relational in that the study was trying to ascertain the degree of influence that the participants' biographies were having on their practical and experiential passage through their PGCE and, at the same time, how their gendered dispositions were challenged, altered, reinforced and/or legitimised by the *practices* of the *field* of PETE they had entered as a student PE teacher. This work led to a number of publications (including Brown 1999, 2005; Brown and Rich 2002; Brown and Evans 2004).

Theory and findings

Bourdieu has long been an exponent of a position occupied by Kant (1787/2003) in the *Critique of Pure Reason*, sometimes referred to as the 'togetherness principle' (Hanna 2005: 211) in Kantian logic. This complex position is illustrated simplistically by his often recited statement, 'Thoughts without content are void: intuitions without conceptions, blind.' Bourdieu adapted the idea, stating that 'theory without empirical research is empty, empirical research without theory is blind' (Bourdieu 1988a: 774–5). The integration of both theory and data in the analysis conducted in David B's 2005 article 'An economy of gendered practices?' reflected an attempt to co-present empirical data and theoretical exposition. The life history study data was 'blind' of a more general interpretation without theory and yet the theory would have been 'empty' without the practical and lived sensitivities supplied by these data. The integration began by positioning the embodied biographical experiences of the study participants within the social spaces of UK sports and PE cultures and how these two elements conjoined *reflexively* through everyday *practice*. For the purposes of the article, the life history data selected is the case of only one participant that resonated with and illustrated commonalities of position shared by most of the participants. The idea of specific case study is very much at the heart of Bourdieu's epistemic *reflexivity* to which we referred in the introduction to this chapter. Bourdieu further argues:

> To break with empiricist passivity, which does little more than ratify the pre-constructions of common sense, without lapsing into the vacuous discourse of grand 'theorizing,' requires not that you put forth grand and empty theoretical constructs but that you tackle a very concrete empirical case with the purpose of building a model (which need not take a mathematical or abstract form in order to be rigorous).
>
> (Bourdieu 1990c: 233)

This principle of *reflexivity*, along with Bourdieu's key constructs, was applied to a particular case to construct a conceptual *and* empirical view of gender relations in PE in England and Wales as one of a *cultural economy of gendered practice* in which the notion of economy is taken to mean a system of exchange of the valued resources in PE. The argument presented retains, considers and applies the interdependent concepts of *field*, *habitus* and *capital* that lie at the heart of Bourdieu's theoretical gaze. These interrelationships are expressed in the following table:

Table 7.1

Field:	'The structure of the field is a state of power relations among the agents or institutions engaged in the struggle.' (Bourdieu, 1993a, p. 73)
Habitus:	'In order for a field to function, there have to be stakes and people prepared to play the game, endowed with the habitus that implies knowledge and recognition of the immanent laws of the field, the stakes, and so on.' (Bourdieu, 1993a, p. 72)
Capital:	'Capital is effective in relation to a particular field, and therefore within the limits of this field, and it is only convertible into another kind of capital on certain conditions.' (Bourdieu, 1993a, p. 73)
Practice:	'Is the system of structured, structuring dispositions, the habitus, which is constituted in practice and is always oriented towards practical functions.' (Bourdieu, 1990b, p. 52)

However, applying this theory to data indicated that the idea of '*field* of PE' was insufficiently precise. Through studying a range of practical documentary sources[4] it became clear that PE contained a very specific *delimited field* 'that exists to feed and perpetuate the supply and demand cycle for valued cultural goods in PE' (Brown 2005:11). This then was simultaneously an empirical *finding* and a theoretical articulation. Empirically it exposed a well-known practical logic within PE circles, and theoretically the idea of a delimited *field* of PETE allowed the opening of a new space of dynamic positions between the delimited and main *field* of PE. This dynamic space was illustrated as a theoretically articulated transitional process based upon the participants' accumulation of certain valued, gendered, embodied qualities connected with male-associated sporting *practices* that are encapsulated in the disposition articulated by Bourdieu (2002) as being *libido dominandi,* the desire to dominate. The space also showed a symbiosis between these gendered dispositional elements possessed by individuals and those required institutionally. This oscillation between the empirical data and theory gradually saw David B arrive at the realisation of a *gendered cultural economy* described as follows:

> Over a period of engagement with the overlapping fields of PE, sport, and education, a gendered *habitus* is generated that becomes recognized as physical capital. This capital then becomes converted in the dual sense that it contributes strongly towards the formation of a sporting social identity and powerful scheme of valued, internalized dispositions for action that both qualify and pre-dispose the individual for entry into future fields of physical activity and sport. Having entered the de-limited field of Physical Education Teacher Education (PETE), student teachers then refine and reinforce their gendered habitus in ways which closely 'fit' those demanded by the field.
>
> (Brown 2005: 3)

These findings were represented schematically as follows:

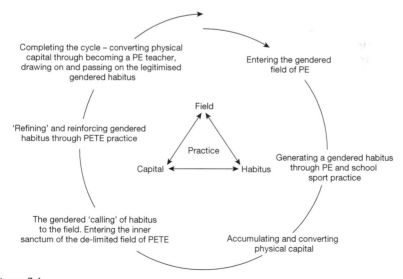

Figure 7.1
Adapted from Brown, 2005: 5

As a social process the gendered *cultural economy* of producing educators does undergo minor developments and changes over time and for this reason the schema does *not* depict a perfect cycle of reproduction nor that the *habitus* of the participants is in any way (pre)determined to result in these courses of actions (i.e. the circle/cycle should not be viewed as a closed reproductive process). In representing the gendered *cultural economy* in this way, David B was drawing upon Bourdieu's relational ideas of *habitus*, *capital* and *field* as constructed in and through *practice* to serve as a 'barometer' that indicates what should happen if the delimited *field* is to fulfill its practical logical remit of meeting demand with a supply of suitably 'trained' male PE teachers. Nevertheless, there is an important distinction to be drawn between this use of Bourdieu's theory and readings of this theory that depict, 'The model of the circle, the vicious circle of structure producing habitus which reproduces structure *ad infinitum'*, which Bourdieu argues 'is the product of commentators' (Bourdieu 2005: 45). The intention of the analysis was to highlight the reproductive *orientation* of relations in this *field*, in particular through better understanding these relations as a process of the construction and conversion of a gendered practical sense engrained as *habitus* into physical, cultural, social and finally gendered *symbolic capital*. Gender reconstruction is thus embedded within this process and proceeds on the basis of a practical necessity, which partly helps to explain why gender relations have been so hard to change in this subject. These understandings, it was hoped, might begin to reveal areas for addressing change, as concluded in the article:

> Making the gendered economy of practices transparent in the fields of PE and PETE constitutes an important step, but it is only the first one. Change will require the construction of knowledge that challenges stereotypical understandings of gender and practices that represent new conditionings that empower individuals with a modified form of habitus through which they can teach.
>
> (Brown 2005: 19)

Addressing these practical issues involves taking a theoretical position on social change and continuity which as Tonkiss (1998: 35) argues, 'is one of the most basic and difficult concerns for sociology'. This topic will occupy our focus for the remainder of the chapter.

Changing the gendered cultural economy in PETE

In what follows, we are guided by Wacquant's (1992: xiv) principle that 'a reflexive sociology ... cannot, on pain of self-destruction, demand a closure of thought. Therefore, an invitation to think with Bourdieu is of necessity an invitation to think beyond Bourdieu, and against him whenever required.' In this section we reflect on how we might engage with changing the economy of gendered *practices* in PE in England and Wales. First, we posit that social *practice* is *the* modality for promoting and understanding change in the social world, and that changing PETE will necessitate revising *practices*. Second, we revisit the vexed question of how *habitus* changes, in order to highlight potential spaces for intervening and disrupting the gendered cultural economy in PE with such revised *practices*. While we think with Bourdieu throughout this discussion, at times we also begin to diverge from the logic of Bourdieu's own intellectual *practice*. This divergence is driven by practical application of theoretical constructs to a specific context and the resulting emergence of revised interpretations.

Changing revised recruitment and training practices

Practice, Bourdieu argues, is 'the site of the dialectic of the opus operatum and the modus operandi; of the objectified products and the incorporated products of historical *practices*; of structures and habitus' (Bourdieu 1980/1990: 52). *Practice* is thus an 'irreducible' modality and a potential driver for both changing and reproducing socialised individuals deliberatively. We require a brief digression here to underpin the significance of this point. Ericsson, Prietula and Cokely's (2007:3) psychological studies of 'experts' demonstrated that the common denominator was immense investments in focused *practice* and accompanying social support. To apply Bourdieu's terminology, they conclude that experts are not born but *made* through *practice* in *fields* of culture that facilitate that *practice*. Elsewhere, neuroscientific developments on the topic of neuroplasticity demonstrate the biological impact of sustained social *practices*. For example, Bogden *et al* (2004) found MRI scans of groups of participants who learnt three ball cascade juggling revealed structural changes (augmentation) in parts of the brain normally associated with visual motion processing and storage. Educative *practices*, such as juggling, physical rehabilitation *practices* and meditation *practices* have all produced similar evidence of neurological change. Following neuroanthropologists such as Downey (2010), these developments are transforming understandings of the embodied impact of education, training and, by implication, everyday repetitive lifestyle *practices,* in ways which have implications for Bourdieu's theory. Such psychological and neurological conditioning might be viewed as other ways of understanding the incorporation of *habitus* through *practice*. Seen in these terms, it is easier to understand the significance of why Bourdieu (1980/1990: 73) claims that '"what is learned in the body" is not something that one has, like knowledge that can be brandished, but something that one is.' These additional understandings of *habitus* help us to understand why changing the *habitus* is so difficult and why gendered social advantage, disadvantage and notions of 'gendered ability' nurtured through social *practices* become tangibly observable and naturalised (Brown 2006).

Taking the above ideas into account, it is possible to see the deeply embodied significance of the *habitus* of PE teachers through the filter of the social *practices* they have engaged in throughout their gendered physical activity careers. Importantly, changing the gendered *cultural economy* in PE will involve carefully altering both recruitment and training *practices*. However, achieving this change will involve challenging some of the inherent logics on which these *practices* are based, which is a challenging task because, as Bourdieu (1980/1990: 89–90) considers, 'Practical sense "selects" certain objects or actions, and consequently certain other aspects, in relation to "the matter in hand" an implicit and practical principle of pertinence.' The core practical 'sense' or logic of the delimited *field* of PETE is one of supply and demand. The demand is instigated by current regimes of school PE and sport, which are historically, legally and pragmatically divided around the gendered division of experience. Therefore the 'matter in hand' is for PETE programmes to find the best 'fitting' teachers for the next generation of teachers with the structured practical needs of *field* of PE at this time. However, the *field* of PE lacks autonomy and is highly permeable to outside influence. Such a relationship is defined by struggle, suggesting that change is possible. Following *habitus*, PETE recruitment might consider the gendered *habitus* of applicants and student teachers more closely, using it as a tool for understanding what is to be done. For example, the relative absence and over-representation of gender-associated *practices* required for the role of both male and female PE teachers and the expertise in alternative activities and the alternative incorporated dispositions that these may bring. This process would then involve embracing, through the screening process of applicants, embodied histories; paying attention to a broader range of physical cultural activities for that gender. This may be achieved by valuing and targeting a broader range of dispositions identified by the embodied biographies of applicants, showing investment into dance, watersports, BMX riding, martial arts etc. In addition, following the logic of *practice*, PETE would need to offer sustained opportunities to *practice* activities where gaps in the *habitus* are identified. In this way, the demands of the *field* could be met but the gendered *habituses* of prospective teachers might be systematically broadened and thus provide a more expansive *generative grammar* empowering teachers to engage comfortably in alternative *practices* themselves, thereby valorizing a wider and less gender associated set of PE experiences to pupils.

'Once bitten twice shy': the changing habitus *and changing the* Habitus

The view of social *practice* we are proposing is that *practices* are not epiphenomena of *fields* or agents actions. Instead, *practices* constitute *fields* and agents at the same time as *practices* are constituted by the actions of agents and the logics operating within *fields* – a symbiotic relationship. In spite of determinist readings of Bourdieu's conception of *habitus*, Bourdieu (2005: 45) argued that 'the habitus is not a fate, not a destiny. I must insist on this as I have done many times before.' Bourdieu's reasoning for this seems to revolve around two key points. The first is that 'habitus must not be considered in isolation. Rather it must be used in relation to the notion of field which contains a principle of dynamics by itself as well as in relation to the habitus' (Bourdieu 2005: 47). As evoked by the idiom 'once bitten twice shy', *habitus* is best seen as a part of an ongoing reflexive process of engagement with the social world. The *habitus* becomes a *generative grammar* or an 'open system of dispositions that is constantly subjected to experiences, and constantly affected by them in a way that either reinforces or modifies its structures' (Bourdieu and Wacquant 1992: 133). As it is symbiotic, the generative and cumulative phenomenon *habitus* is also constantly emergent in potentially unpredictable ways. There are a few important implications for such a view in research into physical culture and for challenging the gendered cultural economy in teaching PE.

The first is that small changes in *fields* of physical culture are initiated as changes in *practice* that will construct a 'dialectic of confrontation' (Bourdieu 2005: 47), via *practice*, between the *field* and the *habitus* of existing or potential participants, including teachers and pupils. For example, the increase in provision of previously masculine associated sports to female pupils in PE has encouraged and in some cases necessitated different forms of *habitus* for many existing and emerging female PE teachers, thereby attracting different candidates to the *field* with quite different embodied biographies (Rich 2001)[5]. These include a feel for increased levels of physical contact, overt competitive displays, the celebration of strength and power, and a whole suite of emotional displays normally legitimated through competitive male-associated sport and physical culture. Such scenarios illustrate Bourdieu's (1989b/1996: 340) view that:

> Pedagogical action can thus, because of and despite the symbolic violence it entails, open the possibility of an emancipation founded on awareness and knowledge of the conditionings undergone and on the imposition of the new conditionings designed durably to counter their effects.

Therefore, practical awareness might be raised by design as part of the pedagogic process. The stimulus for such moments is often where the practical logic of an individual or an entire *field* is presented with a challenge or a crisis, such as an injury, a major policy–practice shift and so on. This kind of crisis might be induced as a learning aid. For example, male student teachers might be subjected to the experience of 'learning' a new activity under conditions that replicate a hegemonic masculine teaching approach, and then asked to reflect on this experience. In one scenario, a handball class might be taught in a way in which the teacher educator behaves in a dominant masculine *associated* manner; invading and dominating the learners' physical space; making elementary skill learning competitive; openly judging and ordering learners' performances comparatively and hierarchically with reference to stereotypical gender associations of physicality; and using their voice in a loud, impersonal, overbearing manner etc. Male students would then be asked to reflect on this experience.

Lastly, the notion of *habitus* as a composite term is discussed by Bourdieu in *Distinction* (1979/1984) as a *scheme of dispositions*. In better understanding change and how to influence it in *fields* of physical culture such as PETE, research might go beyond a focus on *habitus* to consider the composition of these dispositional schemas in more specific terms. David B has, elsewhere (Brown and Jennings, in press) begun interpreting *habitus* schemas as dispositional continua, with orientations emerging from individually identified dispositions ranging from *focal* to *peripheral* in the way in which these generate resources for action. By *focal* we mean those dispositions that are central orientating principles for action for a given individual; by contrast, a peripheral disposition is one which, while clearly present, generates a lesser or secondary sense of focus for action. Such a view can help identify the common gender-associated dispositions formed through *practice* in sports cultures and PE teaching, while simultaneously allowing for variation in the prominence of a disposition with a given individual *habitus*. This 'disposition-specific' approach has the advantage of being able to highlight gender-associated dispositions held by all teachers regardless of their gender/sex status, without recourse to generalising about an individual's teaching *habitus* as either masculinist or feminist. An example of this might be that while the competitive disposition appears omnipresent in physical educators, for some it may represent a *focal* orientation due to their own embodied biographies, while for others it may represent something of a peripheral or background disposition. This disposition-specific approach would open a space for an examination, with students, of where their competitive disposition reveals itself in the teaching process and how it is connected to their biographical experiences. The dynamics opened up by viewing dispositions as a continuum from focal to peripheral must be seen alongside another dynamic, which is that teachers simultaneously occupy *multiple fields of cultural activity*. Theoretically at least, each of these *fields* will also contain its own practical logic and disposition-forming *practices* that intermingle continuously with (in terms of this discussion's frame of reference) the masculinised PE teaching/sporting *habitus*. The potential for such intermingling to generate an awareness of the problematic nature of the prevailing heteronormative dichotomised gender *doxa*, in this field and one's own position in relation to it, can be used to stimulate revised actions that prioritise other core dispositions such as collaboration and cooperation. An obvious example for the male PE teacher may be fatherhood, or the termination of a competitive sports career and its replacement with recreational activities. Each of these might provide impetus to reorder or modify focal dispositions surrounding control, competition, contact, physical ability and emotional expression amongst others. These kinds of reflexive engagements with aspects of one's *habitus* beyond the immediacies of sport and PE *practices* might also provide a specific focus in PETE programmes and is something we sought to incorporate into more recent work (Aldous and Brown 2010; Aldous, Sparkes and Brown 2012).

Closing comments

In this chapter we reflected upon one engagement with Bourdieu's work in attempting to better understand the hegemonic, heteronormative and dichotomised gender relations reconstructed through the process of becoming a PE teacher in England and Wales. We interpret this process as a *cultural economy* of gendered *practice*. We reflected that changing this situation might involve close attention to two fundamental Bourdieuian ideas inserted into a specific context: that of the importance of changing *practices*, and a focus on how *habitus* changes. Both of these insights help us to illuminate particular moments in the process, *practices* and areas of dispositional focus that might be helpful in promoting change.

We began this chapter by highlighting that Bourdieu's distinctive sociological *reflexivity* is one that refuses to collapse the *practical logics* of the social worlds we observe into the theoretical logics of the analyst, and that the two logics should be developed together. We see merit in continuing this reflexive principle, allowing contextualised case study accounts to inform practical action, future research and theoretical insight. In this way, Bourdieu's ideas move beyond a conventional theory and start to resemble a *theory-practice-method* at the same time. Wacquant (2011: 82) has recently argued this in relation to the focus on the *habitus* that can become 'The tool of investigation', further noting that 'the practical acquisition of those dispositions by the analyst serves as technical vehicle for better penetrating their social production and assembly'. We agree strongly, and would further suggest that the *theory-practice-method*, appropriately situated in a *field* of physical culture, might also become a tool for practical interventions to challenge the practical masculinist logics that continue to dominate physical cultures such as PE in a variety of settings.

Notes

1 The term 'reflexivity' also connotes the idea of 'reflex' action. In Bourdieu's sociology this is encapsulated in the idea of *habitus* informing 'conditioned' responses from socialised social actors. However, the degree of conditioning and the predictability of the response should not be misinterpreted as pre-determining agency but rather as resourcing it for a field-specific action.

2 In England and Wales a PGCE (Post Graduate Certificate in Education) PE is a one year university and school based course. Students must possess an undergraduate honours degree in a sports related subject.

3 *Habitus* was used as a theoretical purposive sampling strategy. Selections were based on the sporting backgrounds of participants (a mixture with elite single and non-elite general sporting backgrounds), and a mixture of school types attended and regional backgrounds.

4 GTTR forms are the application forms students complete in the PGCE application process. Students must list their practical competencies in specific detail and these are assessed against the 'requirements' of the profession at the moment of entry. PGCE programme-specific documents also outline desirable and essential qualities, skill sets and experiences.

5 While beyond the scope of this chapter, the specific issue of the female PE teacher adopting more masculine associated dispositions, through engaging in sporting practices in male associated sport, while empowering to a degree, does little to challenge dominant masculinist orthodoxies in the subject. That said, the significance of such changes for both gender relations may take time to properly understand.

8 Skirting the issue

Women boxers, liminality and change

Elise Paradis

Keywords: *Gender, bodies, boxing, change, liminality*

Introduction

On 13 August 2009 the International Olympic Committee (IOC) announced that it would allow women to box for the first time in London in 2012. To make room for women's three weight classes, the IOC cut men's from eleven to ten. Although far from equality, this new arrangement was perceived as a major victory for women's boxing. On 18 September 2010, merely a year after this major milestone for the sport, the International Boxing Association (AIBA) 'invited' women athletes to wear a skirt as part of their uniform for the 5th Women's Boxing World Championship in Barbados. Only Poland and Romania made all their athletes wear the skirts (Bourgon 18 January 2012). As a result, only 14 out of 40 competing athletes wore the skirt in Barbados 11 of whom stated fear of retaliatory action (Rivest 18 September 2010). Rumours circulated that the skirts may become mandatory at future international events, as AIBA considered different possibilities for women's official uniform.

In a classic essay, Messner (1988) wrote that female athletes are contested ideological terrain, their bodies a site where social anxieties about the gender order are projected. In the case of boxing, our cultural view/myth of women as fragile, pacific beings in need of protection does not sit comfortably with images of muscular women hitting one another in the head, shedding blood and getting knocked out. While women have been boxing since the eighteenth century (Hargreaves 1997), until very recently their existence has either been denied, illegal, hidden or eroticised. Their recent inclusion at the Olympics was a watershed.

In this paper, I use Bourdieu's theory of *practice* and the concept of *liminality* to discuss what has been perceived as a major setback for women boxers after their inclusion on the 2012 Olympics programme: what I call AIBA's 'skirt issue.' I analyze media coverage of this initiative to expose the different coexisting logics of the *field*, which range from 'women shouldn't box at all' to 'warriors shouldn't wear skirts'. These differences illustrate the crisis that is currently occurring in the field of boxing and its associated condition of *hysteresis*.

This paper is written using a content analysis (Krippendorff 2004) of the response to AIBA's initiative to mandate the wearing of skirts by women boxers at international events. A Google search conducted on 23 January 2012 and repeated 23 May 2012, identified media responses to the issue published between 23 September 2010 (after the initiative was first announced) and 3 March 2012 (the date when confirmation that women would not need to wear skirts was posted on the AIBA website). Documents about women's boxing in the Olympics and about the Women's Boxing World Championships were also collected from the AIBA website, along with women boxers' profiles. All documents (n = 28) were read and coded before being categorised by type of argument.

Bourdieu and the gendered body

My theoretical approach combines insights from Bourdieu's theory of *practice* and the concept of *liminality*. This conceptual apparatus enables us to see the body as a stratifier that shapes and constrains lived experience and its representation. It also helps us to understand how structural factors such as a changing gender order and the mythology of boxing can lead to the contemporaneous existence of feminist advocacy and attempts at disciplining women's bodies. Indeed, Bourdieuian ideas of *doxa*, *crisis* and *hysteresis* help connect individual-level resistance and structural change.

Bourdieu's theory of practice

Bourdieu's key concepts of *field, capital,* and *habitus* have been covered earlier in this volume. My argument in this chapter is dependent on three other Bourdieuian concepts: *doxa, crisis* and *hysteresis*. *Doxa* is a 'set of fundamental beliefs which does not even need to be asserted in the form of an explicit, self-conscious dogma' (Bourdieu 1997/2000: 15) and which lead social agents to behave in a particular way. It exists at the intersection of *field* and *habitus*: it is embodied intuitive knowledge of the game that is played within a specific *field*, knowledge developed through interactions in a *field*. Consequently, it is *doxa* that guarantees that most agents in a *field* will share a similar *habitus* (Hardy 2008: 125).

A *crisis*, defined as a break in the 'immediate fit between the subjective structures [*habitus*] and objective structures [power relations]' in a *field* (Bourdieu 1977a: 168-9), enables the reconsideration and re-evaluation of the taken-for-granted or unspoken and may lead to *doxic* change. In a stable *field*, objective structures, field logic, *habitus* and *doxa* align. Social agents feel like 'fish in water' as the world makes sense; they know how to play the game they are asked to play frictionlessly. In a *field* in *crisis*, however, field logics and objective structures are being disrupted and the legitimacy of the *doxa* is reconsidered. According to Bourdieu (1977: 83): 'The hysteresis of habitus, which is inherent in the social conditions of the reproduction of the structures in habitus, is doubtless one of the foundations of the structural lag between opportunities and the dispositions to grasp them.' In other words, because it is embodied and durable but not inflexible, *habitus* has inertia; in contrast, *fields* and their associated logics are disembodied and can change rapidly (Bourdieu and Wacquant 1992: 130). *Hysteresis* will happen when an agent's *habitus* has been fitted to a structure that does not exist anymore. Consequently, 'practices are always liable to incur negative sanctions when the environment to which they are actually confronted is too distant from that to which they are objectively fitted' (Bourdieu 1977: 78).

Bourdieu and gender

Gender is a key determinant of social agents' cultural and symbolic capital and thus an important factor in their position in the *field* (Bourdieu 2002; Paradis 2012). As such, it creates a symbolic order that constrains the possibilities of actors and results in a deep gendered divide within society. Bourdieu's concept of the *habitus* is seen by feminists as a critical mediating element between structure and action (Laberge 1995; McCall 1992). For Moi (1991: 1019), Bourdieu's approach 'enables us to reconceptualize gender as a social category in a way which undercuts the traditional essentialist/nonessentialist divide'.

For Bourdieu and Bourdieuian theorists, the development of a gendered *habitus* is the result of an internalization of external social *practices* that position women as different from and dominated by men. In Bourdieu's (2002: 55) own terms: 'The masculinization of the male body and the femininization of the female body ... induce a somatization of the relation of domination, which is thus naturalized.' Sport participation contributes to the embodiment or internalization of cultural norms, that shapes gendered and classed relations of domination (Bourdieu 1978). Furthermore, as Bourdieu notes, the female experience of the body is 'the limiting case of the universal experience of the body-for-others, constantly exposed to the objectification performed by the gaze and discourse of others' (Bourdieu 2002: 63). To further theorize this aspect of gendered bodies I turn to the concept of *liminality*.

Liminal bodies

Anthropologist Arnold van Gennep (1908) first introduced the idea of liminality in relation to rites of passage among small-scale societies. The concept got purchase through its development by Victor W. Turner (1967), who extended the concept. Individuals who are parts of various minority groups can be seen as liminal: situated 'betwixt and between' socially prescribed positions, living in a space where there are no established rules, pre-prescribed ways of being and doing (Turner 1967).

Women boxers inhabit a liminal space, a contested position. They are both women and not 'real' women, both boxers and not 'real' boxers: they do not have the right capital to claim either full womanhood or full boxinghood. Their bodies are bodies-for-others, scrutinized and often dismissed as appropriate for neither boxing nor full (heterosexual) womanhood. Their strength, muscularity and aggressiveness detract from their feminine capital; their femaleness detracts from their pugilistic capital. Yet as we shall see in the next section, women have become less and less liminal in sport over time; there is also evidence that the masculine, misogynistic and homophobic *doxa* of fighting sports is changing.

Women and fighting sports

Sport has been theorized as a space that defines social relations, creates hierarchies among men as well as legitimating the domination of men over women (Messner 1988). Women who participate in what are seen to be stereotypically masculine sports, such as hockey, football, basketball and boxing, have been ostracized in a wide variety of ways (Bolin 2003; Muller 2007), partly because sports serve to reinforce a faltering ideology of male superiority (Messner 1988). Even as women have been 'allowed' to participate in any sport they 'choose', hegemonic gender relations still shape which sports girls and women choose, as well as the status they obtain from participation (Fields 2008; Messner 2011).

Women's boxing and doxic *crisis*

While women have been boxing since at least the eighteenth century, it is only recently that they have been legitimately doing so in the United States. They started being officially licensed as professional boxers only in the 1970s (Hargreaves 1997) and were not allowed to box as amateurs until 1994, when Dallas Malloy, backed by the American Civic Liberties Union, won her case against US Amateur Boxing (*Malloy v. U.S. Amateur Boxing*). These two historic moments have arguably led the sport into a state of crisis that had still not been resolved in 2009 when the IOC allowed women into the 2012 Olympics.

The *hysteresis* experienced by individuals in the field is still visible today. The historically masculine, misogynistic and homophobic *doxa* of boxing has been only imperfectly replaced by a more welcoming one imposed partly from without. Women boxers face both implicit and explicit harassment or discrimination, in the gym and beyond (Mennesson 2000; Paradis 2012). Lafferty and McKay (2004: 263) found that men and women boxers alike relied on 'inborn biological differences' between men and women to 'explain why men's boxing was inherently superior' to women's. Hargreaves (1997: 45) wrote that 'In general, promoters and boxers alike want to present an essentially feminine clean, tidy sporting image ... They oppose women who ... wear khaki shorts and shirts and "look like blokes".' Based on ethnographic work, Mennesson (2000) has argued convincingly that class and (heteronormatively-appealing) beauty interact to shape the different realities of women in the sport. 'Butch' women were sometimes violently mistreated by men who purposefully hurt them, while attractive ones were rarely challenged to their skill level to protect their face. Similarly, Paradis (2012) highlights how women boxers experience boxing systematically differently: excluded from certain rituals and reminded they are outsiders and dependent on coaches whose *habitus* may not condone women's boxing.

Finally, the liminality of women fighters can be seen in academic scholarship, where they have been pushed into the margins. Indeed, despite women's inroads into contact sports over the past 20 years in the United States and elsewhere (Boyle, Millington, and Vertinsky 2006; Cahn 1994; Fields 2008; Hargreaves 1997; Paradis 2010), most recent sociological accounts of fighting sports do not feature women. But for a few exceptions that focus on women's experiences (Halbert 1997; Hargreaves 1997; Lafferty and McKay 2004; Mennesson 2000; Mennesson and Clément 2009; Paradis 2012), women's presence in accounts of fighting sports tends to be minimal (e.g. Abramson and Modzelewski 2011; Woodward 2006) or altogether ignored (e.g. Beauchez 2010; de Garis 2000; Green 2011; Wacquant 1995a, 1995b, 1998b, 2004). Furthermore, as noted by Woodward (2008: 548), there are very few women among the authors of the *field*'s key ethnographies and boxing books, maybe in part because the *field* tends to be difficult for women to access (Lafferty and McKay 2004; Woodward 2008).

Female boxers, as liminal beings and as newcomers looking for legitimation in a field in crisis, consciously manage their presentation of self to navigate the difficult gendered waters between what is perceived to be too masculine (with ensuing negative stereotypes and sanctions) and too feminine (with ensuing negative stereotypes and sanctions). While several of boxing's powerful agents have embraced women's participation in the sport, others lag behind, begrudgingly tolerating women among their rank: their *habitus* has not evolved to match the new field structures. The skirt issue, as I will show, exposes the tensions experienced within the field as the distribution of capital has shifted, as the rules of the game have evolved, and as the old heterodox idea of women in boxing has become orthodox.

Skirting the Issue

In August 2009, AIBA celebrated the decision by the International Olympic Committee to include three weight classes for women on the London 2012 Olympic card. Yet merely a year later, a rumor emerged to the effect that AIBA would *require* women boxers to wear skirts during competitions. Michael Rivest, a boxing commentator writing for timesunion.com, shared the 'disturbing news' that AIBA officials 'prefer women boxers to be in skirts, rather than in their typical team uniforms' (Rivest 18 September 2010). The issue received little press coverage until Elizabeth Plank, a Canadian-born amateur boxer studying in London, brought to life a petition on Change.org asking AIBA to 'play fair' and not 'ask female boxers to wear skirts' (Change.org December 2011 – January 2012). Worldwide, commentators took to their keyboards. Commentators can be separated into two groups: those for whom skirts are no problem and those who are outraged.

Skirts? No problem

The first set of commentators sees no problem with women boxers wearing skirts. For some of these people, it is about a display of the gender-appropriate image. Cuba's head coach thinks that Cuban women 'are made for beauty and not to take blows around the head' (Jacobs 21 September 2009), and one reporter quotes the

Polish national team's coach: 'By wearing skirts, in my opinion, it gives a good impression, a womanly impression' (Creighton 26 October 2011). For others, the issue can be reduced to the pragmatic question of comfort. High-profile Canadian boxer Mary Spencer is often cited in support of the skirts: 'I actually wore a skirt at the world championship last year,' she said, and 'found them to be much more comfortable than shorts' (*The Canadian Press* 11 April 2011). For a final subset of commentators, the skirt issue is of comparative insignificance. According to Iorfida (20 January 2012), the 'fashion crime' represented by the skirts pales against other issues in the sport (it has become boring) and larger injustices faced by women boxers (who have only three weight classes to men's ten). This exemplifies the dilemma faced by the field: women are legitimately participating in the game, yet the distribution of *capital* has not become even between men and women.

Skirts? Outrageous!

Another set of commentators sees the skirts as a serious setback for women boxers. Some arguments against skirts are rooted in sport psychology. For example, in the text of the Change.org petition, we read: 'forcing female boxers to wear a uniform they are not comfortable in may have direct consequences on their performance. Research has repeatedly shown the reality of stereotype threat on individual performances' (Change.org December 2011 – January 2012). Another argument centes on the legitimacy of women boxers. Says Marianne Marston, professional boxer who runs women's boxing classes across London: 'Unfortunately it's sometimes difficult for women to go into boxing gyms and be taken seriously' (Rawi 17 January 2012). A third set of responses focuses on our cultural ideas about femininity. Plank asks polemically: 'What is it about the strength of women that still shocks us? … While men are taught to apologize for their weaknesses, women are taught to apologize for their strengths' (Plank 22 January 2012). A final set of comments stresses how the skirts are a way to sexualize women boxers and an attempt to 'sell' the sport. The short skirt is seen as a symbol of sexual availability and as the sport industry knows well: sex sells. According to Bourgon, the subtext of the AIBA initiative 'seems to be that more people will tune in to watch women fight if they look more like, well, women' (Bourgon 18 January 2012). Some women athletes concur, including British lightweight champion Natasha Jonas, who thinks that the 'only people who would want to see women in skirts are men' (Creighton 26 October 2011).

Discussion

In this paper we have seen a wide range of responses to the AIBA skirt issue, including that of the AIBA's President, who stressed viewers' inability to tell men and women boxers apart. Commentators within the field of boxing took extreme positions, which is quite surprising. Indeed, while we might expect strong reactions from people outside the field, the range of responses from boxing insiders seems odd: if we like boxing as a sport, why should we care whether men or women are in the ring? Isn't it cause for celebration that women athletes have become so good at boxing that they box as well as men? That they look as strong and focused and muscular as men?

How do a Bourdieuian perspective and the concept of liminality help us make sense of all of this? First, it is obvious that the skirt issue is not merely about a piece of fabric. It is a clear indication that the boxing field is in a *crisis* triggered by the inclusion of women into this historical male preserve. The *field* structure has been transformed by the inclusion of new, legitimate agents: women. Consequently, the masculine, misogynistic and homophobic *doxa* of the *field* has been disrupted. While some agents have adapted to the new *field* structure and welcomed a more inclusive *doxa*, others have suffered from *hysteresis*: their *habitus* has not yet adapted to the new environment and women's presence.

That AIBA should invite women to wear skirts is a sign that the organisation itself has not fully adapted to women's newfound legitimacy. It is the attempt to mark the bodies of female athletes as feminine, a means to reassert their difference from the unmarked male body, that has constituted the *doxa* of boxing for centuries. Our social understanding of the female *habitus* is at odds with the boxing *habitus*. The concept of liminality here helps us make further sense of this issue: sitting at the uncomfortable intersection between woman and boxer, demure and powerful, in need of protection yet aggressive, female boxers' bodies are neither here nor there, betwixt and between to social positions that make sense independently but not together. The skirt, then, can be seen as an act of positioning, an attempt by AIBA to reconcile these two positions.

Clearly, 22 years after Messner's (1988) classic essay, the female athlete's body is still contested terrain. The AIBA initiative, less than a year after women's admission to the Olympics, betrays the profound anxieties associated with women's progress in boxing, anxieties about the gendered contradiction that women who box represent for several officials, coaches, men athletes and the general public. Using a Bourdieuian perspective, we understand how AIBA stood between a rock and a hard place: women threaten not only the masculine *doxa* of boxing but also its very logic, its mythology; at the same time, women boxers threaten the domination of men over women, and thus the mythology of both manhood and womanhood.

In short: the skirts skirt a broader issue. Women boxers threaten a gender order where women are the weaker, demure sex: submissive, passive, nurturing and in need of protection. The fact that women's boxing prowess is such that it can't be easily told apart from men's when the clearer signifiers of face, hair and gender-typical clothing are hidden by a gender-neutral uniform threatens the idea that men are inherently better, tougher, more muscular, more athletic. To punch like a girl used to be an insult; now these 'girls' can punch so well that the audience can't tell them apart from men.

On 20 February 2012, Elizabeth Plank declared on the Change.org website that petitioners had 'won', making it clear to AIBA that the public did not approve of skirts as a mandatory uniform (Change.org 20 February 2012). Although a fight was won for women in boxing, the war they are waging for recognition and for greater gender equality is far from over. Until recently, being female meant exclusion. Since 2009, however, female boxers have gained legitimacy through amateur sport's greatest event: the Olympics. However, different and contradictory *habitus* still coexist in boxing. The crisis is far from over, as the fact that national team coaches can publicly claim in all impunity that women are made for beauty and shouldn't box shows. Social agents will continue to clash to define the new rules of the game, to gain privileged positions in the field. Wearing a skirt or not, women boxers are redefining the *field*'s *doxa*: they are redefining what it means to be a woman and a boxer, redefining what a real woman looks like and what a real boxer looks like. Yes, they can.

9 Entering the field as a sports coordinator

Negotiating the micropolitics of the profession

Erin Christensen and Anthony Rossi

Keywords: *beginning teacher, staffroom, capital, field, habitus*

Introduction

The significance of the first year of teaching has received much attention in educational literature. Many researchers have emphasized the reality shock or abruptness that confronts first year teachers as they transition from teacher education programs into school (Lacey 1977; Lortie 1975; Veenman 1984). Additionally, this transition is acknowledged as being significantly influential on beginning teachers' career paths and choices (Huberman 1989; Ingersoll and Smith 2004). The challenge of beginning teachers not only concerns the transition into and management of the classroom environment, but also the negotiation of the school's 'bewildering organizational landscape' (Curry *et al.* 2008: 661). The 'cultural codes' beginning teachers are required to understand in order to fit in are typically informally passed on to newcomers via established staff members (Schempp *et al.* 1993) and are consistent with many of the conventions surrounding the notion of learning at work (Illeris 2011). As such, the staffroom,[1] characterized by a collection of newcomers and established staff members, presents a 'micropolitical reality' in beginning teachers' job situations (Kelchtermans and Ballet 2002b) in which beginning teachers must navigate, position themselves and learn customary and desirable behaviors and perspectives of the teaching profession. Ball (1987: 216) regards schools and subject departments as 'arenas of struggle' but suggests that 'to a great extent the backstage realities of organizational life are neglected by theorists and researchers' because they are 'deterred by the messiness involved in the analysis of the personal and emotional aspects of organizational functioning'. It is precisely the 'backstage realities of organizational life', the political positioning experiences of beginning teachers, that this chapter is concerned with, the transition, learning and *practice* of beginning health and physical education (HPE)[2] teachers within the 'messy' processes and interactions of the staffroom.

This chapter therefore attempts to address the significant silence within the literature regarding beginning HPE teachers' positioning experiences of the staffroom (works by Curry *et al.* 2008; Kelchtermans and Ballet 2002a, 2002b; and Schempp *et al.* 1993 have explored beginning teacher micropolitical experiences of the school). For HPE pre-service teachers, staffrooms have been reported to function as communities of practice and as sites of workplace learning (Sirna *et al.* 2008) that influence pre-service teachers' understanding and identity formation (Sirna *et al.* 2010). The staffroom is considered a space where the constraints of the HPE department seem to offer only limited possibilities for pre-service teachers in terms of developing and learning to become a HPE teacher (Rossi and lisahunter 2012). For beginning HPE teachers, Keay (2005, 2009) highlights the possible hindrance of beginning teachers' professional development through the unequal positioning of beginning teachers identified in the physical education (PE) subject department. Staffrooms act as important places where professional learning occurs; 'recognized and named physical spaces that house functional, social and representational spaces' (lisahunter *et al.* 2011: 35). lisahunter *et al.* (2011) conceptualized transition from university to full-time employment as a teacher to be a process and/or product of professional spaces and the staffroom as a place where beginning teachers participate and interact to understand who they are and what they do professionally. While these studies point to the significance of the subject department for pre-service and beginning HPE teachers, there remains much that is unknown in relation to their political positioning experiences in staffroom spaces.

The study reported in this chapter (Flanagan 2012) followed seven beginning HPE teachers into a variety of urban and rural, departmental and general staffrooms in Australia (four teachers were in urban departmental staffroom settings and three in rural general school settings). We were interested in the beginning teachers' positioning experiences of the staffroom space into which they transitioned. We understood the staffroom as a physical space in which the field of education is played out, and used a narrative inquiry approach (Clandinin and Connelly 2000) to understand how beginning HPE teachers positioned themselves politically in the staffroom and how this influenced their learning and *practices* in their first year of teaching. Bourdieu's interconnected notions of *habitus, field, practice* and *capital* (Bourdieu 1977, 1998a, 1997/2000) articulated well with this focus, offering a new and fresh way to understand and unpack beginning teachers' positioning experiences of the staffroom.

Within the HPE context, Pierre Bourdieu's conceptual tools have been used to explain durable norms and *practices* (see for example Brown 2006; Gorely *et al.* 2003; Hunter 2004; Light and Kirk 2000). For Bourdieu (1998a), the term *habitus* most closely refers to a set of durable dispositions, tastes and ways of thinking, acting and being that are shaped through individuals' experiences in various social settings. The body is pivotal to *habitus* because, through *practice*, social and cultural norms become inscribed in the body as gestures, deportment, perspectives, behaviours and tastes. Individuals interact and engage in various overlapping social settings that Bourdieu (1977) describes as *fields*. Such *fields* or social spaces are infused with power struggles and organising structure (Bourdieu and Wacquant 1992). The relationship between *habitus* and *field* is dynamic in that, through *practice* in the social *fields*, individuals both shape their *habitus* and contribute to shaping the *field*. Through this ongoing experiential process *habitus* is formed. Over time through *practice* in a *field*, socially constructed ways of thinking become embodied in individuals and 'naturalized' (Bourdieu and Wacquant 1992).

We conceptualized the staffroom as a space in the *field* of teaching, where the *field* is enacted in a particular way. The staffroom is a contested *social* [work] *space* (Bourdieu 1989a, 1980/1990, 1998a) where individuals are offered, or claim, different modes of participation based on power dynamics and perceptions (Billett 2001). The interactions and positioning within the staffroom are influenced by the relative amounts of valued *capital* that individuals (teachers) are recognized as embodying (Bourdieu 1984a, 1997/2000). The value or *capital* granted particular resources are particular to the context and may be cultural, social, physical, symbolic or economic. In HPE departmental staffrooms, such as those seen in urban school settings in Australia (see for example Flanagan 2012), these are played out through, for the most part, the physical culture of HPE, the cultural *practices* surrounding sport, the body, exercise and fitness (see Sirna *et al.* 2008, 2010), and the moral gaze that these factors tend to attract.

This chapter employs Bourdieu's conceptual tools of *field*, *habitus* and *capital* to explore beginning HPE teachers' positioning experiences and learning in staffrooms (i.e. staffrooms shared with staff from different subject departments in the school). While the HPE departmental staffroom tends to be a bounded space with unwritten rules and expectations that guide *practice* within that space, in this chapter we shall suggest that general staffroom spaces are also bounded by (possibly different) unwritten rules and expectations, some of which are from outside of the staffroom. This is particularly so, as we found in Larry's story, in small rural Australian settings. The approach we use here is to present one beginning teacher's story of the staffroom at the rural Johnson School (a pseudonym), in the form of a narrative to open up for reflection how the logic of the professional *field* plays out more broadly in the rural context than in the urban context. Importantly, we acknowledge that not all the participants in the study experienced beginning teaching in the same way. However, what can be said with confidence is that for all of the participants, their position in the politics of the staff as negotiated in the staffroom as a beginning teacher presented significant challenges (see Flanagan 2012 and Christensen [née Flanagan] 2013), amongst them negotiating the professional micropolitics, negotiating *capital* and moving beyond the boundaries of the physical space, but not the professional space.

Negotiating the staffroom: a story from the field

This narrative account is drawn from a variety of field texts that were created with Larry such as conversations, emails, text messages and photographs. Conversations referred to throughout the narrative account are taken from conversations with Larry during the first week of the school year (Week 1) and 6 months on (Six months on).

Larry: Be a 'professional'

During his initial weeks at the challenging Johnson School, the only high school in the small town (2,500 residents), catering for 140 students, a sense of busyness and unity encompassed Larry's consideration of the mixed subject staffroom. As a 23-year-old graduate, Larry described feeling particularly fortunate to be sharing this small staffroom space (a 3 metre x 9 metre room) with 12 other teachers, 9 of them under the age of 28 years old and of those, 5 under 25 years, and seven of whom, like him, were first appointed in a rural school. He explained:

> [E]veryone is so helpful because they all know what you are going through ... They've all been shipped out to a rural place. ... Getting all this stuff that you have never seen and done before. Everyone has been through the same thing.
>
> (Week 1)

Larry perceived a sense of unity within the staffroom, and depicted that everyone was working towards the same goal; everyone was busy taking on different responsibilities and doing their bit for the school, such as learning coordinating, running the gifted and talented program, and facilitating the student council. Larry proudly reported that he was responsible for 'all things sport'. He sensed that sport was positioned positively and perceived well by the majority of the staff at Johnson, with the HODs (Heads of Departments), principal and the majority of staff being supportive. Larry explained that 'there are just a couple who are just not sporty people and no matter what I say it is not going to change so I just work around it' (Week 1).

While it didn't take Larry long to feel comfortable in what he described as 'the united staffroom', he was very particular in how he described his approach to being the beginning teacher, or what he termed 'the freshy' in the staffroom:

> [W]e are all there to do your job but at the same time, you just have to be aware that you know, you are the new person, you are the one that people don't know and that sort of thing. So I just went in there and introduced myself, be kind, be respectful towards others and try and get along with everyone as best as you can. You know make an effort to talk to people and things, matters outside of school too.
>
> (Week 1)

Larry also had a heightened sense of awareness in relation to being a young teacher in a small community where 'everyone knew everything about everybody else'. As a teacher, Larry considered himself a role model not only at school but also in the small community. He disclosed that in his first few weeks at Johnson this was constantly on his mind, 'Like not paranoid but you've just gotta be aware of what you're doing. Because when you are a teacher you have to set an example' (Week 1). This had become particularly apparent to Larry in the first week of school:

They are always out there, like when I was in my car the other day down at the shops. Kids yellin 'spin it up sir, spin it up'. And then the next day, 'Oh did you spin it up sir' like that you know. Or like on Friday night you have like one beer and then all of a sudden on Monday 'Were you pissed on Friday sir?' It just all gets blown out of proportion.

(Week 1)

To overcome this visibility in a small town, Larry 'let his hair down' on the weekends outside of Johnson. He often went camping, four wheel driving and fishing with two other young new teachers from his staffroom to escape 'feeling like a teacher seven days a week'. Larry's awareness of the transparency of a teacher's life in a small community spilled over onto his approach in the staffroom. While he had formed friendships inside and outside of school with some of the other male teachers, he kept his thoughts about the school and staffroom members, functioning, dynamics and happenings to himself. He didn't feel comfortable confiding in anyone in the staffroom or the community 'cause I know if you say something around here to the wrong person everyone knows', and because he would be spending three years in this small town he explained that 'you have to look after yourself in the long term' (Week 1).

Being 'professional' pervaded Larry's approach to being a teacher in the classroom, staffroom, school and community. Through conversations with Larry throughout the year, his ongoing and unwavering references to his particular image of professionalism were striking. On moving to Johnson, he had made it a priority to portray this image of being professional, which for Larry was

just doing your job. Making sure that you go to an effort to get along with people to do the right thing, to not do or say things that piss other people off. You've got to always think about what you do, think about what you say. Make sure you're doing your job correctly, you're doing the best by the students, you're doing best by the school, you're doing the best by yourself. You're just being the best that you can. You're sort of being highly organized, highly punctual. You know, just all the facts of professionalism.

(Six months on)

Larry expressed that this image of professionalism, which he sought to embody, was imperative to how he defined himself:

I think your job's your job. And how you act at work is what defines you. So if you take your job seriously, if you're being professional, people are going to take you seriously and they're going to give you respect and they're going to look at you in the right way. Whereas if you don't be professional, you don't give a damn, people aren't going to look at you in the right way sort of thing. And in a small community, that is so important.

(Six months on)

Larry spoke of the small community in which he lived: 'It's funny how people up here don't differentiate between school and like outside' (Six months on). Larry considered the staffroom as an extension of this small community with the priority of professionalism particularly important in this place he shared with 'a completely different range of people who have got different morals, different values, different ways of looking at things' (Six months on). Larry was resolute in his lack of respect for a number of teachers within the small staffroom who did not fit his image of a professional. However, he always endeavored to act professionally:

> [T]here are people on staff who I look at the way they do things and I don't agree with and I don't necessarily like them, but I make an effort to portray – to be professional and always do things in the way in which I think is right. So if they make a comment that I don't think is correct, you don't stick your nose in and get involved but you kind of – I'm someone who doesn't look for conflict. At the same time, I'm not going to sit there and take it either. You kind of keep things smooth, you know get along with everyone, do your job. If you've got something to say, say it but say it in the right way that's not going to offend other people sort of thing.
>
> (Six months on)

As a beginning teacher, Larry tried to keep his head down, going 'with the grain' unless there was something he felt passionately about. Within the staffroom, Larry considered himself a 'mediator; but when it comes to sport I'm the leader, I make the decisions, what I say goes'. In this way, Larry acknowledged that his position as sports coordinator, as 'the leader of sport' and his commitment to a professional image had facilitated his entry into the staffroom by providing an avenue through which to develop rapport and, in turn, influence and earn the respect of his colleagues. He exemplified his approach in a recent conflict he had been involved with regarding Wednesday school sport. Larry had heard a teacher complaining about Wednesday sport and felt that the teacher was indirectly complaining about him. Larry did not think this was fair or warranted and stepped in to defuse the situation. Speaking to this teacher in private, away from the rest of the staff, Larry reported that he acknowledged how the teacher was feeling and explained that he had not intended for the situation to come to that. Larry felt that he had addressed the problem and had done so 'in the right way, in a very polite way, in a very submissive way. I didn't look for conflict and it all worked out fine' (Six months on).

Having been an occupant for nearly six months, Larry's perception of the staffroom was that it functioned on a shared ethos, a sense of unity and mutual respect between its members; a place where teachers were working towards the common goal of providing a positive learning environment for students from low socio-economic areas. However, Larry depicted that this positive and united vibe shifted dramatically when a small number of particular teachers were present in the staffroom. A significant swing in Larry's perception of the staffroom had occurred since the conversation six months previously in Week 1. Larry perceived that there was a very small number of teachers within the staffroom who did not share nor attempt to embody what he termed the 'unity' of the staffroom. From watching and listening to these teachers, Larry had the impression that they 'didn't care' about their important roles as teachers, respect other people within the staffroom or embody a professional image. This, he construed, manifested in the way the staffroom 'vibe' shifted when they entered the room, 'When you get someone in there [in the staffroom] who doesn't fit the mould or doesn't go with the flow sort of thing, it just stuffs everything up' (Six months on).

Larry's aggravation was clearly evident as he launched into an explanation of an ongoing issue between two teachers within the staffroom. This conflict, Larry indicated, had culminated in three rather large arguments in the staffroom, making everyone else in the staffroom feel uncomfortable. While Larry had never had an issue with these particular people, he was not interested in involving himself in their conflict nor did he agree with what he considered their unprofessional behavior. Larry felt that these two particular teachers could not be trusted and their behavior significantly changed the feel of the staffroom: 'they bitch and whinge about everything and take things out of context. But when they're in there, everyone sort of feels a bit uptight' (Six months on). One of the teachers involved in the conflict was new to the school, and other teachers had mentioned to Larry that the staffroom 'wasn't like that last year', that the incoming of one of these new teachers to the school had changed the whole feeling of the staffroom. Frustrated, Larry believed that all staff had the right to a professional environment in which they felt comfortable, the behaviour of these two teachers was unprofessional and significantly influenced the experience of other teachers within the staffroom.

Making Bourdieuian sense of this story

Larry's is a less common situation in the corpus of stories that made up this study. First, he acquires cultural and social *capital* very quickly as he is assigned the position of sports coordinator. Not only is this position seen as important in the context of the business of school, but within this particular school sport is held in high regard. At the same time, the *practices* of organization, communication and leadership connected with being sports coordinator are entirely consistent with the 'durably installed generative principle of regulated improvizations' (Bourdieu 1977a: 78) that Larry was able to bring to the position. His notion of 'being professional' in terms of his assigned role was connected to organizational skills, self-discipline and usually a high expectation of others. Indeed, as we indicated earlier, Larry described himself as a leader and a decision-maker, and through these self-descriptions he embodied the role of sports coordinator through other expectations of leadership such as dress, punctuality, and even carriage of the self – that is, he wanted to 'look the part'. Hence, the role defined the nature of the *practices* inherent *within* the role, as they were part of what Bourdieu calls the 'objective structure' (1977a: 78). It is this objective structure that necessarily defines the social conditions required for the production of those *practices*. Moreover, these *practices* were legitimated through what Bourdieu (1977) calls *officializing strategies*. Officializing strategies are the production of regular *practices* that presuppose competence and ultimately come to define and represent the *practices* that are then considered to be indispensible – that is, they assume the status of 'role'. This then confers *capital* on the role holder, thus Larry gained capital from his role as sports coordinator. As Bourdieu (1977) describes, this *capital* provides the authority to 'define' a situation and then mobilize the available resources that are considered necessary to deal with the situation. Larry was in a position to define situations and assume the competence to manage them. This was how Larry saw himself 'fitting in' so easily and having a 'feel for the game' (Bourdieu 1980/1990). The dialectic of his role and sense of self were harmonious. As depicted in Larry's story, Larry played the game deliberately and consciously and was 'born into the game, with the game, and the relation of investment, *illusio*, is made more total and unconditional by the fact that' he was aware of what the game was (Bourdieu 1980/1990: 67). This was not necessarily common across the study and inevitably this was not where Larry's challenges lay. For Larry then, acquiring *capital* that was highly tradable around the school, given the status of sport, was relatively straightforward (if not simple). Indeed, given the importance of sport to the sense of community in small country towns of Australia (see Baills and Rossi 2001; Rossi and Sirna 2008), Larry's acquired *capital* far exceeded his expectations. So even though he was aware of the game and even though his *practices* to some extent defined the game, particularly when it came to 'managing sport', his status and kudos available through his playing of the game was unexpected. However, as a consequence of his emerging *habitus* there was a potential dark side. His presupposed competence built through his performance of role probably added fuel to the disdain he felt when others failed to demonstrate what he considered to be the expected level of professionalism.

What Larry experienced was the blurred lines between school and community. This was one of the challenges that Larry faced. The staffroom (expected to be experienced as a bounded space in the *field* of teaching) that might normally be defined by the HPE departmental office for HPE teachers was, as Larry had expected, far less bounded and much less than his contemporaries and peers were reporting in other schools around the state. As a consequence, the broader 'objective structure' i.e. the community at large, brought about certain *practices* that Larry considered were desirable given his subjective position and role in the school. So he was careful with consuming alcohol and in the way he drove his car. Bourdieu's claim, then, that the 'habitus is the universalizing mediation' (1977: 79), may warrant further consideration. Whilst his professional *habitus* was durable across the overlapping nature of *field*, other less bounded *fields* induced a reflexive adjustment in *practices*. So when Larry went camping and fishing it was because he did not want to be a teacher seven days a week and wanted his subjective position to be something different. This is insufficient reason to dismiss *habitus* and nor would we want to. Rather its permeability to adaptation, in this case beyond the bounded *field*, is worthy of attention and perhaps the idea of *subject position* is a more flexible and indeed useable concept by which '*practice*' can be described and accounted for. Though his *practices* within the bounded context of the school and the staffroom were consistent with his professional dispositions, he understood that such *practices* had to be maintained beyond the physical boundaries of the school but within the looser boundaries of the town. This is what Larry meant by 'being a teacher seven days a week'. Hence, the taxonomies of social order represented by the professional citizenry of the town reproduced *practices* that Bourdieu calls *doxa*, a set of taken-for-granted beliefs seen as self-evident and undisputed. These stable expectations, themselves a product of historical conservatism, perhaps confirm Bourdieu's (1977a) position in that 'the stabler the objective structures and the more fully they reproduce themselves in the agents' dispositions, the greater the extent of the *field* of *doxa*, of that which is taken for granted' (pp. 165-6). To overcome the restrictions of *doxa*, Larry had to remove himself from the *field*, as can be seen in Larry's narrative when he goes on camping and fishing trips. This further suggests Larry's capacity to compartmentalize the performance of *habitus* according to *field*. Larry knew his life would be under surveillance as a new teacher in a rural town and this is consistent with the work of Macdonald and Kirk (1996). The maintenance of *practice* was consistent with his teacher subjectivity. Hence Larry's solution was to ensure that he was able to move beyond the limits of the *field* as far as he could be confident about doing this as a way of removing himself from the gaze and the reproductions of dispositions that were only representative of one aspect of his life.

Notes

1 Within international and national literature the notion of staffroom as a particular site, location, space and place within the school is quite slippery (see, for example, Ball 1987; Gewirtz 2002; lisahunter *et al.* 2011; Rossi and lisahunter 2012; Rossi *et al.* 2008; Sirna *et al.* 2008; Sirna *et al.* 2010). For the purpose of this chapter the term *staffroom* refers to the office that is co-inhabited by teachers; the staffroom may or may not be a subject department office.

2 In this chapter the terms physical education and health and physical education are used interchangeably. In Australia the subject area is called health and physical education; however, the term physical education is more common internationally. In general the literature on physical education teachers relates to health and physical education teachers.

10 Bourdieu, young people and physical activity

Intersecting fields of social class and family

Symeon Dagkas and Thomas Quarmby

Keywords: *habitus, field, social class, family*

Introduction

This chapter employs Bourdieu's conceptual tools and notions of social, economic and cultural *capital* to explore the way in which they shape young people's physical activity dispositions and practice. We will draw from our empirical work conducted in the past with young people from economically deprived social groupings, in diverse *fields* where social (re)production takes place. As such, we will interrogate notions of social class and family, as *fields* where young people, through their various interactions, develop *habitus* and engage in *practice*. We will provide effective examples that highlight the intersection of these *fields* (family and class) and the disposition of being physically active in the *field* of physical culture in the cultural transmission of values relating to physical activity that could (re)produce existing structural inequalities. Bourdieu's concepts are therefore used to highlight social inequalities across various *fields* where *habitus* is formed, by intersecting forms of *capital* with changes in the *field* of family. Finally, drawing on Bourdieu's key concepts helps us understand how the multifaceted influences that operate in and through combinations of family and social class influence young people's engagement with physical activity.

Understanding the role of physical activity in the lives of young people is important for a multitude of psycho-social and physical reasons. More importantly, epidemiological data underpinning policy often adopts a homogenous approach (Gard and Wright 2005) and overlooks difference within and between social groups from various socioeconomic backgrounds, ethnicities, racial and family formations, thus preventing understanding of the processes of accumulation of physical activity dispositions. As such, descriptive statistics of certain populations (low social class and ethnic minority groups) have fed into worldwide policy on physical activity that negates young people's specific needs and individual agency. Hence, with current economic uncertainties and projected increases in poverty worldwide, especially amongst young people of low social class groupings (Joyce

2011), attempting to understand young people's dispositions through their own voices is of great importance. In this chapter we will draw on the use of social theory to (de)contextualise young people's dispositions toward physical activity and the impact of structural inequalities in distinctive yet overlapping *fields*.

(De)Contextualizing Bourdieu in our research

Used correctly and together, Bourdieu's key concepts provide a method for simultaneously analysing 'the experience of social agents and of the objective structures which make this experience possible' (Bourdieu 1988b: 782). Bourdieu argues that action or *practice* is linked to the reproduction of social structures and the maintenance and reproduction of unequal social relations. Bourdieu's (1984a) framework outlines the substantial links between structural conditions at the macro level and individual actions on the micro level, particularly as related to the reproduction of class *practices*, behaviours, tastes and values. Before we embark on this chapter it is crucial to introduce the notion of *field* as it has been used in our research. Broadly, *fields* are defined as distinct cultural and social realities, sites of cultural reproduction with particular norms and boundaries within which various interactions and events take place.

Bourdieu (1993b) defined *field* as a site in which certain beliefs and values are established and imposed on the people within it through the various relationships and *practices* that occur. In this sense, *fields* are sites of ideological reproduction (Bourdieu 1993b, 1996). Bourdieu and Wacquant (1992: 17) argue that a *field* 'is simultaneously a space of conflict and competition', structured internally in terms of power relations. The relative power that determines positions of dominance and subordination and locates individuals and groups within *fields* is determined by the distribution and accumulation of *capital* in the form of cultural, social, or economic resources (Bourdieu 1986). Individuals try to distinguish themselves from others and acquire *capital* that is useful or valuable within that arena and as such, *fields* are seen to be hierarchical. However, the boundaries of a particular *field* are demarcated by where its effects end. Consequently, such boundaries can be difficult to locate and thus overlapping *fields* (family, schooling, physical culture etc.) can affect the internal dynamics within them (Laberge and Kay 2002).

Bourdieu sought to use the concepts of *capital* and *habitus* to understand how the objective structures of society influenced subjective behaviour. For example, physical activity participation is seen to be shaped by social structures, and, essentially, how young people's *habitus* is influenced may shape their initial and ongoing involvement in physical activity and even the nature and reasons behind engaging in activities in general. Our research findings from various projects would suggest that the dispositions (which make up *habitus*) to engage in physical activity arise from a complex interplay of various economic, cultural and social factors associated with the *fields* in which individuals are positioned. All these factors constitute an individual's dispositions towards physical activity. They are embodied, and therefore may operate at a subconscious level and are only evident as a feature of the way a person appears or acts (Bourdieu 1999a). Such dispositions comprising an individual's *habitus* are therefore socially constructed and acquired through interactions across a range of social contexts. With regard to this chapter, the two main *fields* in question are those of 'class' and 'family'. Social class operates as a broader *field* within society, given its hierarchical structure that is determined by the distribution and accumulation of *capital* in the form of cultural, social, or economic resources (Bourdieu 1985b). In this sense, individuals are positioned and defined in particular groupings that Bourdieu conceptualises as 'class'. For Bourdieu (1996) the family is viewed as the primary socialising structure, a social *field*, a site in which *capital* is accumulated and dispositions (of *habitus*) are acquired. He argued that different forms of physical, economic and, above all, symbolic power relations exist within the family *field* (Bourdieu 1996) and help to organise and shape the structure of the *field* and thus, agents' actions within it. Hence, it could be argued that at the micro level an individual family is nested within the overlapping *fields* of family and socio-economic status. Studying *fields* therefore draws attention to the interactions and relationships between social agents occupying different positions within a given social space (e.g. a family), that shape understanding and subsequent dispositions of *habitus* (Bourdieu 1989a; Bourdieu and Wacquant 1992).

Socioeconomic status and intergenerational *habitus*

As mentioned earlier, our research has focused on the structural factors of social class and family formations. According to Evans and Davies (2006), social class is a set of social and economic relations that influence, dominate, and dictate people's lives. They maintain that the term social class implies 'not just a categorization or classification of people with reference to some quality, but an invidious, hierarchical ranking of people which is inherently value laden' (Evans and Davies 2006: 797–8). Social class is, therefore, a set of social and economic relations that influence, dominate and dictate people's lives (Evans and Davies 2006). It is also important in the context of this discussion to reflect on Bourdieu's (1984a) argument that different social classes tend to develop different orientations towards their bodies and, we might infer, towards engagement in physical activity for health, physical education (PE) and sport. Socioeconomic status (SES) has often been used as a synonym for social class, representing groupings in society based upon occupation, education and housing. While Bourdieu (1984a) described social class as groupings of society not just influenced by socioeconomic status but by a synergy of socio-cultural factors, we have chosen to adopt the term socioeconomic status, as a form of economic *capital* and one component of social class, to be used to inform our discussion. For instance, there is evidence that higher SES is linked to higher levels of involvement in physical activity. In our research, young people from low SES groups experience greater barriers to participation in sport than those from middle or high SES. Such barriers can be classified as financial, logistical and geographical (Dagkas and Stathi 2007). While participants from high SES areas reported a plethora of opportunities both within and beyond school, young people living in low SES areas often commented on the restrictions they faced due to their geographic location and lack of facilities:

There's not much to do here. (Boy low SES)

Well I like playing basketball but there's nowhere round here to go. (Boy low SES)

Maybe if there was a gym close by I might have gone to that. (Girl low SES)

In other words SES, as used in this chapter, is a pervasive factor determining not just choice and preference in physical activity, but also the capacity (physical and material) to realise those choices and preferences.

In the context of PE and sport, high SES parents expect teachers and schools to build on parental 'investment' in their children through their embodied *practices* (Dagkas and Stathi 2007). Such *practices* appear to illustrate Bourdieu's (1984a) concept of *intergenerational habitus,* as parents implicitly impart to their children values, attitudes, predispositions and their embodied *practices* of involvement in physical activity . For instance, those young people reported engaging in whole-family activities during weekends, such as going for country walks or visiting local leisure centres. As two students explained:

> We [referring to the whole family] are members of a local private gym just down the road, which is great ... and they [leisure centre] have a really good swimming pool. (Girl high SES)
>
> We do it [participation in physical activity] as a whole family sometimes by going to the gym. My parents enjoy it as much as us [referring to himself and his brother]. (Boy high SES)

The resulting *habitus* has the potential to influence the PE *field*, especially in schools representing high SES. Our data has demonstrated (Dagkas and Stathi 2007) that levels of parental involvement in physical activity and school sport are reflected in (their) children's participation and choices, leading to the 'consumption' (participation) of activities 'appropriate' to (their) SES. As such, hierarchical powers in the primary socialisation *field* (family) influence *practices* and agency in the secondary *field* (school). In addition, our data has shown (Dagkas and Stathi 2007; Quarmby and Dagkas 2010) that schools tend to nurture these trends by providing *practices* and pedagogies appropriate to their students' SES. In this sense it could be argued that there are structural inequalities built into PE and youth sport environments. In different schools, for example, children experience different activities that are sometimes undertaken in very different environments. Some schools have extensive grass playing fields, sports halls and a range of other facilities (think of public schools who pride themselves on such facilities), whereas others may have only poorly maintained hard surface areas.

Intersecting class and family

Having contextualised the use of Bourdieu's conceptual tools in our research, we turn now to discussing the way that we have addressed *'field(s)'* in our research and their importance in shaping individual agency. We have demonstrated and defined different *fields* that create social barriers in which power relations exist and actors acquire *capital*. As such within the school, the *field* of 'PE' is made up of a 'structured system of social relations between the educational authority, PE teacher educators, PE curriculum writers, health and sport professionals who have influence over curriculum and practices, individual school administrators, PE teachers, and PE students' (lisahunter 2004:176). The *field* of 'family' is made up of a structured system of social relations that maintain physical, economic and symbolic power relations between members (Bourdieu 1996). Such family *fields* are hierarchically structured in terms of economic *capital* (usually lying with the parent(s)) and cultural or social *capital* and its symbolic value within that *field*. However, different family formations may mediate the internal structure and power relations evident within some *fields*. For instance, in comparison to other family formations (such as married couple or cohabiting families), lone-parent families tend to be severely disadvantaged with weekly household wages being substantially lower (Office for National Statistics 2004; Save the Children 2011a). Approximately a quarter of all children living in lone-parent families are classed as being in severe poverty (Save the Children 2011a), while half of all children in poverty reside in lone-parent families (Save the Children 2011b). Lone-parent families are therefore most likely to experience social and economic deprivation, especially with regard to their material circumstances (UNICEF 2007), and are more likely to be associated with lower social class groupings (Pryor and Rodgers 2001). As such, the various structures within the family *field*, nested within similar social class groupings, may influence individual agency differently. Importantly, Bourdieu (1990b) argues that it is the intersection of *habitus*, *capital* and *field* that produces the *logic of practice*. Moreover, drawing on Bourdieu, we suggest that those who occupy the same SES position within the *field*, and the same family structure, with similar objective living environments, may share similar *habitus* and through *practice* reproduce their social position within the shared *field*. This was evidenced by the young people in our research who, despite acknowledging the importance of physical activity, began to exhibit diminished desires to engage in physical activity and made unconscious choices that reflected the behavior of their SES circumstances and family formations, e.g. sedentary behaviors that could incorporate TV viewing, computer games etc. Moreover, economic and social resources restricted the possibilities to enact *practices* in line with their underlying physical activity dispositions (Dagkas and Quarmby 2012). This was particularly evident for Jerome, whose mother's lack of free time prevented his access to physical activities alone and with her and meant that he developed a taste for more sedentary activities that would occupy him:

> Most of the time I'm like on my XBox but sometimes I do like to go round to my friends and we like play some football or something but normally just play Xbox... there's not much else to do like really 'cos mum's always busy.

This was equally the case for Naomi, who reflected on the nature of her family structure and indicated that there were few opportunities to engage in anything other than sedentary pursuits:

There's nothing to do like with just me and my mum, we just sort of sit at home and watch the telly. Don't really speak or anything... Apart from watching like TV... no not really... maybe we used to do little things together when they [mother and father] were together ages ago but she's not got the time now so yeah we just watch TV.

However, entry to a new *field* can be seen as providing the opportunity for *habitus* to change as individuals are confronted by the unfamiliar. Such changes in *field* also alter stocks of *capital*, which, alongside *habitus* and *field*, are vital in determining *practice*. More specifically, in many cases in our research it was evident that changes in the family environment (one *field*) directly influenced changes in the dispositions towards physical activity that impacted on individuals' *habitus* (Bourdieu 1984a), the development of the body either in terms of physical development or in terms of physical activity behavior. For example, Taylor (a 13-year-old girl) identified her father as influential in shaping her desires for physical activity because he initially taught her how to swim and stated that if he 'didn't get me into sports then I probably wouldn't do it at all so I think it's good that I spent at least like 6 or 7 years just doing sports with him'. However, Taylor now lived with her mother and stepfather and was only able to see her biological father on Wednesdays and every other weekend. As a result of the change in family structure and limited contact with her father, Taylor's desire to engage in activity when with her mother and stepfather was reduced:

Well, some weekends I'll be like I just can't be bothered to do anything, I just do my work on Friday and then the rest is just to relax but erm, like if my grandma and granddad come up, my granddads got like something in his legs which means... I think arthritis... So he can't walk very far but he can cycle, but my grandma likes to be really active, even though she's, I think she's 79 now, but she walks 3 miles every day, and erm, she does lots of different sports, so like sometimes she'll come down for the weekend, or we'll go up hers for the weekend and we'll just like, we'll take a picnic and we'll just walk all day. And like she lives by C [area of residence] so we go to the [outdoor centre], which is an outside swimming pool which I love and we spend all day there in the summer.

Taylor's activity dispositions evidently came alive when she encountered a different environment that was supportive of her own desires (swimming). Such dispositions remain embedded long after the initial conditions have gone but can be re-ignited when the environment is more conducive.

Without wanting to paint a disheartening and homogeneous picture regarding young people's physical activity in specific *fields*, some young people also reported increasing their engagement with physical activity as a result of a change in their family *field*. For Claire, a change in family structure from a two-parent family to a lone-parent family had meant that her mother now provided more support and encouragement to engage in dancing than previously when her mother and father lived together:

I do dancing but my mum comes with me and sorts everything out for me like costumes and things like that... She's always with me helping whatever I do... Yeah, she's very encouraging!

It was clear that for Claire, given time, the change in family structure allowed her to become aware of alternative possibilities that were afforded to her by her mother. Hence the change in the dynamics and make up of her *field* (family structure) lead to changes in Claire's *habitus*. So it is clear from our research evidence that the family, as a particular social *field* and site of social reproduction that struggles with physical, economic and symbolic power relations (Bourdieu 1996), allows for the development of physical activity tastes and preferences.

Concluding thoughts

We have demonstrated in this chapter the use of Bourdieu's conceptual tools in research that deals with the intersectionality of social class and family formation in acquiring physical activity dispositions related to SES. We maintain, therefore, that early family experiences intersecting with socioeconomic variables 'produce the structures of the *habitus* which become in turn the basis of perception and appreciation of all subsequent experience' (Bourdieu 1977: 78).

While Bourdieu's work has been critiqued as being deterministic, dwelling too much on reproductive aspects and focusing on continuity rather than change (Shilling 2004), we would argue that there is still potential for change as effected through the exercise of agency and the interaction of *habitus* and *field*. For example, Shilling (2004) would point out that Bourdieu viewed social life as patterned, regular and stable and while emphasising the importance of agency, *habitus* rarely accounts for change. Morrison (2005) too would argue that the main problem centers on the notion that *habitus* encapsulates structured structures and structuring structures. Morrison (2005: 313) suggests that the *habitus* is 'both a result of social structures and yet also structures; that is, changes and influences, behavior, life-styles and social systems'. Indeed, Bourdieu himself stated (1990c:133) that new experiences are 'perceived through categories already constructed by prior experiences'. However, while there are limits to *habitus* operations (Bourdieu 1977; 1980/1990), Reay (2004) suggests that an individual's *habitus* is malleable and responsive to its current circumstances and therefore continuously restructured by its encounters with the outside world. Like *habitus*, a social *field* is not fixed and it is possible to trace the history and shape of a *field* in support of understanding how change happens (Thomson 2008). Hence, Bourdieu's concept of *field* still allows for the potential of change and has helped us uncover structural inequalities that exist in society that directly affect young people's *habitus*, taste and agency in relation to physical activity participation.

11 The paradox of physical activity for Qatari women

Researcher *hysteresis* and *reflexivity*

Kelly Knez and lisahunter

Keywords: *Qatar, abaya, physical activity, reflexivity, hysteresis*

This chapter is a dialogue between: a culture, Qatar; a Qatari woman, Dana; an expatriate researching physical activity while working in Qatar, Kelly; a co-author who brought Bourdieu's social theory to Kelly while visiting Qatar, lisahunter; and Bourdieu's interconnected concepts of *practice, field-habitus, capitals, reflexivity,* and *hysteresis.* The chapter's pedagogical intent is to invite you to use Bourdieu's conceptual tools to make your own positioned reflexive analysis alongside ours (see Chapter 1). The chapter authors embody Australian and mixed-Western resource-rich cultures, valuing exercise (Kelly) and movement (lisahunter). We ask you, as a reader, what culture/s do you embody and what worldviews do you hold, and why is this important when analysing narratives from other cultures?

What follows are: brief descriptions of the socio-historical context of contemporary Qatar and the project that informs this chapter; Dana's narrative of being female in Qatar; and Kelly's analysis of the relationship between physical activity and females in Qatar from her Western social scientific standpoint. We draw from project interviews and field notes. As *you* read the narrative, notice what you think might be going on – a common social researcher's question rooted in sociology, ethnography and narrative inquiry. Also notice how you interpret the narrative. What does it tell you about your own culture? Employing a Bourdieuian lens to understand 'what might be going on' for Qatari women and physical activity, we had extensive discussions reading Dana's story and offer two foci of analysis in the final part of this chapter. The first is the negotiated paradox of physical activity for Qatari females, as embodied by Dana. The second is researcher *reflexivity*, who and where 'we' are, experiencing *hysteresis* as social researchers from another culture in relation to Dana's field texts. We finish by commenting on the efficacy of Bourdieu's concepts and theoretical framework for understanding physical cultures and ourselves in physical culture … our own, and Qatar's.

A (very) brief background to the State of Qatar

How would you write such a background for your own cultural context?

Qatar is a small country on the Arabian Peninsula, sharing its only land border with Saudi Arabia to the south. Ruled by an absolute monarchy, the royal family, who include the current Emir Sheik Tamim bin Hamad Al Thani, his father (and previous Emir) Hamad Bin Khalifa Al-Thani, and his mother, Sheikha Mozah bint Nasser Al Missned (henceforth referred to as Sheikha Mozah), are credited with facilitating the rapid transformation of Qatar over the past 15 years. This includes tangible changes, the seemingly overnight development of innovatively designed skyscrapers as Doha's central business district, construction of lavish shopping malls, a vast modern highway infrastructure, and Qatar Foundation, which houses Education City (accommodating six North American university campuses). Less tangible but significant changes for Qatari women include the acceptance of obtaining a driving licence (early 2000s), increased access to tertiary education through Qatar University and Education City, and increasing cultural acceptance of employment of Qatari women. However, amidst this development and change, Qatar remains highly structured, conservative and patriarchal, partly through the power and preservation of tribal organizing patterns that have far reaching influence, including in the *fields* of business, education, social groups, family, housing, politics and sport. Coupled with prevailing local customs deeply rooted in Islamic heritage, young Qatari women negotiate the well-worn paths of previous generations with the new opportunities and developments of a quickly formed contemporary Qatar.

A highly visible marker of traditional and contemporary local custom is Qatari national dress – one of the first things visitors notice when arriving in Doha. Women and girls wear the *abaya,* a long black gown, and the *shayla,* an accompanying black headscarf. Some Qatari women also partially or completely cover their face. Traditionally, the *abaya* was a loose, formless, black covering but it has recently been modified through innovations and elaborate designs. Men and boys wear a *thobe,* a long white garment, and an accompanying head dress. Our description of Qatari women's national dress is in no way intended to reinforce narrow yet commonly held stereotypes of gender equity in the Middle East, nor to reduce Qatari women's rich and varied life experiences to a single piece of clothing. This would oversimplify a complex interplay of culture, tradition, citizenship and agency. However, discussions of Qatari women and physical activity cannot be separated from meanings inscribed, and practices embodied, as a direct outcome of the wearing of the abaya and shayla.

In line with Qatar's rapid progress, the country markets itself globally as a 'Sporting Nation'. Recent developments include the successful bid for the 2022 World Cup and hosting of high profile international sporting events. Further to this, the second Tuesday of every February is declared by Emiri Decree as National Sports Day, a day for citizens and expatriates to participate in various state and community organized recreational activities and sport. The paradox faced by Qatari women, however, is the extent to which they are able to participate in regular physical activity within this newly developed 'Sporting Nation'.

The project

The body of literature associated with Muslim women's participation in physical culture is rapidly growing, the majority being conducted 'on' Muslim women living within non-Muslim majority countries, with very little research conducted within the Arab world, even less within the Gulf Cooperation Council (GCC) (see Benn, Pfister and Jawad 2009; and Dagkas, Benn and Knez 2014), and nothing within Qatar with Qatari women. This exciting and unique opportunity posed issues for us, especially as cultural outsiders, issues that invited us to use Bourdieu's tools for explanatory power in an empirical analysis of 'what was going on here' – for Qatari women, and for us.

The project behind this chapter considered the physical activity and health experiences of Qatari women. Methodologically, the project was grounded within a poststructural framework. Ten physically active Qatari women aged between 18 and 28 were interviewed about participation in physical activity from childhood through to adulthood. We discussed the influences of key *fields*, including family, tribe, schools and social networks. Interviews were conducted in English and transcribed verbatim, with participants selecting a pseudonym and checking the transcription for accuracy. Ongoing field notes by Kelly added background information. What follows is one participant's narrative.

Dana tells her story

I'm 27 with a Qatari father, Mom's Western. I have a few siblings, quite unusual for Qatari family often with more than six. We all live together, our house is huge – nine bedrooms, each with an en-suite. We have a maid, her husband is our driver. I always wanted to be an athlete, but because of the society and the environment, it just never worked out as a profession. As a child, there wasn't opportunity for me to pursue sport seriously. The infrastructure wasn't in place. Qatar loves sports, especially with the big events they have here, but I don't think it's taken seriously by the community like it is abroad. I think of a treadmill when I think of physical activity. If I lived anywhere else in the world, I would have chosen the word running, but I can't just go outside and run, so to me, associating running is with the treadmill. I can't run anywhere because of the abaya, it just wouldn't work. It's a sun magnet, you would heat up and burst! Not to mention the likelihood of tripping over it and hurting yourself. I don't know of any Qatari women who would run outside without an abaya. I hardly know any Qatari women who don't wear the abaya. So if they wear an abaya in social life, they wouldn't ever take it off and run. Covering is their social responsibility. I cover, but I don't cover religiously. I cover socially and culturally. The idea of social responsibility might be hard for some non-Arab-Muslim women to understand. You're treated differently when you are covered here, especially when you are a Qatari. Because I know of some girls who don't wear abaya, we never associate with them, it's about your reputation, it's just not good to be seen in public with them.

Of course it's not impossible for a Qatari woman to be physically active, but it's challenging for me to have physical activity in my life all the time. I really have to make the effort to exercise every day, I force myself to find time because it is so important to me, it keeps me balanced, grounded. I'm lucky I can do a lot of it at home, as well as in the hotel fitness centers, like the Ritz or Four Seasons, so I can always fit it in if I want to. But in Qatar it really is hard to be physically active, especially when you are working all day, and then you have – you HAVE to spend some time of your day with your family, every day. Family in Qatar is also a responsibility. It's like you have to go to your job, you have to spend time with your family. And then there is Friday, the family day. Cousins, aunties and uncles, there is always something going on, like at my grandmother's house. And you have to go every Friday, or else you are sick, because if you are not sick, then where are you?

Life is just different in Qatar compared to the West. A lot of marriages in Qatar are arranged by the parents for example. You would think you have to look a certain way to get a good husband, but it's not really a problem. I've noticed men here like women with meat, with curves and some meat on them. They don't like skinny girls, and they don't like muscular athletic looking girls. But I still think that being skinny in Qatar is definitely easier than being overweight. It's about image here, how you look, what you wear, not only your abaya, but your shoes, your handbag, what is under your abaya, your make-up, all of it. And everyone wants to be skinny.

Who are the role models for Qatari women? Sheikha Mozah. If it wasn't for Sheikha Mozah being the woman she is, I don't think Qatar would have grown this much, this drastically. I think it would still be like it was when women weren't allowed to drive, which was only 14 or so years ago. Sheikha Mozah made it okay to continue your education. People used to think 'you don't need to go to university because you are going to get married'. She made education important to girls, not to families, but to girls. She put this idea into girl's heads that your education matters.

Even though there are more sporting associations and federations for women now than before and women can join them, I don't really see them competing. It's not looked at as proper, culturally. I was playing tennis when I was at school, they asked me to compete in tournaments but when I asked my Dad he said 'no'. Mom, she didn't want to hear it, she told me to not make trouble. So if I'm dealing with that and I'm mixed nationality I'm sure that in other families, they probably don't even discuss it. It's not a possibility, not even up for discussion. I think it's cultural, mostly. It's just not looked at as a profession.

Westerners often focus on how we dress, and notice that we walk slowly – yeah we walk slow. It's the way we dress! Qatari's make life complicated. We are in high heels, elaborate abayas, big handbags, and we move slowly, just to look elegant. If you see someone walking really fast you are just 'why are you walking really fast?' I mean, even men walk slow. When I travel I wear whatever I feel like, but decent of course. When I leave the country and I take the abaya off, especially when I'm in western countries, but I'm looking for it because I'm physically used to it. I'm just like 'Oh, okay it's not there'. 'Cause even physically, your habits are so used to it, in the abaya I sit better, like my posture is better. When I'm just wearing jeans and t-shirt, I slouch, and I don't even realize it. But in the abaya you always have to look elegant, you always have to look classy, so you think about your posture, the way you are sitting, you don't lean that much, you are always proper. So that's what that clothing does.

So I wear the abaya, but I'm not really religious, but I'm very connected to Allah on a daily basis. I find that physical activity grounds me, it creates a quiet time to think. But, from what I know, the prophet Mohammad, peace be upon him, said that you should teach your kids three different things, like how to swim, ride horses and archery. So to me, those are things that are just practical, you need these things for daily life. But I've never heard of anything about sports and Islam. But in Islam you are responsible for your body. You are responsible for your health, you're responsible for what you eat, the way you treat your body. I guess for women, playing sport and being active, as long as you are not mixing with men, it's fine.

But I know what you are thinking – are there any real restrictions that I face as a Qatari woman, in relation to sport and physical activity? There are not that many facilities, and sport and physical activity is not such a big deal in this society, because education is now the big deal for women, and business. So it's not that it's not allowed, it's not forbidden, it's just not… a priority now, in life, according to the culture and to the society.

Reading Dana's story with the help of Bourdieu

Dana's story allows us to consider empirical *practices* of physical activity for Qatari women without losing sight of the complex daily interplay between cultural tradition and rapid contemporary change, and without privileging one over the other. Bourdieu's analytical framework of *practice* that includes *field-habitus*, *capitals, doxa* and *hysteresis* help us make meaning of Dana's experiences without moralizing issues of gender equity from a position of 'outsider'. Dana challenges dominant culture through her *practice* in daily physical activity. Despite this, however, she is still bound by *doxa* (Bourdieu 1990b), the implicit rules, what is expected of her as a woman by her family and the society through which she moves. Rapid economic and infrastructural change, juxtaposed against dominant *doxa,* that work to maintain a highly conservative culture, create a paradox of physical activity for many Qatari women. Firstly, we explore key elements of the primary *field* that work to reproduce the conservative Qatari culture with direct reference to the body and possibilities for physical activity. The macro *fields* of Qatari society and the family/tribe are clearly significant here, as is the abaya – both practically and theoretically. Secondly, we consider how Dana, as a *social agent*, is able to negotiate and re-position herself amidst this conservatism to be able to *practice* physical activity on a daily basis. Along with the immense change that Qatari women have experienced, we propose that this exercising of *agency* has been facilitated through Dana's *cultural capital*, sense of *practice* and cultural trajectory.

Cultural reproduction

Cultural reproduction works through societal structures or *fields*. Bourdieu argued that the primary *field* is the family (1977, 1998a) as the first and dominant socializing structure. Within Dana's context, 'family' and 'tribe' are used interchangeably. Qatari society denotes citizens or 'nationals' of Qatar, and it is these nationals, 12 percent of the population, that hold the newly acquired oil wealth of the country. Qatari citizenship is closely guarded through a patriarchal familial system, granted automatically to children of Qatari fathers, but to other individuals only under exceptional circumstances. There is much *economic* and *social capital* to be gained by maintaining tribal membership, and for nationals like Dana there is pressure to conform to the *field* of the tribe, through dress, social interactions and her behaviour, including participation in sport. Dana's actions and decisions are a reflection of her immediate family, and larger tribe; 'social responsibility' is pivotal to the tribe and Qatari society/culture, as highlighted when Dana refers to attendance requirements at family gatherings, her parents' comments when she asked to play competitive tennis as a younger child, her adoption of the abaya, and avoidance of women who choose not to wear the abaya. Such markers of social responsibility provide powerful examples of the pervasive workings of cultural reproduction that work to maintain a highly conservative society within a country experiencing unprecedented cultural and urban shifts.

However, despite outward shifts in many cultural *practices* (i.e. women driving, obtaining tertiary education), the maintenance of traditional dress – in particular the abaya and shayla for women – is viewed by many outsiders as a sign of continued oppression. Such moralizing lacks a sophisticated and nuanced understanding of Qatari culture, and works to reproduce fabled understandings of an exotic, oriental other. Looking past this, Dana's accounts provide insight into how the abaya shapes daily movement, and in doing so provides us with an alternative narrative to the way physical movement is culturally valued and understood. According to Dana, image is 'everything' and comprises of make-up, hair, handbags, shoes, what is under the abaya. The desired outcome of this work on the body is 'elegance'. Dana describes the way the abaya shapes and inscribes bodily comportment, that is, movement and posture, for example. There is significant 'work' that is required to develop and maintain this look, to successfully 'pull it off'. While the predisposed *practices* of appearance tend to reproduce *doxa,* there is also evidence of *agency* that incorporates particular forms of Western exercise/physical activity in Dana's *habitus*.

Such is the effort invested in the *bodily hexis* associated with the abaya, that a Qatari woman can identify if a woman wearing the abaya is from Qatar, a neighbouring GCC country, or a non-GCC. This inscription and re-inscription on the body, the *habitus*, is a slow and prolonged process, not something that can be learned over night. The dominant and legitimized, slow and elegant, daily movement patterns and *practices* of Qatari women are produced and reproduced. We would argue that such movement, akin to systems such as Tai Chi, Yoga and Qigong, has been marginalized in Western notions of physical activity. At the same time Western movement and exercise forms are now being increasingly valued in Qatar. Oppositional forms of movement, and ultimately dispositions, are in negotiation in the very mundane *practices* valued in this emerging Qatari culture. Such a paradox has serious implications for governing authorities seeking to enhance Qatari women's engagement in physical activity and provide the world with a particular image of sport, exercise, and ultimately success. Despite Dana highlighting the obvious impracticalities of matching the abaya with conventional (read – Western) forms of physical activity, there are significant social and cultural rewards, or *capital*, for adopting the national dress.

Negotiating practice of daily physical activity: the rewards of strategic conformity

Indeed, the rewards of conforming are enticing, especially when they translate into maintaining a high ranking social and cultural positioning. For Dana, such rewards may also facilitate opportunities for daily physical activity, rather than impede it; for example, she has the *economic capital* that allows her to work out in the gyms of high-end hotels and resorts. Dana's legitimate positioning as a Qatari woman of good social standing affords her the opportunity to draw upon this *capital* to participate in physical activity on a regular basis. She is able to do this, we suggest, without challenging the *doxa* of the tribe and Qatari culture, through participating within gender-segregated environments, or at home, whilst maintaining the position of legitimate Qatari woman in both her professional and private life. Further, Dana is able to draw upon religious text in support of women's participation in physical activity. Such knowledge could arguably be identified as a marker that holds significant *cultural capital* in a conservative Islamic state.

What we found to be striking in Dana's narrative was her sense of *practice* – her reading, knowledge and playing of the social game. She knew what rules to abide by, and which ones she could challenge. For example, she conformed to the *doxa* of the tribe and Qatari culture, but challenged cultural attitudes through participation in daily physical activity. She is able to do this in culturally sanctioned ways (gender-segregated environments) that are powerfully supported by religious text. Finally, Dana's cultural trajectory with cross-cultural *habitus* may have afforded her the *agency* to work within traditional spaces to reshape over time what is possible for the Qatari women whose individual history is shaped only by conservative or traditional *practices*. It will be interesting to monitor how such *agency* reshapes modern Qatari society, the positioning of women, and the legitimization of the nature of physical activity and for whom.

A note on *hysteresis* and *reflexivity* as research tools

Qatar embodies major transition in one lifetime, from a traditional, largely nomadic culture to one that is marked by both modernism and urbanism. Dana embodies this transition, she is constituted by one parent's Western world and another's Arabic world. As researchers, we moved between these different worlds, but are positioned differently to Dana, creating a moment for reflection. For Bourdieu, rapid transitions between traditional and modern societies triggered a need for *reflexivity* (Deer 2008). Unlike Dana, *we* were unable to negotiate the two cultural spaces, feeling quite like fish out of water, and experiencing what Bourdieu referred to as *hysteresis*, where the *habitus* is not appropriate to the *field*. In our theory of *practice*, our attempt to understand what might be going on for females in Qatar in relation to physical activity, we are interpreters analysing our world to guide our *practices*. Our analysis is situated in a particular context of which we are part, as will your analysis if you have attempted it. The challenge for us was to adjust in such a way as to avoid imposing our worldviews onto a system of logic quite different to our own.

Bourdieu's posthumously published book *Esquisse pour une auto-analyse/Outline for a Self-analysis* (2004c/2008) provides an account of how particular social and intellectual trends of our own context influence our work as scholars. Our project created a mirror to look at how our own family backgrounds, career trajectories, socio-historical contexts and ideas of our own lives shape what we research, how we research, who we research with, and how we make sense of the research. This *reflexivity* characterizes much of the contemporary work of social researchers; however, this has not always been the case, nor is it yet the case for some. Bourdieu recognized (Bourdieu and Wacquant 1992) that *reflexivity* should be a central part of social researchers' work, but often it is not. This made *reflexivity* a methodological focus of his work – see work that spanned his career from *Sociologie de l'Algerie* (1958) to *Science of Science and Reflexivity* (2004a). For us, *reflexivity*, as methodology and epistemology, represented the empirical–theoretical dialogue, and it was one that we kept coming back to in this project. While not all researchers doing ethnographic work will have the opportunity for *hysteresis* to force *reflexivity,* it is an important reminder of the need for *reflexivity* when doing qualitative research.

Conclusion

Legitimation of education and active public life by Sheikha Mozah, a woman who embodies education and demonstrates agency as a female, may be just what is needed to facilitate *practice* for female participation in physical activity. However, let us be careful about which assumptions drive shifts and the analysis of such shifts. *Habitus-field* changes are manifested in the *practices* of those like Sheikha Mozah and Dana. Conceptually we framed the project using Bourdieu's tools, employing the concepts as part of our method. Reflecting on our own worlds in relation to those we research and how that informs where we put our research energies and politics is another way we have practiced Bourdieu's work. What *practices* do you participate in? What questions do you ask of your world and your self? Where do such energies come from and go to? How do you know? These are some of our challenges we hope you will consider.

For us as 'outsiders', the appeal of Bourdieu's work, over others, is the comprehensive methodological and epistemological nature of his theory. He also demands of us as researchers to be *reflexive* and, in doing so, to consider the complex relationship between our own *habitus*, the research *field* and the agents that occupy it. Bourdieu encourages praxis based on specific situations and issues. For us these are useful points to guide our work and to look for ways to be agentic in our research. We hope this chapter has provided useful illustrations to translate into the work you intend to do. Having read the introductory chapter in this book and employed Bourdieu's tools to read Dana's narrative, what sense do you make, how, and why? While at the one level we have introduced an illustration of the paradox of physical activity for Qatari women, we also hope that the chapter's pedagogical intent has triggered some useful learning in the form of *hysteresis* and researcher *reflexivity* for you to take into your own areas of research.

12 Understanding *dis*/ability in physical education through the lens of Bourdieu

Hayley Fitzgerald and Peter Hay

Keywords: *Physical Education, ability, disability*

Conceiving ability within schooling and PE

Ability is a term that is widely employed within the education community, in a manner that appears to assume its enduring and inherent constitution. Evans and Penney (2008) noted that the performative culture of contemporary neoliberal education systems has been particularly influential in positioning ability as a measurable entity with definable and discriminating properties. The intersections between ability and measurement are most acutely observable in the pursuit of meritocratic standardised assessment regimes that purport to capture and recognise the inherent 'abilities' of students. Belief in even the plausibility of a meritocratic assessment regime is informed by a particular view of ability. Clearly, one's perspective on ability has an impact on 'how the purpose of schools, the educability and achievement potential of students, the role of teachers, the curriculum that is offered, and the manner in which it is offered is viewed' (Hay and Macdonald 2010: 1). The way in which abilities are conceived of, sanctioned, measured and conferred on students in subjects such as PE has a notable impact on how individual students are valued in those subjects by teachers and other students, how students view themselves and their own educational potential, and how willing students are to learn and pursue recognition for that learning in education *fields*. Of course, discourses of ability circulating through schooling seep into other social spheres such as family, and these (re)produce the meanings and values afforded to the abilities of students within and beyond the education community. In particular, it should be recognised that for young people PE is one of a number of sites of practices involving physical culture (including physical activity, exercise, sport and recreation) and each informs how bodily practices and associated abilities are valued. Whilst this chapter focuses on a PE context, it should therefore be recognised that it is these broader sites of physical culture that also need to be explored if we are to better understand how ability is imposed, pursued, and acquired.

As a key site of physical culture, PE is not immune to the performative imperatives of the broader education system and, consequently, the notion of ability is similarly characterised by discourses of measurement, standards, and the valuing of performing bodies in reference to defined appearances and capacities. The body, including its appearance and its actions, is particularly significant to contemporary definitions of ability. The valuing of students' bodies within PE continues to be underpinned by a biological paradigm, and according to Evans and Penney (2008) students' bodies are objectified by defining optimal measures of physical ability associated with performance (such as skills), body shapes and 'looks'. By legitimizing ability through these measures a discourse prevails that assumes an 'able body' has the potential to achieve the optimal performance and secure valued *capitals*. For students who do not match up to the characteristics associated with valued abilities, PE can evoke considerable anxiety and become an alienating experience (Brooks and Magnusson 2006; Hunter 2004). Indeed, *dis*abled students are one group that have fared less favourably in PE because they continue to be subjected to normative assumptions about their abilities (Fitzgerald 2005; Fitzgerald and Kirk 2009a). The scientific and objectified nature of PE has led Evans (2004) to conclude that PE had become 'disembodied', reducing discussions about the nature of PE 'to a dribble of *unproblematic assumptions* either about motivation and health-related behaviour, or "fitness", or "*talent" for "performance"* in the interest of health and/or participation in *organized sport'* (p. 96, emphasis added). He complained that very little critical attention had been given to the concept of ability that underpinned these assumptions, or to understanding the way in which the notion of ability has been complicit in the perpetuation of inequities in PE.

In this chapter we build on the work of Evans (2004) and seek to develop critical dialogue that moves beyond *unproblematic assumptions* concerning ability within PE. Along with Bourdieu, we believe that 'what is problematic is the fact that the established order is *not* problematic' (Bourdieu 1998a: 56). Therefore, we *make* the established order problematic by exploring ability as socially constructed and in this way seek to move beyond current narrowly conceived notions found within PE. We specifically focus on insights from *dis*abled students and PE teachers in order to explore embodied conceptions of ability. We consider there to be a number of distinctive features offered when *dis*abled students are foregrounded in discussions of ability, including enabling the dichotomizing of ability. That is, *dis*ability is equally a means of recognizing ability, given that ability and *dis*ability are relative terms that are dependent on one another for meaning. For example, the prefix 'dis' in the word *dis*ability provides a constant reminder of the perceived subordinate relationship between *dis*abled and 'abled' people within society. In foregrounding *dis*abled students in our discussions we also recognise, like Edwards and Imrie (2003), that Bourdieu's work offers a means of thinking beyond dominate medical and social model conceptions of *dis*ability. Indeed, the medical model of *dis*ability has been criticized for a biologically underpinned orthodoxy. More recently, commentators have argued that the social model excludes 'the body' from experiences of impairment (Goodley 2011). Bourdieu then offers the possibility for recognizing the interrelationships between the individual and wider socio-cultural practices within society.

Given these differences in understandings of *dis*ability, we could expect there to be some tensions around PE and the relationship with *dis*ability. That is, how do the performative imperatives of measurement, standards, and the valuing of particular physical capacities (mis)recognize the abilities of *dis*abled students in PE? In beginning to explore this question we next consider how Bourdieu's conceptual tools can provide a useful means for rearticulating ability within PE. We then briefly introduce the research projects from which data was drawn to illustrate how students and teachers make sense of ability within PE. In concluding, we discuss the implications of these understandings for students and the practice of PE.

Bourdieu, ability and PE

Like Evans (2004), Hay and lisahunter (2006) and Hay and Macdonald (2010) we deploy Bourdieu's thinking tools in order to make sense of how ability is imposed, pursued and acquired within and through PE *practices*. In critiquing dominant beliefs about ability and their representation in the message systems of education, Evans (2004) drew on the theoretical work of Bourdieu to provoke readers to consider ability as a social construct and the recognition of 'able' as a process of social construction. Evans proposed that the embodied dispositions of a person, which Bourdieu described as their *habitus*, could be considered as abilities when 'defined relationally with reference to values, attitudes and mores prevailing within a discursive field' (Evans 2004: 100). *Habitus* in Bourdieu's work demonstrates the 'ontological complicity' that defines the relationship between agents (such as teachers and students) and their social worlds (such as schooling). It is when individuals participate in *fields* (including PE, sport and the family) that they embody beliefs, action and appearance cultivated within these *fields* and these features scaffold what becomes (mis)recognized as ability within PE. Here Bourdieu's (1990b) notion of (mis)recognition is used to reflect the *practices* within PE that marginalize, but yet remain a legitimizing feature of PE, and this becomes an integral part of the reality of the *practices* within this *field*. Evans observed that one's identification as 'able', or 'talented', served as a form of cultural '*capital*' that could be traded for other forms of *capital* such as high achievement grades in a school subject, or selection for culturally esteemed sporting teams or programs. To this end, within the *field* of PE, Bourdieu's (1990b) notion of *capital* provides a means of articulating the value afforded to how different abilities are recognized, acquired and valued by students and teachers, and through the *practices* of PE. That is, what gets (mis)recognized as valued abilities and who is deemed to be 'less able' becomes implicitly and explicitly evidenced through the actions and beliefs of those agents experiencing PE. In beginning to utilize Bourdieu's conceptual tools to shed light on conceptions of ability within PE, we focus on conversations from *dis*abled students and PE teachers about ability.

Conversations about ability and PE

This chapter specifically focuses on *dis*abled students and PE teachers in order to explore embodied conceptions of ability within PE. As we have already suggested, *dis*abled students offer an interesting vantage point for considering ability, given that *dis*ability is often conceived of as the opposite to ability. Alongside *dis*abled students we also consider PE teachers' conceptions, as they are powerful mediators reproducing and reproduced by ability discourses. This chapter draws on broader thinking developed from a number of research projects (Fitzgerald 2005; Fitzgerald and Kirk 2009b; Hay and lisahunter 2006; Hay and Macdonald 2010). In particular, we utilize extracts of interviews from a study focusing on ten young *dis*abled people and their experiences of physical education and sport (Fitzgerald and Kirk 2009b). Interviews were undertaken in two secondary schools in the Midlands of England. The research participants were selected because they experienced mainstream (regular) physical education. Within this mainstream context it should be recognized that concerns around inclusion have increasingly been promoted nationally and indeed internationally (Gabel and Danforth 2008). That is, it is implicitly assumed that PE teachers will (re)consider their practices in order to support inclusive PE experiences. The two young *dis*abled people featured in this chapter are James and Adam. James enjoys PE at school. He is considered by his teammates to be a good boccia player. James has cerebral palsy and uses a walking frame. Adam does not like PE and is generally negative about school. He enjoys watching and playing football with his brothers away from school. Adam uses a wheelchair.

Data is also presented from a study including one teacher and six Year 11 students (in their penultimate year of compulsory schooling) at two demographically distinct schools across twenty weeks of the school year (Hay and Macdonald 2010). Over this period, information was collected about the influence of teachers and students on the nature of the *field* and the contributing factors to ability recognition and differentiation. Mark was the Head of Department at a large, high-fee, coeducational private school, while Anthony was an experienced senior teacher at a state secondary school situated in a relatively low socioeconomic area. Mark and Anthony were asked to identify six students in their PE classes in three deliberately broad and loosely defined ability categories (high, middle and low). Unaware of the identification process, these students were then invited to be participants in the study. Drawing on the different studies summarized above, a number of short illustrative extracts follow in which two students and two teachers talk about ability in PE.

Ability talk in PE

My walking frame makes me different in PE (James, aged 12)

> With my [walking] frame it makes PE different for me. I mean it's the same in that I'm in my class with my mates. I get to do it all. It's just like any subject we do… Like I'm with my friends and do what they do. I would say, I have more things to think about you know. You know, it's like I've got more equipment to think about. I'd say it makes me very skilled, at an

advanced level. I have to think about how I use my frame. So I've got to do what everyone else does and to do this have to figure out how to move, like figure out how my frame will help me. It's easy for the boys who run normally and they shouldn't get credit from winning, that's just easy. Give them a frame and see what they think then. Mr Davies has no idea 'bout me and what I can do cause he's just looking at the good boys, the ones playing for the school teams, the ones who look good, who do what he tells them, they win. I can't do that. I can't be like them.

(James)

James' excerpt prompts consideration of the extent to which he perceives his PE teacher to be inclusive in relation to how his ability is conceived of and recognized. James acknowledges that physical performance is important within PE. To this end, James perceives his ability, in relation to skill, to be superior to other students. James indicates this is because of the additional consideration needed to move with his walking frame. As he describes, he is 'at an advanced level', possessing what he deems to be valued *capital* within the *field* of PE. However, the valuing process does not seem to extend to other powerful agents within the *field* and James is acutely aware that his skills are not recognized or valued by his PE teacher. James conveys a familiarity through his *habitus* about what counts as valued physical *capital* within the *field* of PE. For James the symbolic power of normative (non-*dis*abled) skills and competences form a significant marker of ability within PE. And James' ability to skillfully move with his walking frame does not inscribe him with the comparable status given to 'playing for a school team, looking good and winning'. James also recognizes that he is not able to work towards these kinds of valued measures of ability within PE. In this respect, whilst inclusive agendas may have extended practical PE experiences to James, they seem not to have restructured the *field* with regards to valued *capitals*.

Me and My 'A' grade brothers (Adam, aged 12)

Within schooling the school report is a key resource that serves as a means of transmitting values and beliefs about achievement and ability. In this sense, the school report rewards those that accumulate the *capital* valued within specific *fields* such as PE. In this excerpt Adam, like James, has a strong sense that his physical *capital* associated with ability is absent in his school report.

'The Report'. It's the one thing I really hate about school. I can remember every grade I get in every subject, but only one matters. English B, Maths B, Science B, Art A, RE C, attendance 100%, works hard, likeable young man, popular amongst peers, blah de blah de blah. And then the mark that counts, PE, C. Exactly the same, mixes well, tries hard, but that's not enough, never good enough. Why? 'Cause my brothers always get As in PE; top of the class, key member of the team, crucial performances in last game, blah de blah de blah. And PE's the most important subject for dad... 'Well done son' doesn't mean the same as 'Well done lads, chips off the old block' ... I hate [school] reports, if I could change one thing about school it'd be reports. It's not like I'm bad at school, I'm okay, my report is okay.

(Adam)

For Adam, his lack of achievement seemed to be all the more evident because of his awareness of his father's expectations and the comparisons made with his brothers. According to Bourdieu (1998a) the family is a key *field* in which various forms of *capital* can be accumulated and converted. Indeed, Adam's short extract illustrates how normative conceptions of physical performance within PE and the family are powerfully reproduced between both *fields*. Key family members (in this case Adam's father), like PE teachers, serve as key mediators for recognizing the possession of valued *capitals*. Having reflected on the excerpts from students James and Adam, next we consider reflections from two PE teachers.

Achieving their potential (PE teachers, Mark and Anthony)

As part of the Hay and Macdonald (2010) study, the teachers were asked to explain the basis upon which they assigned students to the ability categories of low, middle and high. Anthony highlighted the significance of the grades, the students' conduct and their motivation, and physical prowess as characteristics informing their ability categorization.

Yep, um, purely on their first term results [selection of students in their ability groups]. Largely, I looked at their physical performance first and based on that then I looked at their academic achievements or their academic um... well, basically how well they're conducting themselves in an academic setting. You know, looking at their motivation.

(Anthony)

Similarly, Mark highlighted the significance of dispositional factors as well as the relational engagement of students with the teachers. The students' physical capacities were also significant:

Mmm... um, well, first of all, when you start teaching, when you first get them together, just their demeanour in the classroom for a start, gives you a bit of an indication. Whether they're switched on, whether they respond to your questions or your teaching ... It's fairly easy in the physical side when you put them out on the volleyball court and you ask them to play a game of volleyball, which we do very early in the piece, without too much tuition. We ask them to get out there on court and play a game and we video them and then they assess themselves, too, at that stage ... But as far as the academic side of things is concerned and the classroom work, it's a matter of how they interact with you in the class early on.

(Mark)

Ability was an important factor in Anthony's mind in relation to achievement potential and achievement realization. On numerous occasions Anthony suggested that students, in the main, achieved standards that were consistent with their abilities and that motivation was both indicative of student ability and the key to good grades. Although he believed it was possible that students could achieve grades both beyond their abilities and below their abilities, he thought that this was unlikely. Anthony indicated:

> No I don't think so. I don't think there were any surprises. The mark they were actually awarded was one they deserved based on their abilities I s'pose. So, it's um… I think they got what they deserved, basically.
>
> (Anthony)

In this way Anthony demonstrated a strong meritocratic view of student achievement that positioned students, their abilities and their work ethic as the significant factors contributing to their achievement. In general, he believed that the physical capacities of the students were high and that their academic quality undermined their potential to achieve in PE.

Both Anthony and Mark referenced the students' abilities against their own capacities, interests and investments in PE and associated discourse communities such as sport. For example:

> I would like the kids to come out knowing what I know and be able to do what I do. So it's about knowing and doing a sport, a physical activity. Um, that is a dream and that will never happen. Um, I guess for that to happen the kids have got to eat, breathe… they've got to live the sport to be able to learn it.
>
> (Anthony)

> I guess I quite like doing it [teaching Senior PE] 'cos I feel comfortable. I feel that it's my subject. It's something that I am experienced in. I think I know what I'm doing.
>
> (Mark)

As mentioned earlier, *fields* are constituted by, among other contributors, the expectations, beliefs and values of the most powerful agents – in this case, the PE teacher. Indeed, the teachers were clearly influential in the structuring/restructuring of the *field*, as well as the conditions of engagement in it. The teachers' sense of agency within the *field*, indicating their capacity to structure or restructure the *field* was strong and this had implications for recognition of the varying levels of ability.

Concluding remarks

By drawing on Bourdieu's thinking and the accounts from *dis*abled students and PE teachers, we argue that understanding ability as embodied social constructs offers possibilities for reconceptualizing the abilities of young people in PE.

Indeed, by scrutinizing the structures, *practices* and mechanisms of PE a fuller picture emerges regarding the ways in which this values and (mis)recognizes ability. The two teachers bring to the fore the values, beliefs, and expectations of those with most power over the defining features of PE and their particular influence over what is understood, promoted and recognized as ability in PE. In particular, the extracts highlight the prominence of dispositional and attitudinal characteristics (e.g. motivation, demeanor, enthusiasm), an emphasis on physical performance and other physical *capitals*. The excerpts from the two *dis*abled students highlight an explicit awareness of how *fields* (such as PE and the family) and key agents (such as PE teachers and parents) serve as a resource in which the emerging *habitus* contributes to recognizing ability within PE. To this end, the brief transcript excerpts and associated analysis draw out a number of key issues concerning notions of ability.

First, the teachers were less interested in the development or alteration of the bodies of all the students in the class, and more interested in engaging with students already possessing the valued physical and dispositional attributes. This was emphasized by Anthony, who indicated an excitement when students demonstrated potential. For the other teacher, Mark, the inequitable engagement was more subtle, but no less constraining, as he was resigned to the limited effect he believed he could have on the students' corporeal capacities. These accounts serve as a gauge for the kind of body the teachers believe they can work with in PE, a body that is unlikely to be characterized as *dis*abled.

Second, ability seemed to be a relatively stable concept in the mind of both teachers even though their perceptions of the sources and expressions of ability were different. Anthony believed that lower abilities of students were associated with their limited aspirations and motivations, themselves antecedents of their familial conditions. Mark, on the contrary, believed in the inherent nature of ability and referred to the students' possession of 'God-given talents', expressed in a context of high expectations and standards. Not only was ability stable, it was a strong predictor of achievement in the sense that both Anthony and Mark believed the students achieved in line with their abilities. Mark indicated further that he was able to tell whether a student was going to achieve within the first few weeks of engagement because of his perception of their work ethic and physical capacities. Indeed, it was physical competences that the two *dis*abled students also recognized as important markers of ability, that is, playing for a school team or achieving an A grade in a school report. Interestingly, James and Adam were aware of the ways in which they did not match up to these ideals and, in different ways, each expressed frustration at their inability to work towards valued abilities recognized by their PE teachers and within their family.

Finally, and related to the first two issues, the teachers were clearly influential in the structuring/restructuring of the *field*, as well as the conditions of engagement in it. These kinds of conditions were essentially premised on normative ideals that assumed non-*dis*abled recipients of PE. To this end, the *dis*abled students were aware that their PE experiences failed to match up to such non-*dis*abled norms. Yet James was able to articulate how he believed his physical competences related to maneuvering with his walking frame should be valued within PE. This seemed not to be recognized or valued by his PE teachers. Like Evans (2004) we would argue it is this kind of (mis)recognition of valued abilities that serves to perpetuate inequalities experienced by many students, including *dis*abled students within PE.

In this chapter we have focused on how abilities are conceived of, sanctioned, measured and conferred within PE. Our encounter with Bourdieu's conceptual tools including *habitus* and *capital* provides a useful means for rearticulating notions of ability within the *field* of PE. That is, Bourdieu offers the tools to unravel and expose the shortcomings of defining ability through neoliberal discourses of measurability. Such discourses are implicitly restricted to an 'able body' and seek to quantify ability through measures defined by optimal performance (focusing on sporting success) and standards associated with fitness levels (focusing on health agendas). Moreover, by drawing on Bourdieu's thinking to queer the relationship between ability and *dis*ability, we believe that understandings of ability as the embodied social constructs become more sharply attuned. Indeed, by attending to the relationship between ability and *dis*ability conventional conceptions of ability within PE can be brought to the foreground and ambiguities recognized. It is this amplification that could most helpfully guide the prospect and (im)possibilities for transforming how ability is recognized within PE. Of course, Bourdieu's thinking also offers the possibilities of accounting for the interdependency of social practices between different sites of physical culture. And whilst this chapter has focused on a PE context, we are mindful that this shapes, and is shaped, by other discursive *practices* evident through physical culture more broadly. For example, the experiences of physical culture encountered by the two students and teachers featured in this chapter would have illuminated further these kinds of insights. It is to these contexts that our attention also needs to turn if we are to better understand how ability is imposed, pursued, and acquired within and through physical culture.

13 *Symbolic capital* and the hetero norm as *doxa* in Physical Education

Karin Redelius, Birgitta Fagrell and Håkan Larsson

Keywords: *Heteronormativity, gender, doxa, symbolic capital, symbolic violence*

Introduction

A number of scholars have pointed out that physical education (PE) seems to be characterized by rather stable gender norms when it comes to patterns of behavior and perceptions of the subject (Brown 2005; Flintoff 2008; Penney 2002). These norms could also be labelled *doxa* because they are ideas, interests or practices that seem to be experienced as 'natural' and 'self-evident' (Bourdieu 1977). In this chapter, we would like to draw attention to these dominating and stable patterns and to *doxa* concerning gender and sexuality.

Some might regard 'gender' as an issue that is related to girls, and 'sexuality' as one that is related to homosexuality. This is, of course, not the case, since *doxa* concerning gender and sexuality influence the lives of each of us. Prevailing norms often support a certain way of being and moving and are therefore both enabling and restricting in many ways. This is also true for the so-called hetero-norm, or heteronormativity. In simple terms, heteronormativity designates the (often implicit) assumption that everyone is heterosexual 'until proven otherwise', and that the 'natural' way of life is heterosexual (Rosenberg 2002). In our culture, there is a tendency to interpret social interactions from the given standpoint that everyone is heterosexual, and that heterosexual desire is related to girls and boys being different and 'opposite' (Butler 1990). Practically, this means that actions, e.g. ways of moving, that are seen to signify heterosexuality are promoted, while ways of moving that are interpreted as 'gay' or 'queer' are marginalized or excluded.

In PE, the taken-for-granted norms, or *doxa*, condition the participation of all students, regardless of gender or sexual identity. All students are exposed to *doxa* with regard to things like appearance, how they should move and what kind of person they should be in the gym. All these reflect interests with a gendered slant, in terms of what girls and boys should look like and how girls and boys should move. The aim of this chapter is to highlight girls' and boys' terms and conditions in the subject of PE, with a special focus on gender, sexuality and normality. By using some of Pierre Bourdieu's concepts (*doxa, symbolic violence, field* and *symbolic capital*), we demonstrate how these can be employed to analyze and understand a school subject characterized by physical exercise and bodily movement.

Gender and sexuality as *doxa* in PE in Sweden

PE is one of the most popular subjects in Sweden. However, the prevailing *doxa* and gender structures are notable in that this popularity is not evenly distributed among pupils of different gender (Larsson and Redelius 2008). With regard to gender, it is also the case that boys feel that they can influence the teaching to a greater extent than girls, which means that boys' attitudes are more positive than those of girls, boys report a higher level of physical activity during the lessons compared to girls and boys have higher grades than girls. Having said this, it is important to note that the groups of girls and boys are not always homogeneous. In some cases there seem to be greater differences in attitudes to the subject within groups of boys or girls than between the groups (Larsson and Redelius 2008). However, the general picture indicates that masculine norms dominate the school subject (Quennerstedt *et al.*2008).

This general picture of gender patterns has served as a starting point for several of the studies that we have conducted in recent years. These studies have been directed towards students in their later years of compulsory schooling in Sweden (15-16 years of age) and their teachers. The methods used have primarily been in-depth interviews and observations (and in some studies video recordings). The major attempt has been to explore, and in some ways challenge, *doxa* concerning gender and normality. More specifically, the aims have been:

- to explore the relation between movement and heteronormativity in PE as experienced by the students (Larsson *et al.* 2011);
- to illuminate how games place girls and boys in different subject positions (Fagrell *et al.* 2012);
- to illuminate the *symbolic capital* as it appears when teachers talk about grading criteria, and to discuss the way it contributes to the construction of gender (Redelius *et al.* 2009);
- to outline a perspective that might be able to produce new ways of conceptualising and understanding what is happening in terms of gender power relations in PE classes (Larsson *et al.* 2011);
- and finally, to scrutinize the hetero-normative character of the discourses and *practices* that, from the point of view of PE teaching, constitute gendered positions and subjectivities in PE and make them susceptible to change (Larsson *et al.* 2009).

A brief account of the results of these studies show, for example, that the observed teaching was underpinned by essentialist and functionalist assumptions about gender, exposed through a pragmatic approach to teaching. Although the teachers were aware of the dominance of (some of the) boys in the gym, this dominance seemed to be regarded as *doxa*, i.e. as something normal or natural and something to be managed logistically rather than challenged. It seemed equally important for the PE teachers to treat the students in a way that promoted physical activity for the majority. In doing so, they relied on traditional ideas about gender in relation to sport and physical activity and avoided challenging gender stereotypes. These strategies, which we label benevolence towards girls and a tribute to masculinity, are successful in so far as the students adhere to the same traditional ideas and do not resist the gender stereotypes used by the teachers. As we see it, the strategies of benevolence towards girls and the tribute to masculinity among boys are different ways of reproducing ideas about the sexes as naturally different and attracted to each other. In other words, such strategies are based on hetero-normative assumptions. In view of this, any real attempt to challenge gender stereotypes in PE should also challenge heteronormativity.

The results of the studies also showed how different kinds of activities, notably dance and ball games, position girls and boys in different ways. In order to act as 'normal', girls and boys seem to have to conform to a heterosexual matrix (Butler 1990). This means that if boys are skilled dancers they are more likely to be viewed as queer or strange and, conversely, that if girls are skilled ball players they are more likely to be regarded as queer – and that this is undesirable. Since the *doxa* of heteronormativity is embodied in and through movement, another conclusion is that any effort to challenge the hetero-normative culture within PE would have to consider which kinds of activities to include in the PE curriculum and make it possible for the students to move in new ways.

Other results from our studies, mentioned above, showed that the *logic of practice* (Bourdieu 1980/1990) governing the lessons was the 'proper game', i.e. more or less playing according to the official rules. Combined with hegemonic masculinity (Connell 1995) and the passivity of the teacher, this kind of logic resulted in the game being dominated by several boys who had been socially conditioned to dominate even though they might not want to, and by the ball-playing girls either being positioned or allowing themselves to be placed in situations in which they consistently underperformed due to this same social conditioning. The social space of PE or the *field* of PE as practiced in the school gym is a contestable space in which the teachers hold more power to determine the prevailing *logic of practice*; therefore the actions of both the boys and the girls are, among other factors, an outcome of the hetero-normative expectations of the teachers. Many attempts to 'adjust' the conditions for girls and boys actually reinforced the traditional gender order, where boys are seen as 'naturally' physically gifted and girls 'lie low' during the lesson.

How, then, might the results that reinforce the earlier findings that PE and the gym setting are sites for gender (re)production and hetero-normative cultures be understood? Here we find the work of Bourdieu both inspiring and useful, especially when it comes to understanding and analyzing power relations. Bourdieu was interested in how power and status relations are maintained in a society in a 'stealthy' way by, for example, the education system and the organization of sport and leisure. He is described as a theorist whose general theme is to

> analyse the role of culture in the reproduction of social structures and how power and status relationships in society are maintained and reproduced in almost all social practices, for example, in fashion, art, literature, architecture, sport, language, education and marriage.
>
> (Johansson and Miegel 1996: 202)

In this sense, Bourdieu's work is fruitful for analyzing how gender norms (or *doxa*) are reproduced in the school setting of PE. Let us therefore turn to his work and key concepts in order to acquire a deeper understanding of the prevailing *doxa* and why it seems so difficult to challenge and change.

Theoretical framework and key concepts

A starting point for us is that the dominating *doxa* for boys and girls in PE are culturally arbitrary. In other words, the origins are not natural, but naturalized to 'make sense'. Instead the prevailing conditions are part of what Bourdieu labels a paradoxical *doxa* that is upheld by *symbolic violence* (1990b). In his book *Masculine Domination* (Bourdieu 2002) he starts by describing the 'paradox of *doxa*'. We include his words at length because they not only captures the essence of *doxa* in a vivid and clear way, but also outline what is meant by *symbolic violence*:

> I have always been astonished by what might be called the *paradox of doxa* – the fact that the order of the world as we find it, with its one-way streets and its no-entry signs, whether literate or figurative, with its penalties and obligations, is broadly respected; that there are not more transgressions and subversives, contraventions and 'follies' ... or, still more surprisingly, that the established order, with its relations of domination, its rights and prerogatives, privileges and injustice, ultimately perpetuates itself so easily, apart from a few historical accidents, and that the most intolerable conditions of existence can so often be perceived as acceptable and even natural. And I have also seen masculine domination, and the way it is imposed and suffered, as the prime example of this paradoxical submission, an effect of what I call symbolic violence, a gentle violence, imperceptible and invisible, even to its victims, exerted for the most parts through the purely symbolic channels of communication and cognition (more precisely misrecognition), recognition and even feeling.
>
> (Bourdieu 2002: 1)

The term *symbolic violence* is used in order to understand how this paradoxical *doxa* is reproduced and continues to affect us. *Symbolic violence* can be explained as 'the violence which is exercised upon a social agent with his or her complicity' (Bourdieu and Wacquant 1992: 167). It is the imposition of certain thoughts and perceptions on dominated social agents who then take the social order to be just. *Misrecognition* is an important term in this context, since it is 'the fact of recognizing a violence which is wielded precisely inasmuch as one does not perceive it as such' (p. 168). The dominated in fact take their position to be 'right'. Below, we present an example of how *symbolic violence* might appear in PE. The extract is from an interview with a girl who was on the pitch while playing basketball but remained mainly on the periphery and was hardly engaged in the game. She did not receive any passes and almost never touched the ball. In fact, it is doubtful whether her team-mates even noticed her presence:

> Researcher (R): How was it today? What did you think about this lesson?
> Girl (G): It was good…
> R: I was sitting and watching the passing and such. Did you get any passes?
> G: No. Not from the guys.
> R: How does that feel?
> G: …Doesn't matter, you know…
> R: Don't you get irritated?
> G: No… I don't care.
> R: No… Did you get any passes from the girls?
> G: Eh … There were no girls in my team.
> R: But does it still feel worthwhile playing?
> G: Mm… sort of.
> R: Sort of?
> G: Yes… one learns how anyway.
> R: Yes, what do you think you're learning?
> G: Mm… Well you know, to play basketball (giggles).
> R: OK, so it's about basketball.
> G: We have just learned rules and stuff that I didn't know about. Or rather re-learned them, I knew them, but had forgotten.

Recognizing the limitations of interview data, this girl seems to be dominated or is perhaps allowing herself to be dominated, but nevertheless thinks that the lesson was 'good' and that it 'doesn't matter' that she did not get any passes because 'she learns basketball anyway'. The paradoxical *doxa* that encourages ball-playing boys to dominate lessons in PE is an example of *symbolic violence* that in some sense is much more powerful than physical violence, in that it is embedded in the most modest actions and the structures of cognition of individuals and imposes the legitimacy of the social order. *Symbolic violence* presupposes a kind of active complicity on the part of those subjected to it. In that sense it requires that 'those subjected to it believe in the legitimacy of power and the legitimacy of those who wield it' (Bourdieu 1980/1990: 23).

Let us now turn to another of Bourdieu's concepts – *field*. It is hardly possible to view school as a place where consensus and harmonizing perspectives prevail. On the contrary, fights or struggles about values are always taking place: for example, over the time allocations for subjects, the availability of different kinds of resources and how the education of children and young people should be conducted. These predominant values are also related to gender. In a Bourdieuian sense, it is possible to imagine that PE teachers and students are agents in a social *field*. It is in this spirit that we use the idea of an existing *field* in order to understand what is going on in PE.

According to Bourdieu (1993a), a *field* exists when a delimited group of people and institutions struggle about something that is common to them. PE might be described as a weak autonomous *field*, mainly because it is highly permeable to the influence of other *fields* (Brown 2005). Drawing on Bourdieu (1993b), we suggest that PE might be seen as 'part of the larger field of struggles of the definition of the legitimate body and the legitimate use of the body' (p.122), and that the legitimate use of the body is seldom gender neutral. In an earlier study, Hunter (2004) uses Bourdieu to analyze and discuss the construction and negotiation of pupils' subjectivities within the *social space* of a particular PE class. She claims that the *field* of PE is 'made up of a structured system of social relations between the educational authority, PE teacher educators, PE curriculum writers, health and sport professionals who have influence over curriculum and *practices*, individual school administrators, PE teachers and PE pupils' (p. 176).

The concepts of *habitus* and *capital* are closely related to the concept of *field*. *Habitus* can be described as social structures embodied as corporeal dispositions, or corporeal schemes of values and perceptions, or, in Bourdieu's words: 'systems of durable, transposable dispositions, structured structures predisposed to function as structuring structures' (1977: 72). For a *field* to arise there have to be stakes to play for and people with a *field*-related *habitus*, including both knowledge about and recognition of the inherent laws of the *field*, who are prepared to play the game.

In this chapter we make use of the concept of *symbolic capital*, i.e. what is recognized as valuable and assigned a value. By 'valuable' and 'of value' we mean the qualities, assets or resources that those in the field recognize and regard as desirable, prestigious and sought after. In other words, what is ascribed as a value is not an individual concern, but it is related to different social groups' interests and views. Used in this way, it can be linked to masculinity and femininity and what is assigned a value in different contexts and what is not. Hunter (2004), for example, found that *capital* was defined in relation to sport/health/fitness, to being a good student and to the gender and bodies of students. In order for a value to be recognized and assigned, there have to be people in the *field* who are predisposed to perceive specific qualities as desirable (Bourdieu 1984a). One might say that *symbolic capital* is an embodied disposition that enables us to orient ourselves in this world.

In Rosenberg's (2002) words, heteronormativity has many connotations and functions and could be labelled as *symbolic capital*. Heteronormativity designates sexuality in an expected form, heterosexual, and means that certain privileged groups of people are in a position to define certain kinds of heterosexuality as to be desired and wished for. Tiina Rosenberg puts it like this:

> [T]he invisibility, the stereotypes and being perceived as different are engendered by the dominating groups that make themselves, their experiences and their culture universal. ... On the whole, without understanding it

themselves, they project their own ideas and experiences about mankind as such, and make them appear as universally applicable. ... Some people are made invisible, since the dominating groups have difficulties in seeing their own point of view as one among many.

(2002: 123-5, our translation)

In PE, displaying 'real masculinity' would be 'quite literally, to embody force, to embody competence' (Connell 1983:27). This means that using force in any physical activity would be akin to 'doing boy', in the case of girls to 'doing tomboy' or even to 'doing lezzie'. In terms of sexual connotations, displaying masculinity would then constitute opposite things in relation to who is doing what. Displaying 'real femininity' does not mean putting the body into fluid and directed motion or occupying (too much) space. Displaying femininity would then constitute 'doing girl' or 'doing sissy', depending on who does what. As we see it, the girl interviewed above displayed such reluctance towards using (too much) force and embodying (too much) space and competence. Another of the girls we interviewed expressed similar views:

> Researcher (R): It's clear that the boys claim more space and are more active, especially when playing ghost-ball ... and as you say ... they throw harder and so on ... Do you think that matters, or that it has a positive or negative impact? Student (S) 16 years old: No, well, I don't think that it matters very much... Um ... I mean it doesn't do me any harm [giggles].
> R: Do you think that you ... have fewer possibilities to show ... the teacher what you can do then?
> S: No, because I think that I can do that anyway... Well ... eh ... No, I don't think so. I mean, it's not as though they... If I really wanted to, I could play really aggressively and ... be a boy [giggles]... but I don't feel the need for it.
> R: Neat expression, 'and be a boy', what do mean exactly? [both chuckle]
> S: Naah, but I mean, throw hard... fling the ball.
>
> (Larsson, Fagrell and Redelius 2011: 21)

In the same way as this student and other girls are reluctant to embody force and competence, a lot of boys attempt to do just that in order to avoid epithets like 'throwing like a girl' or being called names like 'sissy' (Rønholt 2002). The equivalent (and opposite) way of misogynist and heterosexist naming of a girl is 'lezzie'. It seems to be quite common for sporty girls (often designated as 'tomboys') to be called such names if they are unable to display some kind of heterosexual alibi, or a 'heterosexy image' as Griffin (1992: 197) calls it. As stated above, we contend that it is practices like these that, at least partially, make the gender patterns in PE so stable.

Conclusions

Despite several decades of studies of gender in PE, it is both interesting and thought-provoking that challenging and changing the gender power relations in this subject is so difficult. We believe that stable gender structures are related to a non-challenging approach towards the *doxa* of PE: heteronormativity. This naturally echoes the paradox of *doxa*: 'the fact that the order of the world as we find it … is broadly respected. That there are not more transgressions' (Bourdieu 2002: 1). Not only do some people – and in the case of PE, particularly girls and some boys – hold back and underperform, they also believe that this is all right because 'they are not sporty'. As they are not as good at sport as (some) boys, 'it's only natural'.

Social structures are difficult to change, due in part to the incorporated dispositions that are embodied. Incorporated dispositions, or *habitus*, are expressed through individuals' tastes and the particular 'gut-feeling' that people develop in relation to what is right and wrong in a certain situation. What complicates processes of change is that, due to this bodily dimension, people do not necessarily feel comfortable with change, even though they might, rationally speaking, benefit from it. After all, it is not easy to determine – rationally or otherwise – what people might benefit from. What is beneficial in one sense, e.g. being a girl and embodying force in PE, might be a disadvantage in another, such as being confirmed as a real girl and perhaps also being desirable in the heterosexual game. Displaying femininity, which for a girl means acting 'normally', i.e. making herself intelligible as a heterosexual, would then be a problem in relation to what is valued in PE. In reality, it is impossible to separate the social *field* of the legitimate use of the body and the social *field* of intimate sexual relations and pairing for reproduction.

What can PE teachers do to challenge the paradox of *doxa*? Although we believe that it might be difficult to change the prevailing gender *doxa* by simply making the students aware of gender norms, such practice could nevertheless be part of a pedagogical ambition to challenge *doxa*. However, following Bourdieu, we believe that changing *practice* is much more effective. This is an important, albeit sometimes difficult, educational challenge, because it requires awareness of and knowledge about gender norms and how they are played out in *practice* from the perspective of the teacher. Such awareness could form the basis of a strategy in which *practice* is altered. This means changing activities so that students start to act differently. In the game that was played during the lesson we observed, the students were not given any specific assignment or function, and no one expected them to take on any particular feature of the game either. If they had been given assignments, perhaps they would have been differently positioned.

Bourdieu's work has enhanced our analysis of why social structures – in this case unequal norms of gender and sexuality in PE – are so difficult to change. We have used his tools to understand why gender power relations seem to appear as self-evident and taken-for-granted (*doxa*), why they are sometimes ignored or misrecognized as natural and thereby ensure the legitimacy of inequality (*symbolic violence*), and why embodied dispositions (*habitus*) make some people feel uncomfortable with change even though they might benefit from it. From Bourdieu, we have also learned that a critical approach to teaching is not about 'changing them' (the students), but about changing *practices* in ways that make it possible for students to take up a different position within the social space. Changing *practices* would also involve destabilizing the social positions that the *practices* constitute.

14 Understanding snowboarding bodies with Bourdieu

Some reflections from the snow field[1]

Holly Thorpe

Keywords: *Habitus, Capital, Field, Practice, Distinction*

In *Snowboarding Bodies in Theory and Practice* (Thorpe 2011) I blend social theory and empirical evidence to offer a comprehensive investigation of snowboarding bodies in local and global contexts. My analysis derives from multiple modes of data generation, a type of methodology used extensively by Bourdieu and which he describes as a 'discursive montage' of 'all sources' (Bourdieu and Wacquant 1992: 66). Bourdieu (1980/1990) adds that this is 'the only possible attitude toward theoretical tradition' (p. 252). Throughout this project I seized all types of data, evidence, sources and artefacts to enlighten my inquiry into snowboarding bodies, but my primary methods were participant observations, interviews and media analysis. Between 2004 and 2010, I conducted fifteen 'ethnographic visits' – ranging from one week to one month – in an array of snowboarding communities and ski resorts in Canada, France, Italy, New Zealand, Switzerland and the United States. Attempting to understand how snowboarders experienced their bodies in and across local snowboarding fields, I made observations on and off the snow, including lift lines, chair lifts, resort lodges, snowboard competitions and events, bars and cafes, snowboard shops and bus-shelters. I developed my participant-observations in dialogue with 60 participants (32 female and 28 male) ranging from 18 to 56 years of age. Seeking to understand the diverse experiences of snowboarders, interviewees held an array of positions within the culture ranging from novice to professional athletes. I also used cultural sources such as magazines, films and websites, in conjunction with multi-sited fieldwork and interviews, which helped deepen my understanding of snowboarding's cultural complexities.

In sum, my study seized all types of data, evidence, sources and artefacts to enlighten the following theoretical inquiry into snowboarding bodies. But even the richest caches of primary source materials 'will speak only when they are properly questioned' (Bloch 1953, cited in Hardy 1999: 91). As Bourdieu, Chamboredon and Passeron (1991) remind us, no matter how sophisticated one's 'techniques of observation and proof', if it is not accompanied by a 'redoubling of theoretical vigilance' it will only 'lead us to see better and better fewer and fewer things' (p. 88). In my investigation of snowboarding bodies, the range and diversity of theories structured my evidence, and in so doing helped me to reveal more of the complexities and nuances within the culture. I employed an array of theories from compatible paradigms to help explain various dimensions of the snowboarding body (i.e., cultural memory studies, Marxist political economy, post-Fordism, Foucauldian theorizing, Pierre Bourdieu's theory of embodiment, feminism, sociology of mobilities, and non-representational theory). The aim of this project was not 'finding the "right theory"' or 'demonstrating one's theoretical acumen', but finding 'whatever theoretical positions' will best facilitate the task of 'understanding what is going on' (Wright 2001, cited in Andrews 2008: 57). The various theoretical approaches adopted in this study offered different perspectives on various dimensions of the snowboarding culture. In this chapter I discuss the value of Bourdieu's conceptual schema for explaining the snowboarding body as a cultural and social phenomenon.

Understanding snowboarding bodies with Pierre Bourdieu

Although Bourdieu never spoke about snowboarding, his concepts are 'good to think with' (Jenkins 2002: 176) and offer useful and suggestive insights into how socially competent behaviour is achieved within contemporary sport and physical cultures. In his theory of distinction, Bourdieu (1984) assigns a central place to the body, and through a number of theoretical concepts provides insight into the distinctive corporeal practices employed by individuals and groups within contemporary society. He developed the concepts of *capital, field, class, taste* and *habitus* to analyse the formation and the reproduction of these *practices* and explain their significance as subtle social markers. These concepts remain deliberately vague and malleable, encouraging their questioning and their adaptation to the specific domain to which they are applied. Indeed, Bourdieu's conceptual schema enabled an examination of the intimate cultural details surrounding the meaning and use of the body in the snowboarding culture, and how such practices influence the everyday experiences of participants from different groups and positions within the *field*. Here, I briefly illustrate the value of Bourdieu's concepts of *habitus*, *capital*, and *field* as heuristic devices for understanding the snowboarding body as a possessor of power, a form of status, a bearer of symbolic value, and a form of *cultural, physical,* and *symbolic capital.*

Habitus*: Embodying snowboarding culture*

All participants come to snowboarding with a *habitus* instilled from an early age and informed by a network of social positions (i.e. class, gender, race, sexuality, nationality and region). In my research, however, I was particularly interested in the snowboarding *habitus* which develops through practical engagement with, or rather socialization into, snowboarding culture. The distinctive practices of a snowboarding *habitus* are imprinted and encoded in a socializing process that commences during early entry into snowboarding culture. In the past this was primarily through participation, but for many contemporary participants this is often via exposure to a variety of media sources, including snowboarding magazines, websites, videos, video games, or television coverage of major events (see Thorpe 2011). Nonetheless, it is during this socialization process that the 'practical transmission' of boarding 'knowledge' via instructors' and peers' comments, observation, and magazines and films, become embodied (Ford and Brown 2006, p. 123).

In contrast to the calculated performances of some novices, the *habitus* of core participants differs from imitation due to the 'lack of conscious effort involved in the reproduction of a gesture or action' (Ford and Brown 2006: 125). According to Bourdieu (1980/1990), 'what is "learned by the body" is not something that one has, like knowledge that can be brandished, but something that one is' (p. 73). In other words, the snowboarding *habitus* refers to the full embodiment of snowboarding culture that then (typically subconsciously) influences everyday practices and performances. Professional snowboarder Romain De Marchi identifies the *habitus* of core boarders: 'it's kind of a fashionable thing' to snowboard these days but 'the *real* snowboarders still have the passion and know the soul of snowboarding' (cited in Muzzey 2003: 136, emphasis added). Todd Richards (2003) agrees: 'Snowboarding is something you have to figure out. You have to earn it. You have to make it over different hurdles before it reveals its soul. And when that happens, its soul becomes part of you' (p. 281). The 'soul of snowboarding' constitutes what Bourdieu (1971) calls 'cultural unconscious' and it comes via 'attitudes, aptitudes, knowledge, themes and problems, in short the whole system of categories of perception and thought' acquired by a systematic social apprenticeship (p. 182).

In snowboarding, the *habitus* or 'cultural unconscious' derives from a systematic cultural apprenticeship, and the longer one spends immersed in snowboarding culture the more ingrained this *habitus* becomes (see Thorpe 2011). For Ste'en, editor of *New Zealand Snowboarder* magazine, the enculturation process is 'an all-consuming journey' that typically begins with the novice participant 'falling in love with snowboarding' and then becoming a 'cultural sponge', absorbing information from various sources, as well as learning from the occasional 'cultural faux pas' (e.g. novice snowboarders who tuck their snowboard pants into the top of their boots, or allow a gap to form between their beanie and goggles – known as a 'gapper gap' – often draw sideways glances and snide remarks from cultural insiders). After overcoming 'numerous hurdles' such as 'learning to snowboard on sheet ice, dealing with terrible equipment and sore feet', Ste'en proceeded to 'follow winter from mountain to mountain around the world … for more than a decade' (personal communication [pc], July 2008). As Bourdieu (1986) explains, embodying cultural knowledge 'costs time' and time amounts to an investment (p. 222). Thus, with core participants often dedicating many years to snowboarding, and some making considerable personal sacrifices along the way (e.g. relationships, education, career), it is inevitable that struggles occur when 'outsiders' and 'newcomers' endanger such cultural investments (see Thorpe 2004, 2011).

Adopting a Bourdieuian approach, it might be argued that, for core boarders, the socially constructed *habitus* is a primary influence on their snowboarding practices; choices of equipment, clothing purchased, terrain selected, and the style of riding, are often made on the 'basis of practically oriented dispositions that have already been inscribed in the body and subsequently take place without overtly direct conscious awareness of the principles that guide them' (Ford and Brown 2006: 126). The snowboarding *habitus* is, as Laberge and Sankoff (1988) conclude, 'both the internalisation of the conditions of existence and the practice-generating principle of social agents' (p. 270). As Ford and Brown (2006) write in their discussion of surfing, the 'practical logics' that sustain board-riding culture are, therefore, 'embedded in the body in the form of *habitus*' (p. 126). In other words, while the snowboarding *habitus* is typically unconscious, it informs core boarders' decisions regarding an array of embodied practices including dress, language, equipment, bodily deportment and gait, relationships, lifestyle, as well as approaches to risk, pain and pleasure. Snowboarding culture is, therefore, a productive locus of a particular *habitus* which gives rise to, as Bourdieu (1971) says, 'patterns of thought which organise reality by directing and organising thinking about reality and makes what he thinks thinkable for him as such and in the particular form in which it is thought' (pp. 194–5). Of course, this raises questions as to those snowboarders who do not conform to the embodied 'rules' and 'norms' within the snowboarding *field*, or who challenge the snowboarding *habitus*. As I explain below, while Bourdieu is often criticized for not giving enough room to individual's agency within *fields*, in his later work he did give greater consideration to how (some) individuals come to reflect critically on aspects of their own *habitus*, which may lead to subtle forms of resistance within *fields* (see Thorpe 2009, 2010, 2011).

For many core participants, however, the snowboarding *habitus*, internalized through years of participation, continues to be expressed through durable ways 'of standing, speaking, walking, and thereby of feeling and thinking' (Bourdieu 1987/1994: 70) long after the objective conditions of its emergence have been dislodged. For example, Phillipa describes how, ten years after her transition from semi-professional athlete to 'weekend warrior', she still experiences physiological cravings for snowboarding: 'If I read a snowboarding magazine or think about the snow, my heart races, my blood pulses and I am overtaken by a desire to be back on the mountain' (pc, July 2008). Another ex-core snowboarder notes that her body still 'shows all kinds of scars as a result of the asymmetric nature of snowboarding … the ACL reconstruction on my right knee has left me with problems in other joints on that side of my body, and my left knee is also ready to blow at any time' (pc, November 2008). Put simply, for some ex-core snowboarders, the snowboarding *habitus* continues to influence their everyday bodily experiences long after cultural retirement.

Habitus is a multi-layered concept, capturing both 'general notions of *habitus* at the level of society' and 'differentiated notions at the level of the individual' (Reay 2004: 434). As a highly nuanced and complex concept, *habitus* has been used in various ways in different research contexts. In my research, I was particularly interested in the potential of *habitus* to help reveal how the snowboarding culture is embodied, and also how taken-for-granted social inequalities are embedded in everyday practices. Although many consider *habitus* to be one of Bourdieu's more difficult concepts, I continue to be inspired by the interdisciplinary potential of *habitus*; it reminds us of the inseparability of the past and present, the individual and the group, and the corporeal and the psychological dimensions of human behavior. Of course, *habitus* is a relational concept, and only makes sense when used in conjunction with *capital* and *field*.

Capital: power and privilege in the snowboarding culture

Of specific interest to my analysis were the concepts of *cultural capital* and *symbolic capital* as forms demarcating different kinds of snowboarders, and thus organizing the structure of the snowboarding *field*. Bourdieu (1986) argues that *cultural capital* exists in three irreducible forms: in the objectified state (e.g. pictures and books which are the traces or realization of theories and bodies of knowledge), the institutionalized state (e.g. as academic qualifications conferred on those who reach a certain level of education), and the embodied state (e.g. in the form of long-lasting dispositions of the body and mind). In snowboarding, *cultural capital* in the objectified state refers to snowboarding magazines, films, instructional manuals and DVDs, and books (e.g. cultural histories of snowboarding, autobiographies of athletes or pioneers) which are producers and products of cultural knowledge. *Cultural capital* in the institutionalized state refers to roles obtained in the sport or industry through either formal qualifications (e.g. certified snowboard instructor or competition judge) or informal cultural apprenticeships (e.g. snowboard journalist or photographer). Institutionalized *cultural capital* also refers to prizes and accolades received within the sport (e.g. National Champion, Burton Open Series overall winner).

Clarifying the embodied state, Bourdieu (1986) notes that, 'most of the properties of *cultural capital* can be deduced from the fact that, in its fundamental state, it is linked to the body and presupposes embodiment' (p. 244). Bourdieu (1978) also refers to this embodied form of *cultural capital* as physical or corporeal *capital*, which he treats as a form of *capital* in its own right. During the late 1990s and early 2000s, for example, 'goggle tans' were a popular form of corporeal cultural or *physical capital*. Goggle tans were perceived as visual demonstrations of an individual's cultural commitment. According to *Snowboard Magazine*, 'a sure-fire way to tell the local from the yokel is the goggle tan' (Scott, no date, para. 1), and even held a competition inviting readers to submit photos of their goggle tans with the most dramatic 'raccoon eyes' winning a new pair of goggles. The popularity of goggle tans was particularly evident in places with thriving summer snowboarding scenes (e.g. Mt Hood, Oregon), such that some over-zealous boarders would even wear their goggles on sun-beds to further enhance their tan lines! Shilling (1993) views corporeal *capital* as a particularly useful conceptualisation that shares an important relationship with 'all other varieties of *capital*' (p. 149). Indeed, corporeal *capital* was one of the key concepts I employed to provide insight into distinctive snowboarding bodies, with a particular focus on clothing practices (see Thorpe 2004, 2011).

Clothing constitutes an important symbolic marker of group membership. Bryan Turner (1988) theorizes that, 'dress symbolizes and states one's wealth and political power by indicating one's superior sense of taste and distinction' (p. 68). Similarly, Barnes and Eicher (1992) note that 'dress serves as a sign that the individual belongs to a certain group but simultaneously differentiates the same individual from all others: it includes and excludes' (p. 1). As snowboarding Olympian and clothing company owner Pamela explained: 'Personal style in snowboarding is so important. You can read a person by what they're wearing, before they even strap in [to their board]. Everything in snowboarding is a full expression of who you are ... that's why we wear clothes' (pc, September 2005). Engaging Bourdieu's concept of *cultural capital* facilitated my analysis of the significance of dress practices for distinguishing snowboarders from skiers, and how different meanings have been bestowed on these embodied practices at different historical junctures (see Thorpe 2004, 2011).

Symbolic capital is another name for distinction. It is a 'unique form of motivation – a resource, a reward' (Booth and Loy 1999: 4) closely tied up with the concepts of status, lifestyle, honor and prestige. *Symbolic capital* is highly valued within the snowboarding *field*; participants gain prestige or *symbolic capital* via less visible characteristics such as displays of physical prowess, risk-taking and commitment. In contrast to more explicitly competitive sports, *symbolic capital,* or 'performance capital' as Dart (2002) terms it, is assessed more subjectively by snowboarders in terms of style, capability on challenging terrain, and difficulty and range of maneuvers able to be performed in various found (e.g. cliffs, cornices) and constructed (e.g. jumps, half-pipes) snowy spaces. Snowboarders compete amongst themselves, via the symbolic practices of physical prowess, commitment, skill, courage and risk-taking, for marks of 'distinction' (Bourdieu 1984a). In the words of one male participant, snowboarders earn respect from their peers by going 'bigger and fatter than everybody' (cited in Anderson 1999: 55). These are, of course, practices exclusive to only the most committed boarders. The key point here is that symbolic practices of physical prowess, courage and risk-taking, and the media representation of these practices, reinforce the snowboarding hierarchy, and determine the relative social positioning of agents within the snow field.

Field: the snowboarding hierarchy

Field refers to a structured system of social positions occupied by either individuals or institutions engaged in the same activity (Bourdieu 1977, 1978). The alpine snowfield has traditionally consisted of two main groups: skiers and snowboarders. Although these groups share the same mountain space and comply with the same sets of rules (e.g. ski-resort etiquette), they each have their own institutions (e.g. associations, media, etc.), cultural rules, knowledge, practices and people. Over the past three decades, numerous power struggles developed between these two groups as they fought for territory and eminence (see Humphreys 1996; Thorpe 2004). Snowboarders employed various embodied tastes (e.g. clothing, language) to clearly distinguish themselves from skiers during the 1980s and 1990s. More recently, however, the divisions between skiers and snowboarders are dissolving in some *fields* and among some groups (e.g. freestyle skiers and snowboarders; big mountain skiers and snowboarders) (see Thorpe 2011, 2012b).

Over the past two decades, the contemporary snowboarding *field* has become highly fragmented; various sub-groups include competitive athletes, big mountain riders or extreme snowboarders, jibbers or freestyle riders, alpine boarders, weekend warriors, novices and poseurs. Participants from these groups engage in an array of embodied practices in their attempts to preserve, negotiate and transform the legitimate tastes, styles and allocation of *capital*, and meanings of the snowboarding body. With individuals and groups regularly engaging in embodied struggles over status and access to *capital*, the structure of the snowboarding *field* is in a constant state of negotiation. To paraphrase Ford and Brown (2006), the precise degree of value or *symbolic capital* that a big mountain boarder, halfpipe athlete, or any other kind of snowboarder, possesses will differ in relation to the position they occupy within a particular group in the snowboarding *field*, and the current value of the group tastes and styles in relation to the dominant legitimate norm of the social period in question (p. 127). An Olympic snowboard judge has observed 'all forms of snowboarding ... going through in and out stages', and notes that 'slope-style is in focus now, jibbing has taken a bit of a backseat, and alpine seems to be struggling' (pc, October 2005). Indeed, the alpine racer tends to receive very little *symbolic capital* in the current generation, where freestyle is the most prized form of participation. New Zealand snowboarder Andrew Morrison demonstrated the lack of *symbolic capital* allocated to alpine racers when he defined a participant as 'someone... [who] carves, carves, carves and carves and carves,' adding 'I don't have much respect for those guys' (cited in Humphreys 1996: 17).

Young, highly committed 'core' boarders hold a dominant position in the snowboarding *field* and thus have the most power to define tastes and styles on and off the slopes (Thorpe 2012a). Yet various 'other' groups – e.g. older, gay, disabled, or non-white snowboarders – negotiate space on the margins of the *field*. While marginal participants tend to have limited access to *capital* accumulation within the snowboarding *field*, many find the support they need to enjoy their snowboarding experience by forming social groups (e.g. Black Avalanche), creating websites (e.g. www.graysontrays.com; www.outboarder.com), and establishing specialized instructional programs (e.g. adaptive snowboarding programs are available for individuals with various disabilities at many ski resorts), teams (e.g. First Nations Snowboard Team, a Canadian organization with recreational and high performance streams that seek to support Aboriginal competitive snowboarders and qualified snowboard instructors) and organizations (e.g. Alpino, an organization founded in Colorado that strives to get more people of color to the mountains for both recreation and work). Some 'other' boarders also find pleasure in disrupting stereotypes of snowboarders as young, white, heterosexual males. Marcia, a 58-year-old Canadian snowboarder, for example, has been boarding for more than 12 years and enjoys 'surprising people when I take off my helmet and show my long silver hair' (pc, February 2004).

In sum, the *field* of snowboarding is a highly fragmented and structured system of social positions; it is comprised of a number of groups, all of which give value to the practiced boarding bodies in different ways. With the growing differentiation of the snowboarding culture, participants employ an array of embodied and bodily practices (i.e. dress, language, bodily deportment, risk-taking) to distinguish themselves from non-snowboarders, marginal participants and each other, and ultimately reinforce (or resist) the structure of the snowboarding *field*.

Looking forward with Bourdieu

In this chapter I have illustrated how Bourdieu's relational concepts of *habitus, capital,* and *field* facilitated insights into snowboarding bodies as possessors of power, and alluded to some of the struggles (between and within groups) over legitimate use and meaning of physical *capital*. It is important to note, however, that his concepts remained under-developed in a number of key areas (e.g. understandings of lived experience; masculine and feminine identities and embodied gender relations; the significance of space; potential for resistance and social change). Of course, all theories have their strengths and limitations, and Bourdieu's work is no exception. Recently, however, scholars from various disciplines (e.g. cultural geography, sociology, youth cultural studies, education, feminism) have begun critically engaging with Bourdieu's original work and deploying, rethinking and extending his conceptual schema for their own ends. Drawing upon contemporary feminist engagements (e.g. Adkins and Skeggs 2004; McNay 2000) with some of Bourdieu's key concepts, I have been able to gain a more nuanced understanding of men and women's gendered snowboarding bodies, and to explore how the movement across *fields* can prompt some to engage in critical reflection, and perhaps engage in 'regulated liberties', or subtle practices of resistance within fields (see Thorpe 2009, 2010, 2012b). Theoretical syntheses between feminism and the work of Pierre Bourdieu are also proving valuable for rethinking my roles and responsibilities as a reflexive, critical sociologist moving within and across various academic, social, and sporting *fields* (see Olive and Thorpe 2011; Thorpe *et al.* 2011).

According to Fredrick Jameson, we should 'learn theories like languages, and explore as every good translator does the expressive gaps between them – what can be said in one theory and not another' (cited in Leane and Buchanan 2002: 254). Extending Jameson's metaphor, I suggest that once a researcher has gained a solid understanding of Bourdieu's theoretical vocabulary and is able to speak his 'theoretical language' fluently and with confidence, there is much room for self-expression and creativity. Based on my own experiences, I encourage physical cultural scholars to 'play' with Bourdieu's theoretical schema. Pushing, pulling and stretching his concepts in relation to our empirical data can help us identify the strengths and limitations of Bourdieu's theoretical schema for explaining the cultural complexities within contemporary sport and physical cultures, and for helping us think differently about the body and embodiment into the twenty-first century.

Note

1   The author is grateful to Palgrave Macmillan for permission to reprint parts of Chapter 5 ('Cultural boarding bodies: status, style and *symbolic capital*') of *Snowboarding Bodies in Theory and Practice* (Thorpe 2011).

15 Bourdieu and body

Qiang Gao

Keywords: *Bourdieu, body, epistemology*

Introduction

This chapter compares Bourdieu's theory of the body and embodiment with interpretations of the body from other theorists and other theoretical perspectives, particularly those that draw on modern epistemological thinking. In Bourdieu's theory of practice, it is possible to make two different interpretative readings of *habitus*. The first is considered to be a sociological reading in which Bourdieu emphasizes the relationship between the 'body and society'. In this reading emphasis is placed on embodiment of knowledge rather than the body as knowledge in itself. In this chapter, it is expressed as the 'body and society approach'. A second reading of Bourdieu's notion of *habitus* is one that recognizes the body (or *body-hexis*) from an epistemological stance. In this sense the body is read as being a form of knowledge in itself and is expressed here as the 'body as knowledge approach'. This approach originates from a reading of Bourdieu's work that aligns with modern epistemological developments that consider the nature of knowledge. In this reading, I draw on the work of Merleau-Ponty and Polanyi to exemplify an epistemology of the body. It aims to circumvent the individual/society dualism that concerns sociologists. The epistemological linking of the body and knowledge provides an opportunity to contribute to modern developments in epistemology, and promote Bourdieu's ideas more widely.

The way we study and represent the human body in physical culture has become a central focus for many within the broad academic fields of the social sciences and humanities since the 1980s (Shilling 2005). A diverse range of theoretical perspectives, including those of Pierre Bourdieu, whose social theory occupies a leading position in contemporary sociology, has been invoked to examine the body and embodiment (Featherstone and Turner 1995; Turner 1984). Bourdieu's social framework has become very popular for studying socially constructed representations of the body. In this chapter I present an ontological critique of 'what the body really is' (Shilling 1993) and propose an epistemological reading of the body to complement Bourdieu's practical theory. I draw on the work of Maurice Merleau-Ponty and Michael Polanyi, as well as Bourdieu's representation of the body, to show how the body as a representation of both society and knowledge can act as a bridge between sociology and epistemology. I address the way the body exists as both a social actor and a form of social meaning, a subject and representative object.

Bourdieu's theory of practice and theorizing about the body

It is possible to read Bourdieu's theorizing of the body from two different perspectives. At the macroscopic level, citing Proust, Bourdieu finds in the body the means of transferring schemes of thought, which indicates that 'the technique of body can recall the whole system, e.g. the cosmology, the metaphysic and the ethic, etc' (Bourdieu 1980/1990: 69); at the microscopic level, Bourdieu finds that the language represented in our body posture has a moral and psychological correspondence, which he explained as being 'a sense of the equivalences between physical space and social space' (Bourdieu 1980/1990: 71).

Bourdieu argued that the body is both a form of *capital* and also a 'container' of 'practical sense'. In his theory of *practice* the body occupies a central position, especially as it relates to his conception of 'practical sense'. For Bourdieu,

> Practical sense is a quasi-bodily involvement in the world which presupposes no representation either of the body or of the world, still less of their relationship.
>
> (Bourdieu 1980/1990: 66)

In this statement, Bourdieu proposes that practical sense is a state of embodiment in the world rather than a state of the mind. In this way the body is treated as 'a living memory pad' upon which the pre-verbal taken-for-granted childhood learning is stored; it is a form of inculcation 'of deferred thoughts that can be triggered off at a distance in space and time' (Bourdieu 1980/1990: 68-9). Bourdieu often argued that a sports person's 'feel for the game' best exemplifies the concept of 'practical sense'. A sports person's feel for the game has not only a subjective sense – 'a meaning and a *raison d'être* that provides direction or orientation for the player's actions but also an objective sense constituted by specific regularities' (Bourdieu 1980/1990: 69). What takes place in a *field* such as the *field* of sport is full of sense and objectively directed in a judicious manner.

Bourdieu (1980/1990) argued that in social *fields* we unconditionally embark with the unaware illusion of our investment because we subconsciously embody the social conditions of these *fields*. This investment gives one a practical belief in the *field*, that is, an inherent sense of belonging to the *field*. It is a 'practical faith' or practical belief (Bourdieu 1980/1990: 67) embodied by all individuals who belong to the *field*. However, this form of practical faith should not be equated to Kant's 'pragmatic faith', which requires a more conscious investment in the particular practices of the *field*.

Embodiment can be explained by connecting the concept of *habitus* to body technique and body posture, and this is the key to understanding the position of body in Bourdieu's theory of *practice*. The two different but correlative readings, i.e. the body as a 'container' of 'practical sense' and the body as a form of *capital*, evoke two different approaches. The first approach, which can be named the body and society, is based on how the *habitus* creates the social structure of the social world it inhabits. The second approach, which can be named the body as knowledge approach, is based on how the *habitus* passes in this world from generation to generation.

The 'body and society' approach

As far as Turner (1984/1996) is concerned, the relationship between the body and society is hugely important in modern times, but Bourdieu makes this statement more profound. If we consider the *habitus* to be a corporeal version of the 'objectivity of the first order', i.e. the objective world consisting of 'material resource and sorts of capital' (Bourdieu and Wacquant 1992), then the *habitus* lies in the dialectical relationship between the body and society. To be more exact, in the division between 'objectivity of first order' (that of the object world) and 'objectivity of the second order' (the embodiment of the object world) the body plays the role of intermediary. So the construction of the 'objectivity of second order' which is *habitus*, is the corporeal version of the 'objectivity of the first order', the object world (Bourdieu and Wacquant 1992: 9–14).

Social science research on sport can be used to exemplify Bourdieu's use of *habitus* as the 'body and society' or embodiment of society concept. MacAloon (1988) argued that Bourdieu insisted that sport cannot be understood as 'either a monolithic social institution or class of behaviors', because sport takes not only a structural form but also a *habitus* form. This is similar to Marcel Mauss's (1973) argument that today's sporting body reflects a form of 'bodily technique' that can be traced back to ancient Greece. The 'sporting body' has been passed down, taking education as its instrument, from generation to generation. So in the field of sport, where the approach of 'body and society' makes sense, body technique is central. Moreover, body technique cannot be shown without a practical form, so the two representations made by Bourdieu cannot be ignored. As Bourdieu proposes:

> Because the classification schemes through which the body is practically apprehended and appreciated are always grounded twofold, both in the social division of labour and in the sexual division of labour, the relation to the body is specified according to sex and according to the form that the division of labour between sexes takes depending on the position occupied in the social division of labour and the sexual division of labour, in which the former one is the premise of the later.
>
> (Bourdieu 1980/1990: 72)

Apparently, sexual division between man and woman is the first and most important image that people see when they focus on the body. In his article 'La domination masculine' (1990b), Bourdieu traced and elaborated this thread of thought. Supported by contemporary anthropological works such as David Le Breton's *Anthropologie du Corps et Modernité* (2008), it is possible to understand that Bourdieu recognized that both the social universe and the social division of the sexes are arbitrary, and that progressive naturalization provides its legitimacy (Bourdieu 1980/1990). Masculinity occupies the central position from which both males and females determine the difference between sexes. In this way, the body becomes a system of symbolization which is constructed according to the *habitus* (Bourdieu 1980/1990). Because of the masculine priority in social production and reproduction, the sexual division of labour is inclined to make up the perception, idea and actions of social members (Bourdieu 1980/1990). It is a means by which the masculine becomes the social principle presented directly and indirectly. As a consequence, we find that the conception of *corps propre* determines and is shown in the valorization of honor and principle of conservation (Bourdieu 1980/1990).

So in terms of the body and society, we can clearly see that Bourdieu's application of the masculine principle to the social division of labor draws a picture of the relationship between the body and society whereby the social construction of the body is established and re-established.

In the approach of the body and society, where the role of *habitus* realizes its effect, Bourdieu reveals the process of acquisition via the bodily learning of *habitus* as it is passed from generation to generation. Bourdieu pointed out (1980/1990: 73) that 'What is "learned by body" is not something that one has, like knowledge that can be brandished, but something that one is.' In this way, Bourdieu questions the authority of written knowledge and even rationality, arguing (p. 73) that knowledge:

> is never detached from the body that bears it and can be reconstituted only by means of a kind of gymnastics designed to evoke it, a mimesis. ... the body is thus constantly mingled with all the knowledge it reproduces.

Here Bourdieu not only questions the written and rational essence of knowledge but also recreates the conception of knowledge borne in the body and transferred tacitly, through which the dissolution of the 'epistemological couple', by which social scientific discourse is conventionally constructed – theory and empiricism, macrosociology and microsociology – can be realized (MacAloon 1988). The body, in this sense, becomes the 'body as a whole' encompassing both the objectivity of social structure and the subjectivity of mental structure (Bourdieu 1980/1990).

Body as knowledge approach

The philosophical perspectives of Merleau-Ponty and Bourdieu can be used here to construct a more epistemological understanding of the 'body as knowledge'. Both perspectives take 'the form of the multifaceted actuality of the lived body as the mediating ground' (Marcoulatos 2001). The body is a *de facto* 'carrier form of significance'. The *habitus*, in the form of corporeal knowledge, is no longer a cluster of dispositions but rather, as referred to by Bourdieu, an 'overall actuality of a living human as immediately experienced' or 'the generative principle of regulated improvisations' (Bourdieu 1980/1990: 57). It is 'a system of internalized embodied schemes' (Bourdieu 1984: 467), in which patterns of behavior and perception are cumulatively created.

However, Bourdieu differs from Merleau-Ponty with respect to social phenomenology. Unlike Sartre and Merleau-Ponty, Bourdieu denies constructivism and the notion that ordinary knowledge plays an important role in the continuity of social production; instead he promotes the bilateral social reproduction between objective and subjective construction (Bourdieu 1980/1990: 13–23). The body is not only a subjective construction, a view held by Merleau-Ponty, but also an objective construct linking social institutions and social order. Bourdieu insists on treating the body not as purely epistemological, as Merleau-Ponty does, but rather as a total science that relies on the total social fact (Bourdieu and Wacquant 1992: 25).

Continuing with Bourdieu's approach to the body as knowledge, there are still two phrases to work through. In the first phrase, which is always in the field of education, especially physical education, learning knowledge through the physical is one of the most representative approaches (Mechikoff and Estes 2002: 45; Hunter 2004). Although the body is highly emphasized, it is still treated as a substantial object. However, for Bourdieu learning by body bridges the subject and object divide, enabling knowledge and ways of living to be transferred from generation to generation.

In contrast to the first phrase, the second phrase takes Bourdieu's approach of the body as knowledge as a base of knowledge of the body. As Jackson (1983) states, the right is made to dispense with purely logical concepts but not with the incorporated transference and quasi-postural schemes. Knowledge cannot be explained only by symbol, speech, ideas, words, or other 'logocentric' forms. In agreement with Merleau-Ponty, knowledge in Bourdieu's explanation of the 'body as knowledge' is far more than a 'logocentric' form. Thus, in this approach, understanding the body is more than a somatic way, it is a comprehensive, constructive form.

Used in the second way, the *habitus* is far more than a representation of masculine discipline and social divisions of labor, as I emphasized in the earlier explanation of the 'body and society'. Our body is not a slave of *habitus* but rather our body *hexis* forms and is formed by our relationships with others and with the object world around us (Jackson 1983). Otherwise the *habitus* of previous generations will be disrupted and cannot be passed down to the next generation. The location of the *habitus* in the physical and social world determines what the *habitus* will be and how it correspondingly develops, whether the knowledge it portrays is implicit, as in gesture, skill or perception, or explicit, as in the intentional form it takes.

Conclusion: a shift from sociological to epistemological conceptions of *habitus*

Both of these two approaches, the 'body and society' and the 'body as knowledge', bring us different but valuable vistas. But what is it in nature that the 'body and society' approach represents? The sociological way is to understand Bourdieu's idea of the body. The 'body as knowledge' approach opens the way to an epistemological reading of the body that can avoid the structuralist criticism. For in the 'body as knowledge' approach, the body is no longer a medium in which it is only identified with specific kinds of *habitus* or certain social institutions in which it happens to be tied up.

If it makes sense that Bourdieu's practical theory is a de facto theory of the body (Zeng 2009: 45), then the 'body and society' approach cannot accord any positive proof; only the raising of the 'body as knowledge' approach that, as a form of epistemology, centralizes the body but not the embodied movement or body use, can realize his essential end, thus eliminating the dichotomy in the social sciences and other humanities.

Taking a critical view, Bourdieu's idea of the 'body and society' and the alternative approach of the 'body as knowledge' aim to dissolve the dichotomy, where an epistemological connotation can be found. But even if Bourdieu makes the body the centre of knowledge, meticulously interpreting the use of the body as releasing it from both social physics and social phenomenology, he still took the conception of knowledge in a very general way without clear identification and formulation. As a consequence, the body cannot be liberated completely from the traditional dichotomy introduced by Plato that remains in Western philosophical schools of thought.

So the 'body as knowledge' approach possesses the epistemological tint, but the sociological influence cannot be easily eliminated. To become a more philosophical approach, the 'body as knowledge' still relies on the social wisdom that lacks intellectual knowledge, and its relationship to the other categories of knowledge. In order to connect with modern philosophical discourse, especially in the epistemological field, finding the junction point with modern epistemological discourse, which lies on the ongoing discourse of Polanyi's tacit knowledge, might be a threshold that has to be crossed.

Tacit knowledge or unarticulated knowledge, which is considered to be more fundamental than articulated knowledge (knowledge that can be said), as identified by Polanyi (1969: 138,145), is a way of 'knowing how' apart from 'knowing what' and can be traced back to the 'pronesis' of Aristotle (Prosch 1973). This genre of epistemology is strongly critical of the objective epistemology well re-established by Karl Popper in the middle of the twentieth century. The body is important in Polanyi's theory. As Polanyi suggests, all human knowledge has a bodily root:

> The way the body participates in the act of perception can be generalized including the bodily roots of all knowledge and thought ... Every time we make sense of the world, we rely on our tacit knowledge of impacts made by the world on our body and the complex responses of our body to these impacts.
> (Polanyi 1969: 147–8, cited in Zhenhua 2008)

Bourdieu's conception of *habitus*, in respect of its function in 'learning bodily', or as emphasized here in the 'body as knowledge' approach, connects with Polanyi's theorizing and can contribute to the development of modern epistemology views about the body, which are ongoing.

Part III

Issues and tensions using bourdieu

16 Thinking with and outside Bourdieu

Katie Fitzpatrick

Keywords: *class, ethnicity, social theory, post-colonial theory*

I have employed the social theory of Pierre Bourdieu extensively in my work to date. In my recent ethnographic study of 'marginalized' youth in school and in health and physical education (HPE), I found Bourdieu's theoretical tools enormously useful in enabling me to understand the lives of diverse and socioeconomically disadvantaged young people at the intersection of class, place, gender and ethnicity (Fitzpatrick 2013). Prior to beginning this study, I had consciously avoided Bourdieu and was looking more to the ideas of postcolonial theorists such as Homi Bhabha and Edward Said, and to the poststructuralist ideas of Foucault and the feminist ideas of Judith Butler. I put Bourdieu aside initially because I was concerned that applying the *field/capital/habitus* triumvirate would lead me into a deterministic explanation of the class-located actions, and school achievement, of the youth in the study. This assumption had stemmed from reading critiques of Bourdieu (for example, Giroux 1981), which I now feel put undue emphasis on certain parts of his ideas at the expense of the whole. I was worried, most centrally, about where this analysis would lead me and where, as a result of taking this path, I would not travel. This is, of course, a question to ask about the application of any social theory or mode of analyses. In analyzing the complex lives of youth, I wanted my study to present some kind of 'answer' to the intractable underachievement and social marginality to which these young people are both subject and complicit. I wanted the theory to offer and allow for a way out. Of course, I was asking too much. Social theory may help us to understand social contexts; it is unlikely to offer direct solutions to issues of social justice. Zygmunt Bauman states that 'all theory is selective' and goes on to assert that theory serves to shine a light 'in a way that would assist orientation and help find the way' (2004: 17). I returned to Bourdieu in this study for the simple reason that his ideas worked, they resonated deeply with me – my own *habitus* – and with the approach I took to the research. Bourdieu's theoretical tools offered a way into the young people's stories, while simultaneously highlighting the importance of the wider social and political contexts. My engagement, however, with other social theories also allowed me to see where the edges might lie. Bourdieu's ideas, then, shine a light in particular places to assist orientation around, through and within empirical materials. Conversely, this also leaves dark spaces, corners that remain unlit. Bourdieu himself encouraged us to not limit our thinking to singular ideas, but instead to attempt excavation of 'the unthought categories of thought' which, he noted, 'limit the unthinkable and predetermine what is actually thought' (1987/1994: 178).

In this paper I draw on a few snapshots of my ethnographic study in order to interrogate Bourdieu's social theory in this context. I specifically reflect on what his notions of *habitus, field* and *capital* elucidated and what they obscured. I reflect on Bourdieu by way of comparison with another theoretical lens. In so doing, I draw on Homi Bhabha's notion of hybridity to discuss the limits and possibilities of Bourdieu's theoretical tools. I begin with a brief discussion of how Bourdieu's social theory was also methodological in my study. Indeed, I argue that theory and method cannot be viewed as separate. Second, I introduce a narrative from one of the young people in the study and apply Bourdieuian theoretical tools to provide an analysis. I then re-read this narrative using Bhabha's notion of hybridity and end by reflecting on the limits and possibilities of applying each theory.

Bourdieu and methodology

In 2007 I returned to a school I had previously taught at to conduct a critical ethnography of health, physical education (PE) and diverse youth in school. The school in question, which I call Kikorangi High School, is a suburban secondary school of approximately 1,100 students situated in the southern suburbs of New Zealand's largest city, Auckland, home to about 1.4 million people. The school is in the ethnically diverse and very low socioeconomic community of Otara,[1] and is attended almost exclusively by indigenous Maori and Pasifika students (migrants from the Pacific Islands of Tonga, Samoa, Nuie, and The Cook Islands). The suburb where the school is situated is somewhat 'infamous' in New Zealand for poverty, crime, ethnic diversity and gang activity (see, for example, Collins 2009; *New Zealand Herald* 2009a, 2009b). Schools in these kinds of communities, as Steinberg (2010) argues, are known as urban and are often marginalized culturally and socially. This site was the focus of my critical ethnographic study.

Thomas (1993: 4) describes critical ethnography as 'conventional ethnography with a political purpose', and also explains (p. vii):

> Critical ethnography is a way of applying a subversive worldview to the conventional logic of cultural inquiry. It does not stand in opposition to conventional ethnography. Rather, it offers a more direct style of thinking about the relationships among knowledge, society and political action.

Willis (1977) argued that, in order to understand what is happening in a particular setting, an ethnographer must attend to the culture of the research site, what he termed 'the logic of living' in a particular place:

The logic of living must be traced to the heart of its conceptual relationships if we are to understand the *social creativity* of a culture. This always concerns, at some level, a recognition of, and action upon, the particularity of its place within a determinate social structure.

(p. 121, my emphasis)

Seeking to understand what Willis terms the 'social creativity' of a space is the essence of ethnographic research. In order to do this in this study, I committed to spending significant time becoming familiar with and getting 'inside' the social space of the school I was studying. I developed meaningful, trusting and reciprocal relationships with students and teachers over the course of a school year (Madison 2005). I employed four specific methods to do this. The first was participating in classes with the students and completing set tasks and activities alongside them. This approach was central to developing relationships and building trust. In all, I spent over 300 hours in health and PE classes with senior high school students (aged 16–18 years). Over half of this time was with one class. Second, I set up recorded unstructured research conversations that touched on topics such as relationships, school, community issues and achievement. These conversations were free flowing and open to any of the participants who wanted to join in. Numbers averaged between 4 and 6 at a time. At the end of the year, I invited key participants to take part in individual interviews. Third, I kept a reflective journal (Clandinin and Connolly 2000) throughout the year and noted my feelings, experiences, hunches, questions and concerns. Finally, I 'hung out' with students during lunchtimes and chatted, texted and ate lunch with them.

In the earlier quote, Willis (1977) points out that in order to gain sophisticated cultural understandings, we must contextualize our research within wider societal hierarchies or structures. He notes that understanding culture 'always concerns, at some level, a recognition of, and action upon, *the particularity of its place* within a determinate social structure' (p. 121, my emphasis). Critical ethnographers do attend specifically to social hierarchies and power relations, situating their particular studies within sociohistorical and sociopolitical contexts. This is where the place of social theory becomes key. The social theory is not, however, a layer to be applied after the empirical materials have been acquired. It actually informs the entire research process and is itself structured via *habitus*. Brubaker (1993) argued that all research is underscored by *habitus*, indeed that 'every sociological practice, theoretical or empirical, is governed and regulated by a particular sociological *habitus*' (1993: 213). He explained that, in line with Bourdieu's thinking, 'it is the *habitus* that determines the kinds of problems that are posed, the kinds of explanations that are offered, and the kinds of instruments (conceptual, methodological, statistical) that are employed' (1993: 213). The social theory of Bourdieu and the methodologies of critical ethnography aligned with my own *habitus* in this study. The theory was not applied later, it was enmeshed within the study from the very beginning. Nevertheless, other theoretical tools could have been and were used as well. The intersection of different theoretical positions enabled me to gain greater reflexive insight into both my own *habitus* and the gaps and spaces of darkness the theory allowed.

Bourdieu (1980/1990) insisted that we should not only talk about concepts but should apply them to empirical materials to make them work. He also argued that any social theory or methodology should be viewed as one way to approach research rather than as a better way. Using the example of juxtaposing the ideas of Marx with those of Weber, he pointed out that 'one thinker enables you to see the truth of the other' (Bourdieu 1987/1994: 35). Brubaker (2004: 26), indeed, encourages us to 'think with Bourdieu against Bourdieu' and in so doing to 'examine his schemes of sociological vision'. I have chosen a specific thinker in this chapter to help me think about Bourdieu's work. The post-colonial theorist Homi Bhabha is in many ways concerned with the same kinds of problems as Bourdieu. He was, however, specifically focused on how histories of colonization continue to form complex relations of power in ongoing ways. He argued that individuals affected by these forms of power are never completely repressed by them but, rather, resist in active and creative ways (Huddart 2006).

Each of these thinkers, then, brings a new perspective to the study of which I speak here. Concerned as he was with anthropological research and with culture and education at the intersection of class and place, Bourdieu's methodological and theoretical tools lend themselves well to my study of diverse youth in school. Indeed, other critical ethnographers have also applied his ideas (for example, see Willis 1977; Jones 1991). Bhabha's ideas, however, shift the focus slightly to highlight more specifically notions of identity within post-colonial sites such as New Zealand. His theories put an emphasis directly on both ethnicity and resistance.

To illustrate this analysis, I draw on the story of a student from my ethnographic study to explore and apply the ideas of Bourdieu and Bhabha. After the narrative I then reflect on what the ideas of Bourdieu offer before considering what might be missed.

Sofia

Sofia was a year 12 student in 2007, in her penultimate year of high school and from a Cook Islands Maori cultural background. Although she lived in the community of Otara, Sofia attended an elite public girls' school in Auckland city for the first two years of high school. She had transferred to Kikorangi High School the previous year because she was tired of travelling into the central city each day. Despite choosing to attend the local school, she wasn't sure that Otara was a good place to live: 'I reckon if people were given a choice they wouldn't choose to live [here] … if they were given a way out they wouldn't choose this place.' Sofia easily passed assessments and readily engaged in class discussions, but she thought that she'd rather be working and wished she could leave school. She was frustrated by teachers who constantly talk about assessment for national qualifications instead of 'really teaching us'. Sofia imitated a teacher sarcastically: 'This is worth 3 [NCEA] credits and you'll go to university' before asking, 'Who says everyone in our class wants to go to university, who says they even care?' I asked her if gaining credits was solely for university. She replied:

[I]t's about passing school and making your parents happy, otherwise I would be working. If I had the choice, I'd probably be working and making money. I've had a lot of people talk to me [though], like my boss [at the cafe where I work part-time], she's so cool, she told me ... about her life and how hard it was for her, but [she] got to do things [she] wanted ... 'cause she stayed at school and got her qualifications. As the years go on ... you're going to have to be more qualified and stuff even to waitress.

(Individual conversation)

I asked about her plans post school. She shrugged and replied 'I dunno, I want to be rich, as everyone wants to, visit other countries ... my sister got to ride an elephant, even her kids got to ride an elephant, and what am I riding? I'm riding the bus!'

Thinking with Bourdieu

Sofia's *habitus* was produced within her body by the *field*s of practice she inhabited. She was a student of physical education (PE), and part of a group of students who majored in the subject. She never singled out PE as in any way different to her other subject choices in any of my discussions with her throughout the year. In many ways, she collapsed it in with school in general, which was the cause of her frustration. She felt stuck in her local community and in school, while at the same time feeling short-changed by what she perceived as an assessment and credit-driven curriculum. She, nevertheless, recognized the *capital* value in school qualifications and accepted that she must attain these in order to gain employment. The *field* of schooling, and the way it intersected with her local community, was the site of Sofia's frustration. As Lash (1993: 197-8) explains:

The specific and differentiated *field*s are sites of collective symbolic struggles and individual strategies, the aims of which are to produce valuable cultural goods ... The value of a symbolic good depends upon the value assigned to it by the relevant consumer community.

In this sense, the cultural 'goods' are educational *capital* in the forms of qualifications. These have exchange value both in and outside the *field* of production and therefore have an almost universally accepted high value. Interesting here is Sofia's acknowledgement that gaining qualifications is a struggle. There is a latent sense in her statements that, while gaining qualifications is necessary to please her parents, it isn't easy. Because I had known Sofia for a while, it surprised me that she felt this way; she was considered by teachers to be a 'top student' who articulated sophisticated ideas in class and was confident to speak out. She was often the student that teachers looked to for answers and she gained high marks in assessment tasks. Of interest here are the expectations she has formed as a result of the *field* of production. The school Sofia attended is in one of the poorest urban areas in New Zealand. It had the lowest socioeconomic category given by the New Zealand Ministry of Education and, while students did achieve good results by comparison with other similar schools, achievement rates at this time still differed greatly from schools in wealthier parts of town (Fitzpatrick 2013).

Bourdieu and Passeron (1977/1990) observed that schools tend to reproduce social class because people adjust their expectations of success (or otherwise) according to the *field*. Bourdieu (1997/2000: 216) explained that, in this sense, 'the subjective hope of profit tends to be adjusted to the objective probability of profit'. In Sofia's case, however, there is an extra layer of complexity in how she is reading the *field* at the intersection of schooling and community. She has had experience of other *field*s in terms of the elite school and the lives of her sisters in other parts of the city. This has remade her *habitus* in a particular way. Webb, Schirato and Danaher (2002: 23) explain that 'paradoxically – those with the least amount of *capital* tend to be less ambitious, and more "satisfied" with their lot'. Sofia, by contrast, is not satisfied. She recognizes that things are different in this part of town and she wants to leave.

Bourdieu (1991), however, identified what he referred to as the emergence of a regionalist discourse in places that are marginalized or low status. Although a part of the *habitus*, a regionalist discourse is also performative and more conscious, a form of resistance to outsiders' interpretations of a particular place:

> [R]egionalist discourse is a *performative discourse* which aims to impose as legitimate a new definition of the frontiers and to get people to know and recognize the *region* that is thus delimited in opposition to the dominant definition.
> (Bourdieu 1991: 223)

The dominant definition of Otara is, of course, linked to its status as a poor place, and one in which gangs and crime are rife. Otara youth have their own views about what their place is, and specific regionalist understandings of it. While many of Sofia's classmates defended their place and actively and consciously 'reclaimed' it as positive, she identified the regional differences as limiting.

Sofia's experience could be thought about as a manifestation of her *habitus* formed in the intersection of *field*s, but this analysis puts more focus on the *field*s than on her dynamic engagement with, through, upon and around the *field*s. I wonder if limiting the analysis of Sofia's experience to the notions of *field* and *habitus* somehow misses the nuance and complexity of her experiences and responses. The difficulty here concerns Sofia's singular experience across a range of *field*s. Unlike many of the other students, she attended an elite girls' school in the city and had experienced the difference between the cultures operating therein and the cultures of her local community of Otara. Her sisters were both married to Pakeha/European men and she regularly visited them and their families in other parts the city. Her experience and *habitus* then was played out in the intersection of two quite different versions of the schooling and family *field*s. Brubaker identifies a possible weakness in Bourdieu's theory in the following way:

> Bourdieu's schemes of sociological vision … disposed him to see tension and conflict in systemic terms and as structured by a small number of fundamental

oppositions. This is an enormously productive disposition. But it can incline the theorist to read the social world in too systemic a manner, in a manner that risks imposing a systemic coherence on a messy, unruly, and in some respects unsystematic reality.

(Brubaker 2004: 28)

Shilling (2004: 474) likewise argues that 'Bourdieu is unable to account satisfactorily for individuals who break free from the trajectories assigned them by their background and training.' Bourdieu (1987/1994: 91) himself argued that *habitus* as 'the product of an individual history' was largely unconscious and that as long as the *habitus* aligns with the *field* it 'comes at just the right moment and, without the need for any calculation, its anticipations forestall the logic of the objective world.' In Sofia's case, her *habitus* does not always align with the *field*s she inhabits. This creates a discomfort and an ill-fit. Bourdieu used the analogy of a fish in water to describe this situation. He argued that when the *habitus* and *field* were in alignment, the experience was naturalized, like a fish in water. On the contrary, if the two are unaligned, it is akin to feeling the weight of the water (Grenfell and James 1998). So, while the notions of *field* and *habitus* provide a very useful reading of her experience, such a theoretical analysis as I have applied here does tend to highlight the social context more than her active movement between spaces and cultures. Drawing on other theoretical perspectives might add a different dimension to the analysis. I revisit Sofia's story in the next section, this time drawing on the ideas of cultural theorist Homi Bhabha.

Thinking with Bhabha

Homi Bhabha (1994) used the notion of hybrid identities to understand how individuals interact and work in and against relations of power. He viewed identity as unfixed and fluid, enabling different articulations dependant on context. Bhabha suggests that identity exists in the spaces between definitive identifications. These spaces are liminal, fluid and uncertain and they beget moments when the self is split between and in-between culture/s. He uses the metaphor of the stairwell to explain this notion:

The stairwell as liminal space, in-between the designations of identity, becomes the process of symbolic interaction, the connective tissue that constructs the difference between upper and lower, black and white. The hither and thither of the stairwell, the temporal movement and passage it allows, prevent identities at either end of it from settling into primordial polarities.

(Bhabha 1994: 5)

Bhabha suggests that moments of inbetween-ness are worth examining and exploring, especially because they produce uncertainty, resistance, discomfort. They can thus become a starting place for change. Indeed, he argues, such moments open up 'the possibility of a cultural hybridity that entertains difference without an assumed or imposed hierarchy' (p. 5). In Sofia's case, she is certainly experiencing moments of being in-between. She is very aware of the cultural dissonance between different parts of the city and the two schools she has attended; she feels like she doesn't belong in any of these spaces and identifies travel as a way to move beyond the 'stuck' place she currently inhabits.

Bhabha argues (1994: 246) that socially marginalized communities, like the one Sofia inhabits, can create change because:

> it is from those who have suffered the sentence of history – subjugation, domination, diaspora, displacement – that we learn our most enduring lessons for living and thinking ... social marginality ... transforms our critical strategies.

He notes that 'culture is a strategy of survival' (1994: 247). In the case of Sofia, her rejection of her own local community is a form of resistance, a moment when the self is split between multiple spaces. She is able to take on, actively and consciously, different roles in different places. In this sense Bhabha draws my attention to how Sofia is actively and individually pushing against the contexts she experiences and is creating a kind of productive resistance in the moments of thinking and speaking about different social and cultural spaces.

Limits and possibilities

Reflecting on the above brief analyses of a single narrative, we can see that each of these theoretical lenses allowed the text to take a particular direction. While Bourdieu's notion of *field* allowed me to theorize Sofia's experiences in relationship to the geographical and cultural locations she inhabited, it perhaps underplayed how she crossed *field*s at different times and how her very identity was formed in the spaces *between fields*. It may have obscured the complex and multiple positions and identities she held and how, at times, her responses were explicitly conscious. The post-colonial ideas of Homi Bhabha rather highlighted the potential for change in the way Sofia experienced, resisted and was deeply conscious of the spaces she inhabited. Her awareness and resistance created a kind of productive dissonance that caused cracks in the system to appear to her. These two ways of looking at this narrative are, however, not incompatible.

Each of the above theoretical frameworks then produced a different kind of reading of Sofia's narrative. These, of course, intersect with my own culturally-located experience and how I have created the narrative and the study itself. In Bourdieu's terms, both of these readings are only possible via my own *habitus*. In this sense, what is then also interesting is how both of these theories were actually woven into the methodology of this study, not only into the analyses. Bourdieu's ideas resonated with my critical ethnographic methods perhaps because these connected with his anthropological and empirically-located work. Post-colonial ways of thinking consistent with the ideas of Bhabha were also, however, central to the method. Locating Sofia and the other students within the broader cultural and historical contexts (in this case, in New Zealand with its history of British colonization) was central to the study's method and the building of relationships across cultural boundaries. Interrogating my own position as a Pakeha (European) woman researcher was also key in this regard (see Fitzpatrick 2013).

I want to end here with the acknowledgement that any particular theory is limiting and, as Bauman argues, shines a particular light that highlights and obscures. Bourdieu (1987/1994) himself, of course, argued this directly. All theories, then, are both limited and limiting but our application of any theory in the context of research comes via our *habitus* and the intersection thus produces a uniquely culturally located reading.

Note

1 Discussion of the politics of place was an important part of this study. I have explicitly and consciously named this suburb in all the writing I have published around this project. The suburb of Otara has its own special resonance in New Zealand and it is well known in popular and media discourse for diversity, gangs, poverty and crime. Part of the project of the book, in line with post-colonial theory, was to write back against some of the negative stereotypes associated with this part of the city, and to communicate students' views of their place.

17 Does my research look good in that?

Problems, politics and processes when choosing social theory in research in physical culture

Doune Macdonald and Louise McCuaig

> **Keywords: *social theory, physical culture, physical activity, sport, reflexivity***

Introduction

> All social research sets out with specific *purposes* from a particular *position*, and aims to *persuade* readers of the significance of its claims; these claims are always broadly *political*.
>
> (Clough and Nutbrown 2007: 4)

Throughout this book, researchers have asked questions of physical culture and sought to interpret their data and provide explanations using social theory offered by and from Pierre Bourdieu. The prudent application of social theory is de rigueur in social science research, an intellectual convention that Bourdieu himself reflected upon. Contemporary social theory provides a systematic approach to the study of human social life, focusing on commentary and critique of society (Allan 2006). It extends traditional understandings of theory – 'tested empirical generalisations'; 'unified, systematic causal explanations' – to include 'theoretical orientations or perspectives ... that are approaches to framing problems, solving problems, and understanding and explaining social reality' and critical theory 'which refers to both a way of theorizing and the product of that theorizing' such as social inclusion (Schwandt 2001: 252). As outlined in Macdonald *et al.* (2002: 134):

> Mouly (1978) says that if nothing else, a theory is a convenience – a necessity – organizing a whole slew of unassorted facts, laws, concepts, constructs, and principles into a meaningful and manageable form through its assistance in guiding research design, analysis, and interpretation and revealing gaps, inconsistencies, and future directions. 'Good' theory may be viewed as that which is grounded empirically, allows for deductions arising to be investigated, has a strong explanatory/interpretive power, and is stated simply.

This chapter attempts to stand outside the empirical contributions of our colleagues' chapters and take a somewhat reflexive position asking two questions. We ask 'What is the researchers' thinking behind the adoption of Bourdieu's concepts?' More playfully, borrowing from Bourdieu's interest in taste and consumption, we are interested in the question, 'Does my research look good in Bourdieu?' or 'Should I be trying on someone else's theory?'

Stepping in and stepping out of Bourdieu

In this section we draw on email conversations with four of the authors within this text (David Brown – Chapter 7; Elise Paradis – Chapter 8; Karin Redilius – Chapter 13; and Holly Thorpe – Chapter 14) to provide a counterpoint to our own reflections on why or why not we have sought to try Bourdieu on our research, thereby personalising the patterns presented in the section above. In so doing this section endeavours to reveal the thinking, choices and motivations that have underpinned our use, or not, of Bourdieu in our work as physical education, physical activity and sport researchers. More specifically we are interested here in exploring what attracts us to Bourdieu's work to make sense of research questions and data and enhance our analyses, and what other theories have been used or considered alongside Bourdieu's. In taking this approach we hope to capture a little of what Bourdieu regarded as important in reflexive sociology and go some way towards demystifying the 'scholastic point of view', while acknowledging that we are doing so within the field of scholastic work.

Theme 1: Personal resonance

As we each undertake the daunting task of engaging with the array of theorists and theories laid out before us, our endeavours are typically driven by a desire to discover and utilise 'theory as a lens through which to view the data, recognizing that other lenses may also give useful insights into the topic we explore' (Cammack and Phillips 2002: 125) and make sense of our 'worlds', or as some have argued, to see and feel the 'weight of our water'. It has been suggested that Bourdieu's personal experience as a Rugby player influenced his analogous use of terms such as *game*, *field* and *practice* (Allan 2006), reminding us of the personal dimensions of theory-building. Thus discovering and employing a theory or theorist is often a matter of resonance that emerges at the intersections or alliances of personal biography, professional experience, research curiosity and theoretical perspective.

Elise provides us with a sense of her personal resonance with Bourdieu's work:

> The richness of his analyses of class was readily accessible and widely used by sociologists, but his feminist work and his theory of bodily capital – most importantly his use of sport as a class stratified – have been marginalized. Upon reading this work I felt that it intuitively made sense given my own previous gendered experience in martial arts.

Likewise, David Brown's explanation of his engagement with Bourdieu also suggests a connection to a way of understanding what he was seeing:

> Initially, the attraction for me of Bourdieu's ideas derived from my interest in the involving of the gendered body in the social processes I was observing in Physical Education. Bourdieu's habitus and more specifically the idea of 'body habitus' and 'incorporated capital' and the way it is configured around a process of tacit social learning ... pre-supposes (to me) a dynamic process of socialisation of valued, gendered, cultural artefacts into the body.

Holly also identified a resonance connected with the flexibility of Bourdieu's concepts, being 'clearly a "fan" of Bourdieu's work, and particularly its potential for being "pushed and pulled" in interesting directions'.

As suggested elsewhere, 'it is important that researchers primarily use theories they grasp well and for which they feel an emotional preference' (Alvesson 2002: 133). Louise's reflection is telling in this regard, although her intellectual resonance was with Foucauldian theory. Louise emerged out of the classroom 'coalface' determined to find an analytic lens that facilitated the process of making strange the school contexts, curriculum and pedagogical practices that characterized her experiences as an HPE Head of Department. Guided by her research supervisor, Louise experienced less of a resonance and more of 'uncomfortableness' when she engaged with Lupton's (1995: 4) exploration of the 'shift within secular society from a notion of "godliness" to one of "healthiness" as a yardstick of accomplishment and proper living'. Although this initial engagement with theory was facilitating a new appreciation of the 'weight of her water', it provided little insight into how Louise might pursue this line of inquiry. However, when bookshop browsing Louise discovered *Foucault and the Art of Ethics* (O'Leary 2002) which provided a first encounter with the work of Foucault and his exploration of contemporary conceptualizations of 'an ethical life'. As a result she was quite simply entranced with critical and analytic possibilities posed by the Foucauldian ethical fourfold in relation to HPE's mandate to construct healthy, active Australian citizens.

Such serendipity is not uncommon and simply demonstrates the manner in which a researcher's resonance with a theorist is born out of a need to understand and make sense of a 'real life issue that needs to be addressed' (Crotty 1998: 13). Our reflexive conversations reveal the close relationship between life experiences that challenge or intrigue and our subsequent engagement with those who provide insight. Nonetheless, as Tinning and Fitzpatrick (2012: 57) explain, such resonances 'will be limited by the theories we understand, or at least have some knowledge of'. Research advisors, conference presentations, course reading lists and random book shopping all serve to shape, limit or facilitate whether or not a theorist such as Bourdieu comes into our lives.

Theme 2: Clearly articulated 'tools' for analytic work

A challenge that many researchers face within our field is that of complexity. As we have noted elsewhere, 'much of this complexity can be attributed to physical education and sport sitting at the intersection of differing expectations and priorities related to physical activity, physical fitness, sporting success, health, body weight and citizenship, to name a few' (Macdonald and McCuaig 2012: 16). Not surprisingly, a large number of commentators have presented the theoretical concepts of social theory as tools that can be employed to make sense of complexity (Foucault 1974; Nealon and Giroux 2003). Indeed, as Holly notes:

> Bourdieu's argument that theory should provide 'thinking tools' to be deployed in empirical situations, rather than a clearly defined explanatory framework, leaves open a set of possibilities concerning the use of his concepts for answering an array of research questions in sport and physical cultural contexts.

Further, as a field of study that is often grounded in bodily matters, it follows that many of us resonate powerfully with the emphasis Bourdieu's thinking tools place on notions of embodiment. As Holly states, it is Bourdieu's proposal that key areas of culture are embodied, rather than simply 'in the mind', that is the most challenging and relevant to analyses of physical cultures (Thorpe 2011: 137).

For many, the 'thinking tools' to be found within the Bourdieuian toolbox appear to be particularly useful as a result of their clarity and accessibility for researchers. His theoretical toolbox does not appear, to borrow from Butler (2004: 328), to be 'so rarefied or so specialized that it speaks only to an in-crowd or to a group of initiated people'. Doune has found this to be so with several of her doctoral students, who have grasped Bourdieu's theoretical tools early in their candidatures when they were anxious to have a sense of theoretical competence. In particular the concepts of *field, habitus, capital* and *doxa* have provided a manageable and versatile thinking framework – some wardrobe basics – that students have consolidated, embellished and, on occasions, later rejected. The breadth of research questions for which Bourdieu has been useful is significant: for example, exclusion/privilege in curriculum and assessment; gendering through PETE, PE and sport; and ethnicity (Indigenous Australians, Islamic Australian girls, Chinese Australians) and physical activity engagement. Now as successful, established scholars in physical culture, many will attest that Bourdieu's tools were frequently those to which they returned when the complexity of their projects felt overwhelming.

Not surprisingly, then, many of our colleagues could clearly name a particular concept and explain how and why it was operational for their work. For example, David readily identified that '*practice*' was particularly pertinent:

> [I]t was the notion of 'practice' that I found (and still find) most compelling and *useful* about Bourdieu's particular interpretation of this (gendered) process ...The ideas of reflexivity and practice are powerful analytical tools. Applying the analytical lens of reflexive practice to our observations can make our everyday routine actions seem very strange indeed and sometimes also those strange everyday actions a little more familiar (once we understand the logics of strange practical actions of course).

Using the language of 'taken-for-granted' as did David above, Karin's use of Bourdieu's theory to interrogate gender demonstrates the analytic power of this coherence and comprehensiveness:

> We use his tools to understand why gender power relations seem to appear as self-evident and taken for granted (*doxa*) and why they are sometimes ignored – or misrecognized as natural and thus ensure the legitimacy of inequality (symbolic violence), and why embodied dispositions (*habitus*) make some people feel uncomfortable with changes, even though they might, rationally speaking, benefit from them.

At other times, Bourdieu's framework facilitates a coherent research tale as Elise demonstrates:

> There have been several analyses of the representation of women athletes in the media … The relational approach of Bourdieu's framework makes all the pieces of the story 'fit' together: how new agents shake field structures and hierarchies, redefine the rules of the game, the stakes, etc. in a way that threatens those who used to be dominant and benefited from the old order of things

In responding to the question of what Bourdieuian concepts most contributed to their analysis, our colleagues highlighted the attractiveness of Bourdieu's thinking tools, given their malleability, utility and power to understand others' positioning and perspectives. As Holly noted, '*capital, field, class, taste* and *habitus* remain deliberately vague and malleable, encouraging their questioning and their adaptation to the specific domain to which they are applied' and his concepts are 'good to think with' (Jenkins 2002: 176). Nonetheless, Silva and Warde (2010: 158) warn that 'raids to capture discrete concepts may violate the integrity of the conceptual schema which some detect as core to his work'. Such accusations are often countered when researchers employ the rich orchestration of analytic concepts that are to be found in the coherency of Bourdieu's toolbox, as well as partnering Bourdieu's concepts with complementary theories, as shall be discussed in our fourth theme.

Theme 3: Micro-analysis

'Recent social theory has moved to centre stage the question of how our daily routines, habits and competencies serve to shape our social worlds' (Elliott 2009: 123), raising questions about the relationships between the individual and society, identity and culture. Reflections from our colleagues also drew attention to the capacity of Bourdieu's tools to ensure that analysis and theorizing of the data did not occur in abstract ways but, as David contends, Bourdieu's tools invite and assist the study of daily *practices*, possibly minutiae, that form powerful and reproductive patterns (Reay 2004). In this manner, Bourdieu's concepts are useful in achieving what Greene (1995: 10) refers to as 'seeing things or people as big', viewing them in their integrity and particularity, as David further demonstrates:

> Bourdieu's tools allowed me to see a little more clearly how a young male student teacher becomes involved with the field of physical education. The lenses of reflexivity and practice help me better appreciate his bodily memories deposited from routine practices (like post-PE showers, working with teachers to pick teams, helping teachers in lessons etc) ... Most important of all, it helped me to stitch those mundane everyday personal and institutional practices together to illustrate that it is in the reflexivity of such repetitive actions that gendered fields are both sustained and changed over time.

In the Life Activity Project (Wright and Macdonald 2010), Doune, Jan Wright and her students reported the stories of young people's everyday engagement in physical activity – feeding farm animals, dancing in bedrooms, roaming the neighbourhood, playing backyard football, wandering shopping malls. These stories were validated as worthwhile data given their centrality to the young people's *habitus*. Further, the notion of young people adjusting their behaviours as they moved across *fields*, becoming more or less compliant with expectations about being a 'good' daughter/ son, Muslim girl, Chinese Australian etc., by making small and subtle changes to their comportment, clothing, or conversation, was revealed through Bourdieu's attention to the minutiae that befit different fields (e.g. Lee and Macdonald 2009; Pang, Macdonald and Hay, under review). From the micro data, we could recognize the inherent adult-centric power and understand the subtleties of young people's compliance, resistance and originality in shaping their everyday.

Theme 4: Potential theoretical partnerships

Finally, the complexity of the issues and the contexts within which we research have inspired many researchers to explore the gains that are to be had when we draw elements from across the social theory landscape to enrich analyses and understanding. As with fashion, one may choose to take one piece out of a designer's or label's range or, on the other hand, one can choose to be outfitted from head to toe. In our reflexive conversations it soon became apparent that researchers were prepared to 'cast their net widely', to borrow Holly's turn of phrase. As she further explained:

> I employ an array of theories from compatible paradigms to help explain various dimensions of the snowboarding body, including cultural memory studies, Marxist political economy, post-Fordism, Foucauldian theorizing, Pierre Bourdieu's theory of embodiment, feminism, sociology of mobilities, and nonrepresentational theory. ... I selected the theories that I believed would shed light on various aspects of the snowboarding body and help me capture some of the complexities of the global phenomenon of snowboarding...
>
> (Thorpe 2011: 15).

Karin also partnered Bourdieu with gender and post-structural theories and theorists:

> We have considered using and we have also used other theorists and theoretical frameworks in our studies. Post structuralism and the work of Foucault, for example, have offered us ways of understanding how different kinds of activities, notably dance and ball games, subjectify girls and boys in different positions. Queer theory and the work of Judith Butler have given us tools to interpret gender patterns and point out a pedagogical strategy to counteract heteronormativity and gender stereotypes. … Finally, we have also paid attention to, and been inspired by, Maurice Merleau-Ponty and his phenomenology of the lived body since his work enhanced our understanding of the subject positioning of girls and boys.

As with Holly and Karin, Elise has also introduced other social theories/ists to enhance explanatory power, particularly in relation to gender.

> I did consider other theoretical frameworks, including the idea of liminality, which made it into the chapter. There are different ways to see marginalized identities. Poststructural feminists like Judith Butler would have offered another take on the issue: probably emphasizing the mobilization of boxers and boxer fans worldwide, the disruption of gender norms and stereotypes that come from the muscular bodies of female boxers.

David explained emphatically in relation to the question of why/not Bourdieu that:

> in fact, I make a point of *not* reducing everything to Bourdieu's framework. In all of my work to date I have been keen to retain and develop a strong sense of the *reflexivity* of social life, not in order to preach this belief and all its complexities from some lofty theoretical parapet, but simply because this is how I experience life and how I observe (rightly or wrongly) others experiencing their lives, and so this is how I seek to understand it academically also.

In our efforts to ensure that we do not fall into the trap of simply reducing everything to our favoured social theorist, collaboration with colleagues becomes a necessary and generative strategy. Recently, Louise conducted a research project that sought to investigate the impact of teacher–student pedagogical relationships on students' negotiation of the transition from secondary to tertiary learning contexts. Although emerging out of her Foucauldian analysis of caring teaching as a form of pastoral power *par excellence*, collaboration with a colleague who had a sophisticated understanding of Bourdieu's notion of *capital* and *habitus* was to render a more insightful analysis of the resulting student interview data. Whilst Foucault's pastoral power provided insight into the way in which assessment practices were driving, not breaking, caring teaching, Foucauldian theory was unable to account for the anguish students felt as they transitioned from one educational field to another.

What became apparent across all of this commentary is that often no single theory or indeed theoretical concept was considered adequate to explain the complexity of the social phenomenon of interest, but that Bourdieu provided a strong foundation. Of particular interest in the responses from Holly, Elise and Karin was their paradigmatic eclecticism, in particular moving across structural, critical, feminist and poststructuralist boundaries in order to respond to the challenges posed by the research questions and spaces that they were exploring. Additionally, these eclectic tastes and this cherry-picking, partnering and challenging were seemingly encouraged by Bourdieu. David reminded us of a significant quote in this regard:

> A reflexive sociology… cannot, on pain of self-destruction, demand a closure of thought. Therefore, an invitation to think with Bourdieu is of necessity an invitation to think beyond Bourdieu, and against him whenever required.
>
> (Bourdieu and Wacquant 1992: xiv).

To return to our metaphor, while the authors were very comfortable in their Bourdieu, their alterations, trimmings, coats, wraps and hats from elsewhere made their Bourdieu more interesting, distinctive or, even, possibly more comfortable.

Conclusion

As with any theorist or theories, Bourdieu's work and reach have demonstrable limitations. As examples, his theory has been criticized for the over-simplicity of *habitus* for capturing the complexity of social experience, for neglecting the creativity of individual action or agency, for his light account of economic forces, for seeing a false consensus on what constitutes *capital* and who holds authority to define *capital*, for taking a naïve position on globalization, and for an inadequate addressing of gender relations and the significance of space (Elliott 2009; Thorpe 2011). Yet what is apparent is that Bourdieu's theoretical concepts have a breadth of applications in physical cultural research for both early career and established researchers. The centrality of embodiment to his work has served as a hook to those interested in the social shaping and positioning of the body in and across the fields of physical education, physical activity, sport, families, leisure and tourism in a range of national and global contexts.

Importantly, Bourdieu's concepts provide a theoretical bridge across studies of embodiment and physical activity for scholars from a range of social science backgrounds and lend themselves to being complemented, extended and challenged by a range of social theories that frequently sit outside the structuralist intent. Notwithstanding the importance for researchers to be well-versed in the lineage, language and limitations of a social theorist, Seidman's (2008: 297) warning that 'social theory is changing' to become increasingly post-disciplinary is pertinent. As this volume attests, many of the contributors have generated creative approaches to their theorising, looking good in Bourdieu while also challenging disciplinary and paradigmatic conventions.

18 Bourdieu comes off the bench

A reflexive analysis of the circulation of ideas within the sociology of sport field

Richard Pringle

Keywords: *Reflexive sociology, field of struggles, conservation, subversion, symbolic capital*

Pierre Bourdieu is widely recognized as one of the leading social theorists of contemporary times. According to Wacquant (2002: 549), Bourdieu transcended his social background as the son of a sharecropper to rise 'to the apex of the French cultural pyramid and became the world's most cited living social scientist'. Despite his globally renowned status and scholarly interest in sport (see Bourdieu 1978, 1988a, 1999b), throughout the 1980s and 90s his theoretical tools remained somewhat marginal in the (intersecting) fields of the sociology of sport and sport pedagogy. Over the last decade, however, recognition of his theoretical efficacy has grown and his work has now 'attracted considerable interest among scholars of the sociology of sport, physical culture, and physical education' (Brown 2006: 162). Indeed, citations to his work increased somewhat dramatically after 2003.[1]

I explore the questions of 'Why the popularity of Bourdieu?' and 'Why now?' to reveal the workings of power connected with the transmission of ideas within the *fields* of the sociology of sport and physical cultural studies.[2] This topic of analysis is important to examine, as the employment of different ideas/theories encourages but also conceals particular ways of viewing social reality and associated social problems/solutions. The adoption or rejection of particular social theorists accordingly plays an important role in shaping a field's epistemological and methodological practices or, more bluntly, what is known or not known in a field of study.

This examination of the circulation of ideas/theories reflects Bourdieu's commitment to undertake and promote *reflexive sociology*. Reflexive sociology is *not* concerned with attempts to reveal 'the individual unconscious of the researcher but the epistemological unconscious of his [*sic*] discipline' (Bourdieu and Wacquant 1992: 41). Bourdieu did not believe it necessary to 'make resounding private revelations to explain himself sociologically' (p. 44) because he argued that individual people 'are essentially the personification of exigencies actually or potentially inscribed in the structure of the field or, more precisely, in the position occupied within the field' (p. 44). His understanding of *reflexive sociology* was, therefore, a form of epistemic reflexivity that encouraged researchers to reflect upon the various factors that shaped knowledge production practices within their field of study.

In this chapter, I reflexively examine the reception of Bourdieu's ideas within the sociology of sport. I begin by introducing my theoretical tools of analysis, which draw specifically from Bourdieu's (1975) understandings of power struggles within academic fields of study. I then present the results from my empirical analysis in two sections. Firstly, I examine the *field* struggles evident during the 1980s and early 1990s that effectively critiqued the efficacy of Bourdieuian theorizing. I then examine the various political maneuvrings within the *field* that subverted this critique and allowed, in the 2000s, for the recognition of the theoretical legitimacy of Bourdieu. My underpinning aim is not to produce a definitive history of the rise of Bourdieu but to reveal the games of power within the production of academic truths. I subsequently promote the utility of a reflexive sociological approach.

Understanding the sociology of sport as a 'field of struggles'

Bourdieu (1975: 19) theorized that scientific knowledge is produced in the 'state of the structure and functioning of the scientific field'. Further, he suggested that the scientific *field* could be regarded as a 'social field like any other, with its distribution of power and monopolies, its struggles and strategies, its interests and profits' (p. 19). Bourdieu contended, accordingly, that scientific 'truths' were produced within particular fields of study as shaped by the power struggles taking place within that field. These political struggles, he argued, were primarily underpinned by the desire of individual researchers to maximize 'scientific profit' (p. 23). And this profit was gained, he declared, when a researcher was recognized by her or his 'competitor-peers' (p. 23): such as when a research paper is published in a peer-reviewed journal.

Bourdieu (1978) adopted his understanding of *field struggles* to examine the historic development of modern sport. In a paper first presented at the International Congress of the History of Sports and Physical Education in 1978, he argued that the *field* of sporting practices could 'be understood as the site of struggles in which what is at stake, *inter alia*, is the monopolistic capacity to impose the legitimate definition of sporting practices and of the legitimate function of sporting activity' (Bourdieu 1978: 826). He therefore examined the history of social struggles that eventually allowed certain social *practices* to become known as sports.

In drawing from Bourdieu, I suggest that the *field* of sport sociology can be similarly understood as the on-going site of struggles, with particular respect to establishing the legitimate definition and functioning of this *field* of study. The *field* of sport sociology can, more specifically, be theorized as constituted by the conflict (both historic and contemporary) associated with the workings of power between agents and institutions located in this academic *field* when specific attempts are made to determine what constitutes academic profit or *capital*. Bourdieu (1985: 724) suggested that 'The kinds of capital, like the aces in a game of cards, are powers that define the chances of profit in a given field' and noted that within each *field* 'there corresponds a particular kind of capital, which is current, as a power or stake, in that game'. Thus the agents who possess (or are able to use) the most 'aces' within the sociology of sport *field* have a greater chance of defining and determining the functioning of sport sociology. These agents, accordingly, are those who are able to persuade the majority with respect to what types of research paradigms, methods, social theories and topics of examination are legitimate and valuable.

The agents who possess the highest forms of *symbolic capital* are typically those whose books and journal articles are highly cited, who receive awards and are invited to speak as keynote presenters. These individuals, over time, are characteristically able to use their symbolic forms of *capital* to gain increased amounts of *economic capital* via vocational promotion.

However, *field struggles* are never static. Thus the retention of, or search for, *symbolic capital* can be understood as an ongoing game, with different agents employing different *field* strategies respective to their positioning within the *field*. Bourdieu (1975) suggested that there are three prime *field* strategies associated with *symbolic capital*: conservation, succession and subversion. The dominant within a *field* are typically 'committed to conservation strategies aimed at ensuring the perpetuation of the established scientific order to which their interests are linked' (1975: 29-30). These academics, accordingly, tend to examine particular topics via similar methods and social theories. In contrast, those who are 'new entrants' (p. 30) to a *field*, such as those completing doctorates, may tend to use succession or subversion strategies in attempts to gain dominant positions. Those who adopt succession strategies operate within the established scholarly order and may expect to accrue scientific profits (i.e. *capital*) 'at the end of a predictable career' (p. 30) through making only 'limited innovations within authorized limits' (p. 31). Alternatively, a new entrant may employ the infinitely riskier strategy of subversion: a strategy that attempts to redefine the existing academic order. Bourdieu (1975: 30) appropriately noted:

> newcomers who refuse the beaten tracks cannot 'beat the dominant at their own game' unless they make additional, strictly scientific investments from which they cannot expect high profits, at least in the short run, since the whole logic of the system is against them.

In an established *field* of study, such as the sociology of sport, Bourdieu (1975:29) predicted that 'the degree of homogeneity rises among the competitors' so that the implementation of the various *field* strategies tends to produce 'countless small periodic revolutions' rather than major revolutions. This degree of homogeneity also produces what Bourdieu and Wacquant (1992 : 41) called the 'epistemological unconscious' of a discipline, so that agents operating in the *field* can be understood as being almost naturally disposed to certain values and attitudes as associated with the overall research process.

In the following section, I adopt Bourdieu's conceptualizations of *field struggles* to understand the historic and contemporary reception of Bourdieu's theoretical ideas within the sociology of sport *field*.

Field struggles that placed Bourdieu on the bench

Bourdieu (2000: 222) suggested that 'the sense and function of a foreign work is determined not simply by the field of origin, but in at least equal proportion by the *field* of reception'. Yet he further advised, given that the context of the original *field* is often unknown within the *field* of reception, that the manner within which a foreign text enters a *field* of reception becomes the more important dimension to focus on. In this capacity, he suggested that it is relevant to examine who introduces the text to a new *field*, for what reasons, and whether in presenting the work the individual takes 'some sort of possession of it' (2000: 222). As such, he encouraged analysis of the *field* of struggles in relation to the initial reception of a 'foreigner's' work. So how did sociologists of sport initially receive Bourdieu?

Bourdieu's 1978 publication entitled 'Sport and social class' was his first paper that English-speaking sociologists of sport commented on. Within this paper, Bourdieu introduced himself, somewhat humbly, by stating: 'I speak neither as an historian nor as an historian of sport, and so I appear as an amateur among professionals and can only ask you, as the phrase goes, to be "good sports"' (1978: 819). Yet the paper was not received in a good fashion.

John Goodger (1982: 101), for example, concluded that Bourdieu's work promoted 'a rather unidimensional view of the social composition of sport', was under-theorized and needed further refinement. Jennifer Hargreaves (1982) also critiqued Bourdieu's 1978 paper. Hargreaves stated that although Bourdieu's treatment of culture and his use of empirical evidence were valuable, his work suffered from the same weaknesses of structuralism. She further lamented that Bourdieu's 'theory overall entails a form of cultural determinism within which the agents of cultural practices, social classes, and power relations are properties of the system' (1982:14). In this manner, Hargreaves did not believe that Bourdieuian theorizing offered critical scholars the tools that could help them understand and initiate processes of social change. In turn she promoted Gramsci's (1971) concept of hegemony as more fruitful for exploring the interrelationships between culture, ideology and power relationships.

In re-reading Bourdieu's 1978 paper, I can understand why Hargreaves and Goodger offered their critiques. Bourdieu's paper introduced his theorizing but it appears unsophisticated, given his attempt to develop a grand theory that explains, in a quasi-positivist fashion, the probabilities of why different people, from different classes, play different sports. The application of his theoretical ideas resulted in generalized conclusions about sport participation that appear somewhat deterministic and reductionist. His analysis of petanque, for example, revealed this problematic tendency:

> This sport, the least distinguished and least distinctive of all, since it requires practically no economic or cultural capital and demands little more than spare

time, regularly culminates among the lower middle classes, especially among primary-school teachers and clerical workers in the medical services.

(Bourdieu 1978: 837)

Bourdieu later claimed (2000: 220) that 'in international exchanges, the logic of laissez-faire favors the circulation of the very worst ideas at the expense of the best'. Moreover, he suggested, 'Intellectual life, like all other social spaces, is a home to nationalism and imperialism, and intellectuals, like everyone else, constantly peddle prejudices, stereotypes, received ideas, and hastily simplistic representations which are fuelled by the chance happenings of everyday life' (p. 220). Indeed, Bourdieu's 1978 paper on sport history was not representative of his erudite sophistication. Yet his critics were also too quick to represent his theorizing as 'hastily simplistic'.

Ten years later, Bourdieu published (1988a) a more sophisticated paper in the *Sociology of Sport Journal* (*SSJ*) that appeared to specifically address the prime criticisms directed to his 1978 publication. Firstly, he argued: 'one must be careful not to establish a direct relation ... between a sport and a social position, such as between wrestling or soccer and workers, or between judo and employees' (1988a: 154). Secondly, he warned against solely relying on statistics that stem from participation and income-based surveys, as he indicated that such numbers can conceal a dispersion of *practices*. Thirdly, he asserted that it is problematic to treat sporting *practices* as relatively autonomous spaces. In contrast, he encouraged the study of sporting *practices* in relation to other social *practices*. More specifically, he promoted the importance of a dialectic examination between macro and micro sociologies. Fourthly, he confessed that the logic of distinction alone was insufficient to explain the diversity of social practices in which individuals might participate. Lastly, and importantly, he focused on the body and raised the interesting question of how bodily practices and associated disciplines (e.g. PE) can force individuals to do things that the mind might rationally refuse.

Although this was a very different paper from Bourdieu's earlier (1978) sport paper, Jennifer Hargreaves delivered it a similar critique. She devoted several pages to introducing Bourdieu, which indirectly revealed that she took his work seriously, but still concluded that he 'tends to treat people as if they are properties of the system and fails to appreciate how cultural *fields*, such as sports, contain the capacity for people/women to resist and change social/gender relations' (Hargreaves 1994: 21). Bourdieu was positioned as an uncritical structuralist and his theoretical ideas were deemed unsuitable for the critical interrogation of multiple axes of power within sport settings.

By 1994 Hargreaves had established herself as a leading international scholar of critical/feminist analyses of sport and, as such, held significant *symbolic capital*. Her seminal text, *Sporting Females* (1994), for example, won the 1996 North American Sociology of Sport Society (NASSS) Outstanding Book of the Year award and it has subsequently been cited 857 times (according to Google Scholar, September 2012). Her position in the *field* of the sociology of sport was one of *dominance* and her critique of Bourdieu would have been influential. Indeed, other leading sport feminists supported her critical view of Bourdieu. Ann Hall, for example, critiqued Bourdieu as 'androcentric', classified him as a '*male*stream theorist', and suggested that his 'work foregrounds class relations at the expense of other power relations such as gender and race' and subsequently ignores 'feminist theorizing and scholarship' (1993: 99).

I argue in a *speculative* manner that Bourdieu's alleged inability to theoretically examine issues of gender rendered his theorizing unworthy throughout the 1980s and early 1990s . By the early 1990s, sport sociology had become dominated by critical scholars interested in revealing the various inequities and inequalities associated with the workings of power within sport settings. Gender scholarship correspondingly emerged as a preeminent topic of analysis. Between 1993 and 2002 six of the nine books that were awarded the NASSS Outstanding Book award focused exclusively on gender issues. The rise of the importance of gender scholarship can be understood in relation to other *field struggles* that took place in the sociology of sport in the late 1980s and early 1990s. These field struggles related, in part, to the paradigm wars and the subsequent growth of critical qualitative scholarship.

In this context, a group of once emerging sociologists, including, for example, Jennifer Hargreaves, Anne Hall, Michael Messner, Nancy Theberge and C.L. Cole (and, of course, others), employed a mixture of subversive and succession field strategies to successfully establish themselves in positions of dominance within the sociology of sport *field*. Their dominance can be attested by the *profit* they gained from their 'competitor-peers' (Bourdieu 1975: 23), in terms of citation counts, book awards and editorships of key journals/books. Hall (1993: 99) revealed the zeitgeist of the times by advocating that 'the theoretical underpinnings of a truly radical, gendered (and nonracist) theory of sport lie in the combination of feminism and cultural studies, or more succinctly feminist cultural studies'. Their combined research efforts (which were of significant influence on my own research interests) positioned the study of gender relations and sexualities as important, positivism as problematic, structuralism and sex-role theory as theoretically outdated, and Gramsci and British cultural studies as theoretically valuable. Bourdieu, however, was not considered deserving of sport sociological attention: his theorizing was subsequently marginalized.

Calling Bourdieu off the bench

In this section I examine the question: 'Given the existing dominant critique of Bourdieu, how did he subsequently become established in the sociology of sport?' I do so, speculatively, by drawing from Bourdieu, who advised that to understand how a foreign text enters a field of study it is necessary to identify the 'discoverers' and to determine 'what interest they have in discovering these things' (1975: 222). I will argue that the rise of his work can be traced back to the broader sociological call to 'bring the body back in' and the valuable contribution of predominantly Francophone scholars who illustrated his theoretical capacity for critical/feminist analysis.

In 1991, John Loy, one of the so-called founding 'parents' of sport sociology, co-edited a special edition of *Quest*. The justification for the special edition was linked to concerns about the scientization of the moving body and the recognition that the social importance of the body had been underestimated. Loy's inspiration for the special edition had been spurred, in part, by John Hargreaves' (1987) masterwork, which highlighted the political importance of the body in sport and PE. Hargreaves identified the body as central to sport participation but also as significant for understanding the workings of power, social relationships and inequities within sport. He illustrated, accordingly, that examinations of the body could be potentially tied to *critical gender studies*. This recognition would have helped legitimate the entry of Bourdieu into the existing academic order.

John Hargreaves (1987) was spurred by Bryan Turner's 1984 work on the body and society and had followed his lead in drawing from Foucault. In following this link to Foucault, the *Quest* 1991 special edition included a paper written by French Canadian Jean Harvey and his compatriot Robert Sparkes. Harvey and Sparkes (1991) drew on Foucault *and* Bourdieu to develop a theoretical framework for understanding the role of the state in the constitution of modernist bodily politics. This paper was an unabashed celebration of the theoretical work of Foucault and Bourdieu. Jean Harvey had earlier (1983) detailed the theoretical utility of Bourdieu and Foucault, yet his monograph was published in French and received little attention from English-speaking sport sociologists. Robert Sparkes (1990: 72) subsequently recognized that although it is 'several years since it first appeared … the significance of [Harvey's] study is not diminished'. He added: 'Ironically, given present directions in the social and political theory of sport, the book plausibly stands to have more impact today than at its original publishing' (1990: 72). In other words, he was suggesting that the sport sociology field was not 'ready' to receive Bourdieu's theorizing in the early 1980s.

Another Canadian scholar, Richard Gruneau (1993), favourably introduced Bourdieu via a theoretical comparison with Gramsci and Foucault. Although he acknowledged some interesting overlaps between these theorists, he fundamentally concluded that Bourdieu's work offered 'more scope for imaginative and useful analysis' (Gruneau 1993: 105). The theoretical importance of Bourdieu and Foucault was more widely acknowledged in 1995 by devoting a special edition of *SSJ* to their work. This special edition was almost exclusively dominated by Francophone scholars including Jacques Defrance, Suzanne Laberge, Jean-Paul Clement, Genevieve Rail, Jean Harvey and Pierre Chifflet. The Francophone scholars *perhaps* had a nationalistic interest to promote a French theorist, yet I suggest it is *more probable* that their bilingual skills had simply allowed them to discover Bourdieu's theoretical gifts at an earlier date than English-speaking sport scholars.

The special edition of *SSJ* worked to position Bourdieu as a theorist of similar calibre to Foucault. Yet Bourdieu was slower to be accepted into mainstream sport sociology. No doubt the critiques of Bourdieu by the likes of Goodger (1982), Hargreaves (1994) and Hall (1993) had tainted his reception. Yet I also speculate that *before* Bourdieu's tools could be warmly welcomed into the *field* of sport sociology, it had to be successfully demonstrated that his conceptualizations could be usefully employed for critical analyses, particularly the examination of gender issues.

This became the task of French Canadian scholar Suzanne Laberge (1995). She noted that relatively few feminist scholars had drawn on Bourdieu and cited his androcentric bias as a possible explanation. Laberge, accordingly, attempted to correct this bias via a theoretical integration of the notion of 'gender distinction with the concept of cultural capital' (1995: 132). Her attempt was not without theoretical difficulty, as she noted:

> The problems encountered may hold to various aspects of his conceptual framework, among which there are (a) the too deterministic and too rigid relationship established between social structure (position in the social space) and habitus, (b) the unconscious aspect of habitus, and (c) the fact that, in giving too much power to the perceived biological body, he seems to attribute feminine dispositions mostly to women and masculine dispositions mostly to men.
>
> (Laberge 1995: 141)

Despite these theoretical difficulties, which indirectly supported Jennifer Hargreaves' original (1994) critique, Laberge (1995: 144) concluded that 'there appear to be theoretical and epistemological affinities between Bourdieu's sociology and certain feminist perspectives' and she recommended that 'it seems desirable to explore these and other potential links'.

Laberge's groundbreaking article, in combination with Bourdieu's later publication (2002) on masculine domination and the broader sociological turn to the body, allowed critical sport sociologists to acknowledge that Bourdieuian theorizing could be employed for the legitimate study of critical sporting issues. Bourdieu, accordingly, could now be appropriated into the 'established scientific order' (Bourdieu 1975: 30) and the stage was set for his positive reception.

Of the growing number of sport scholars who have subsequently drawn from Bourdieu in the last decade, it is of relevance that many are critical scholars with an interest in gender (e.g. Brown 2005; Gorely, Holroyd and Kirk 2003; Hunter 2004; Kay and Laberge 2004; Light and Kirk 2000; Thorpe 2010). Moreover, some of these scholars have deliberately used subversion strategies in attempts to promote the legitimacy of Bourdieu. David Brown (2005), for example, critiqued Hargreaves' 1994 assessment of Bourdieu, and drew from his embodied sociology to provide a critical analysis of the place of gender within PE teacher education programs. These scholars have accordingly promoted novel readings of Bourdieu in combination with other theorists to subvert the critique that positioned Bourdieuian theorizing as deterministic and overly structuralistic.

Final words: the importance of reflexive sociology

In this chapter I have drawn on Bourdieuian theorizing to offer a speculative explanation for understanding the belated positive reception of Bourdieu within the sociology of sport *field*. Although there are many possible explanations for his recent increase in popularity, I have offered one account in relation to an analysis of the historic and contemporary *field struggles*. Regardless of whether my narrative account has verisimilitude or not, I have primarily aimed to highlight the operation of politics within academia. More pointedly, I hope to have shown that the 'truths' produced within a field of study are connected, *in part*, to the strategies employed by agents in the *field* to promote particular viewpoints. Although I believe that the overwhelming majority of critical scholars are motivated by honorable desires, their actions can also be understood in relation to the search for academic profit or *symbolic capital*. This view suggests that the academic trajectory of a discipline is not simply governed by altruism and rationality but also by passion, egos and power struggles. The underpinning message is important to reflect on: the importance of undertaking research with a degree of 'epistemic reflexivity' (Bourdieu and Wacquant 1992: 36) and with associated recognition that all disciplines have an 'epistemological unconscious' (1992: 41).

Notes

1 The increased popularity of Bourdieu is evident from the results of a citation search I conducted via Google Scholar (December 2011) within the *Journal of Sport and Social Issues*. The results revealed that Bourdieu was not cited in the 1980s, only 6 times in the 1990s and 34 times since 2000, with the majority of these occurring since 2007. A similar trend was evident within the *International Review for the Sociology of Sport*: Bourdieu was cited only once in the 1970s, 17 times in the 1980s, 35 times in the 1990s and 73 times in the last decade. Overall, two-thirds of his citations have occurred since 2000, yet his most influential work was arguably published in the 1970s and early 80s.
2 The literature I draw on in this chapter stems primarily from before the promotion of physical cultural studies (i.e. pre-2008); I therefore refer to the 'sociology of sport' as the primary *field* of my analysis.

19 Working with, against and beyond Bourdieu

lisahunter, elke emerald and Wayne Smith

Keywords: *beyond Bourdieu, theory, methodology, scholarship, physical culture*

As we outlined in the first chapter, this book is about the work of Pierre Bourdieu as applied to the *field* of physical culture. As scholars and citizens there is much utility in working with others' ideas and learning from past *practices*; in this case the ideas and *practices* from Pierre Bourdieu's life work. He has provided us with a set of ideas that cohere in a way that captures some of the complexity of society and related social spaces and people's lives. Within these spaces he has attempted to illustrate the simultaneity of people's *practices* that constitute, and are constituted by, the *social spaces* they are positioned by, and positioned in, through their *practices*. We are the *social spaces* that also create us; at the same time we are not necessarily cognisant of the degree to which we do or do not have agency in that creation. Contemporary neoliberal times in many so-called 'advanced' societies and their educational institutions, such as universities, increasingly seem to be discouraging the production of new ideas, critique, reflection, creativity and intellectual debate, instead preferring standardization, marketization, conformity, information consumption, instrumental rationalization, and a demonizing of intellectual critique as 'leftist' politics rather than the hallmark of an educated society and citizens. Nevertheless, while we debate the efficacy of ideas as a way of summarizing and making sense of what is going on in our daily and cultural *practices*, and as a way of seeing our worlds differently in order to create new, different and better possibilities, learning to work with ideas through research is one of our challenges as academic workers and arguably as thoughtful citizens!

Bourdieu's work, whether in his early ethnographic and visual documentation of Kabyle society or his later analyses of *fields* such as art, media and education, acts as praxis to provide thoughtful ways of acknowledging what might be going on in cultural spaces where, for example, symbolic or otherwise forms of violence may be hampering people's possibility for a good life, and to provide suggestions/ *practices* for possibilities for change. Through engaging with concepts developed from his observations of life, such as his better-known *field, habitus* and *capitals*, or the less well known *misrecognition, doxa, hysteresis* and *reflexivity*, many scholars have stretched their ontological, methodological and epistemological positions and *practices*. As some chapters in this book have demonstrated, these ideas have aided authors' understanding of what they have been researching or attempting to understand. His work has given them a 'framework' within which to establish unthought categories of thought for themselves. Or perhaps they have employed Bourdieu's work to understand contexts beyond those that Bourdieu had observed, analysed and critiqued. For others, their work has been not just to agree with Bourdieu's definitions, explanations or applications of his concepts, which were often not clearly defined by him as his strategy to leave room for more thought. Instead, they have used his work to refine, differentiate or even take new trajectories in their own work. This has often been facilitated by arguing against his concepts or the explanations of those concepts as provided by other scholars. We remind you that part of his project was to stimulate the unthought categories of thought; to encourage the ongoing questioning of what was knowledge, whose knowledge counted, and how did we even 'know'; and to challenge what was understood to be the work of the scholar and the citizen. His work was by no means sacrosanct and he encouraged debate within and beyond his work; he encouraged us to think with him and against him.

Ultimately, Bourdieu's work was about *practice*, not as separate from theory but as something enacted and captured as ideas that in turn were reapplied to *practice*, in a continuous dialogue or cycle that others might describe as praxis. Understanding the logic of that *practice* was perhaps the basis of all his work. No doubt this influence is found in the extensive use of his *field, capitals, habitus* nexus in the work of scholars, as illustrated within this volume. Some social structures embodied by people within *fields of practice* maintain the status quo of a *field* while others might attempt to relegitimise *capitals* or reposition themselves within a *field* in order to change the game. To even understand 'the game' or the operation of the legitimation and positioning of players within the game can be a difficult task, particularly for those immersed in the game, unable to be conscious of the taken-for-granted assumptions embedded in the game, whether the game and it assumptions are for their own benefit or, paradoxically, their own injustice. Some authors in this volume have also used Bourdieu's work to understand the logic of the *practice* in their own settings or those they are attempting to understand.

As the chapters in this book attest, there is still debate, tension and perhaps even a disregard for Bourdieus' contribution to understanding physical cultures. In the triple cycle of discussions and revisions and resubmissions between authors and editors, we have dealt with many challenges. One challenge has been in the slippages in language and in the interpretations and usage of terms such as *field* and *habitus* by different authors. Even clarifying what constitutes the concept of *field*, as related to *social space* was a matter of considerable discussion between the editors and with some contributing authors. Some of the authors situated Bourdieu's concepts in interesting ways within his own framework. This challenged us as editors to rethink how *we* had situated concepts in relation to other concepts. Establishing the different languaging between authors in other non-Bourdieuian concepts such as physical activity, physical culture, physical education, exercise, leisure, recreation and sport made for insightful dialogue. But this was one of the intents of this book, to increase dialogue rather than establish a hierarchy of who was right or wrong in their application of, and engagement with, Bourdieu's work. Ultimately, each chapter's author/s stand/s on their own explanations, application and arguments. You may wish to keep the dialogue alive by responding to their work.

It was of great interest to us to see to what extent authors had an extensive knowledge of Bourdieu's work or had picked up on one or two concepts without placing the concepts within his broader framework. In today's world of fast scholarship to meet auditing deadlines, it was apparent to us that there is not necessarily the time for scholars to fully immerse themselves in the logic of the theory they may be employing. Like the criticism of Bourdieu's work made by scholars based on only a fragment of his work, it reminds us that we need to be cautious of the criticism of theorists when we have not engaged more broadly in their work. Employing arguments that Bourdieu was structuralist, based on early criticisms by others, fails to acknowledge Bourdieu's response to and critique of such criticisms or the ensuing application of his work throughout his career; applications that were clearly not structuralist. Reading primary sources of his work and struggling with some of his concepts can be far more fruitful in the long run than incorporating secondary sources and adopting criticisms without clarifying whether those criticisms stand up to a fair reading of Bourdieu's original work. Some authors here were, however, able to engage with debates around Bourdieu's work and the use of his work before clarifying and justifying their own position. This is scholarship and debate we would encourage

Another challenge to us as editors was the level of *reflexivity* evident in authors' work. Some explicitly addressed *reflexivity* as a topic of their chapter while others did not mention it. As part of our project in editing this book we used our position as editors and reviewers to challenge some of the ideas and practices of some authors, at the same time questioning our own. Again, this was not to suggest that our understanding of Bourdieu's work was any more sophisticated or nuanced than that of others, but to take up his challenge of engaging in the process of *reflexivity* as an important *practice* in scholarly work. Whether this has come through in all chapters, including our own, does not necessarily reflect the amount of debate, reflection, revision, justification, questioning and critique that has gone on. We hope that you will continue to debate, reflect, revise, justify, question and critique as you read, re-read and engage with the *practices* of authors in contexts that may be similar to, or different from, your own. Such *practices* can legitimate, critique, interrupt, instigate, or provide new opportunities for difference in our *practices*, even change what constitutes research, scholarship and our contribution to physical cultures. Whether it is in continuing to challenge *practices* that oppress rather than educate those who are engaged in movement; asking what it is that they are being educated for; looking for ways to challenge the alienating *practices* of sexism, racism, disablism and ageism in sport and movement *practices*; exposing some of the *doxa* of sport and physical education that disengage people from healthy and pleasurable lifestyles; challenging academic and schooling systems that reify particular ontologies and subject matter associated with physical culture under the auspices of economic progress; creating more sophisticated ways to practice *reflexivity* in the academy and society; or celebrating the positive yet complicated experiences of those engaged in physical culture so that it can be even more positive, there are certainly still many spaces to explore, challenge, create and recreate, using Bourdieu's concepts as methodological and theoretical frameworks.

Ideas and the authors of ideas are found or created in a myriad of ways. Neophyte researchers may inherit their supervisors' conceptual frameworks, unaware of the different paradigms and histories available to them. Some can only access authors because the authors have written in their own language or their work has been translated, making some ideas and knowledge inaccessible to others. Others, steeped in a particular paradigm, may dig deeper within their own *field* of logic, creating new knowledge for their *field* but without challenging that logic. Others will have had a broad and liberal education that has mapped out the ontological, epistemological, methodological, or theoretical smorgasbords and wish to locate themselves with authors working within a particular paradigm. Yet others will have serendipitously tripped over a concept or theoretical framework that 'speaks' to the question or puzzle they are attempting to understand. Regardless of the way the authors in this book have come to use Bourdieu's work, or the uses that Bourdieu's work has facilitated in each of the authors' lives, it is clear to us that conceptual and methodological facilitation has come through an ongoing attention to his work within physical cultures. As our debates about the meaning of his concepts, his logics, the efficacy of his work for new times and contexts ensue, there are new spaces for thinking being made available, with a greater sophistication in the use of his concepts and methodologies. We think this is what Bourdieu intended.

We had many reasons for drawing together scholars who are using the work of Bourdieu in this book: to acknowledge that work; to create a volume that may facilitate those researching in physical culture but not yet familiar with Bourdieu's work; to continue Bourdieu's challenge to work with and against his legacy to enhance the sophistication of a community of scholars' work; and to encourage further exploration of physical cultures as yet untouched by Bourdieu's work. Given the expansive culture that could be represented within the broadly defined *field* of physical cultural studies as a developing *field*, and the tenacity with which particular issues associated with physical culture continue to stabilise, there is the possibility that yet another form of *doxa* results. We hope that your reading of this volume, and application to your own work, may challenge some of the *doxa* determining the nature of physical cultural studies, physical education and sport, in particular.

This book brings together some of the work from scholars in *fields* of physical culture using one social theory. It was not to legitimise Bourdieu any more than other scholars, but to show how one author's work can generate new knowledge and a knowledge community in its own right. As such, we hope to generate new debates, challenges to *doxa* and challenges to various forms of *symbolic violence* inherent in our own practices in our contemporary academy and public scholarship within the *field* of physical culture.

References

Abramson, C.M. and Modzelewski, D. (2011). Caged morality: moral worlds, subculture, and stratification among middle-class cage-fighters. *Qualitative Sociology 34*(1), 143–75.

Adkins, L. (2003). Reflexivity: Freedom or habit of gender? *Theory, Culture and Society* 20(6), pp. 21–42.

Adkins, L. and Skeggs, B. (eds) (2004). Special Issue: Sociological Review Monograph Series: Feminism after Bourdieu. *The Sociological Review* 52 (Supplement s2, October), 191–210.

Aldous, D. and Brown, D. (2010). Framing bodies of knowledge within the 'acoustics' of the school: exploring pedagogical transition through newly qualified Physical Education teacher experiences. *Sport, Education and Society* 15(4), 411–29.

Aldous, D., Sparkes, A. and Brown, D. (2012). Transitional experiences of post-16 sports education: Jack's story. *British Journal of Sociology of Education.* DOI:10.1080/01425692. 2012.741805

Allan, K. (2006). *Contemporary Social and Sociological Theory: visualizing social worlds.* Thousand Oaks, CA: Pine Forge Press.

Alverson, M. and Skoldberg, K. (2000). *Reflexive Methodology: new vistas for qualitative research.* London: Sage Publications.

Alvesson, M. (2002). *Postmodernism and Social Research.* Buckingham: Open University Press.

Andrews, D. (2008). Kinesiology's *Inconvenient Truth* and the physical cultural studies imperative. *Quest* 60, 45–62.

Armour, K. (1999). The case for a body focus in education and physical education. *Sport, Education and Society* 4(3), 5–16.

Atkinson, M. (2011). Physical cultural studies [Redux]. *Sociology of Sport Journal* 28(1), 135–44.

Azzarito, L. (2009). The Panopticon of physical education: pretty, active and ideally white. *Physical Education and Sport Pedagogy* 14(1), 19–39.

Baills, L. and Rossi, T. (2001). The transition from isolated rural contexts to boarding school – can school sport play a part? *Journal of Physical Education New Zealand* 34(1), 40–52

Ball, S.J. (1987). *The Micro-politics of the School: towards a theory of school organization.* London: Methuen.

Barbour, K.N. (2011). *Dancing Across the Page: narrative and embodied ways of knowing.* Bristol: Intellect Books.

Barnes, R. and Eicher, J.B. (eds) (1992). *Dress and Gender: making and meaning.* New York: Berg.

Bauman, Z. (2004). Liquid sociality. In N. Gane (ed.), *The Future of Social Theory.* London and New York: Continuum.

Beauchez, J. (2010). La dispute des forts: une anthropologie des combats de boxe ordinaires. *Anthropologica* 52(1), 127–39.

Bell, M. (1997). The developmental of expertise. *Journal of Physical Education, Recreation and Dance* 68(2), 34–8.

Benn, T., Pfister, G. and Jawad, H. (2009). *Muslim Women and Sport*. Oxon: Routledge.

Berger, T. (2008). Agency structure and the transition to disability: a case study with implications for life history research. *The Sociological Quarterly* 49, 309–33.

Bhabha, H. (1994). *The Location of Culture*. New York: Routledge.

Billett, S. (2001). *Learning in the Workplace: strategies for effective practice*. Crows Nest, NSW: Allen and Unwin.

Bloch, M. (1953). *The Historian's Craft*. New York: Random House.

Bochner, A.P. (2002). Perspectives on inquiry III: The moral of stories. In M. Knapp and G.R. Miller (eds). *Handbook of Interpersonal Communication*, 3rd edn, pp. 73–101. Thousand Oaks, CA: Sage.

Bogdan D., Christian, G., Volker, B., Gerhard, S., Ulrich, B. and Arne, M. (2004). Neuroplasticity: changes in grey matter induced by training. *Nature* 427, 311–12.

Bolin, A. (2003). Beauty of the beast: the subversive soma. In A. Boli and J. Granskog (eds), *Athletic Intruders: ethnographic research on women, culture and exercise*, pp. 107–25. New York: SUNY Press.

Booth, D. (2001). From bikinis to boardshorts: Wahines and the paradoxes of surfing culture. *Journal of Sport History* 28(1), 3–22.

Booth, D. and Loy, J. (1999). Sport, status, and style. *Sport History Review* 30, 1–26.

Bourdieu, P. (1958). *Sociologie de l'Algerie* . Paris: Presses Universitaires de France.

Bourdieu, P. (1964/1979). *Les Héritiers: les* étudiants *et la culture*. Paris: Les Éditions de Minuit. ET *The Inheritors: French students and their relations to culture*. Chicago: University of Chicago Press.

Bourdieu, P. (1971). Intellectual field and creative project. In M.F.D Young (ed.), *Knowledge and Control: new directions in the sociology of education*, pp. 161–88. London: Collier-Macmillan.

Bourdieu, P. (1975). The specificity of the scientific field and the social conditions of the progress of reason. *Social Science Information* 14(6), 19–47.

Bourdieu, P. (1976). Le sens pratique. *Actes de la resercher en sciences sociales* 2(1), 43–86.

Bourdieu, P. (1977). *Outline of a Theory of Practice*. Trans. R. Nice; Cambridge: Cambridge University Press.

Bourdieu, P. (1978). Sport and social class. *Social Science Information* 17(6), 819–40.

Bourdieu, P. (1979/1984). *La Distinction. Critique sociale du jugement*. Paris: Les Éditions de Minuit. ET *Distinction: a social critique of the judgement of taste*. Cambridge, MA: Harvard University Press.

Bourdieu, P. (1980/1990). *Le Sens Pratique*. Paris: Les Éditions de Minuit. ET *The Logic of Practice*. Stanford, CA: Stanford University Press/Cambridge: Polity Press.

Bourdieu, P. (1984a). *Questions de Sociologie*. Paris: Les Éditions de Minuit.

Bourdieu, P. (1984b/1988). *Homo Academicus*. Paris: Les Éditions de Minuit. ET *Homo Academicus*. Stanford, CA: Stanford University Press.

Bourdieu, P. (1985). The social space and the genesis of groups. *Theory and Society* 14(6), 723–44.

Bourdieu, P. (1986). The forms of capital. In J.G. Richardson (ed.), *Handbook of Theory and Research for the Sociology of Education*, pp. 241–58. New York: Greenwood Press.

Bourdieu, P. (1987/1994). *Choses Dites*. Paris: Les Éditions de Minuit. ET *In Other Words: Essays towards a reflexive sociology*. Trans. M. Adamson; Stanford, CA: Stanford University Press.

Bourdieu, P. (1988). Program for a sociology of sport. *Sociology of Sport Journal* 5(2), 153–61.

Bourdieu, P. (1989). Social space and symbolic power. *Sociological Theory* 7(1), 14–25.

Bourdieu, P. (1990a). The scholastic point of view. *Cultural Anthropology* 5(4), 380–91. Formerly 1990c

Bourdieu, P. (1990b/2002). La domination masculine. *Actes de la Recherche en Sciences Sociales* 84(1), 2–31. ET *Masculine Domination*. Stanford, CA: Stanford University Press.

Bourdieu, P. (1991). *Language and Symbolic Power.* Trans. John Thompson; USA: Polity Press.

Bourdieu, P. (1993a). *Sociology in Question.* London: Sage. Formerly

Bourdieu, P. (1993b). Concluding remarks: for a sociogenetic understanding of intellectual works. In C. Calhoun, E. Lipuma and M. Postone (eds), *Bourdieu: Critical Perspectives*, pp. 263–75. Cambridge: Polity Press.

Bourdieu, P. (1996). On the family as a realized category. *Theory, Culture and Society* 13(3), 19–26.

Bourdieu, P. (1997/2000) *Méditations pascaliennes.* Paris: Seuil. ET *Pascalian Meditations*. Trans. R. Nice; Oxford: Polity Press.

Bourdieu, P. (1998a). *Practical Reason. On the theory of action.* Cambridge: Polity Press.

Bourdieu, P. (1998b). *On Television.* New York: New Press; distributed by W. Norton.

Bourdieu, P. (1999a). Structures, habitus, practice, In A. Elliot (ed.), *Contemporary Social Theory*, pp. 107–18. Oxford: Blackwell.

Bourdieu, P. (1999b). The state, economics and sport. In H. Dauncey and G. Hare (eds), *France and the 1998 world cup: The national impact of a world sporting event* (pp. 15–21). London: Frank Cass.

Bourdieu, P. (2000). The social conditions of the international circulation of ideas. In R. Shusterman (ed.), *Bourdieu: A critical reader*, pp. 220–28. Oxford: Blackwell.

Bourdieu, P. (2004a). *Science of Science and Reflexivity.* Chicago: University of Chicago Press.

Bourdieu, P. (2004b). The peasant and his body. *Ethnography* 5(4), 529–99.

Bourdieu, P. (2004c/2008). *Esquisse pour une auto-analyse.* The Hague: Liber. ET *Sketch for a Self-analysis*. University of Chicago Press/Polity Press.

Bourdieu, P. (2005). Habitus. In J. Hillier and E. Rooksby (eds), Habitus: *A sense of place.* 2nd edn, pp. 43–52. Aldershot: Ashgate Publishing Limited.

Bourdieu, P. and Johnson, R. (1993). *The field of cultural production: Essays on art and literature.* Cambridge: Polity Press.

Bourdieu, P. and Nice, R. (2008). *The Bachelors' Ball: The crisis of peasant society in Bearn.* London: Polity Press.

Bourdieu, P. and Passeron, J. (1964/1979). *Les Héritiers, les* étudiants *et la culture.* Paris: Les Éditions de Minuit. ET *The Inheritors, French Students and their Relation to Culture*. Trans. R. Nice; Chicago: University of Chicago Press.

Bourdieu, P. and Passeron, J. (1977/1990). *Reproduction in Education, Society and Culture.* London: Sage Publications. 2nd edn 1990: London: Newbury Park/New Delhi: Sage.

Bourdieu, P. and Wacquant, L.J.D. (1992). *Réponses : pour une anthropologie réflexive*, Paris: Éditions de Seuil. ET *An Invitation to Reflexive Sociology*. Cambridge: Polity Press.

Bourdieu, P., Chamboredon, J. and Passeron, J. (1991). *The Craft of Sociology: Epistemological preliminaries.* Berlin and New York: Walter de Gruyter.

Bourdieu, P., Dauncey, H. and Hare, G. (1998). The state, economics and sport' *Culture, Sport, Society*, Special Issue: France and the 1998 World Cup; 1(2), 15–21.

Bourgon, L. (18 January 2012). Why women boxers shouldn't have to wear skirts. Retrieved 23 January, 2012, from www.slate.com/blogs/xx_factor/2012/01/18/women_s_boxing_ and_the_olympics_why_boxers_shouldn_t_have_to_wear_skirts_.html

Boyle, E., Millington, B. and Vertinsky, P. (2006). Representing the female pugilist: narratives of race, gender and disability in *Million Dollar Baby*. *Sociology of Sports Journal* 23, 99–116.

Brooks, F. and Magnusson, J. (2006). Taking part counts: adolescents' experiences of the transition from inactivity to active participation in school-based physical education, *Health Education Research* 21(6), 872–83.

Brown, D. (1999). Complicity and reproduction in teaching physical education. *Sport, Education and Society* 4(2), 143–60.

Brown, D. (2005). An economy of gendered practices? Learning to teach physical education from the perspective of Pierre Bourdieu's embodied sociology. *Sport, Education and Society* 10(1), 3–23.

Brown, D.H.K. (2006). Pierre Bourdieu's 'masculine domination' thesis and the gendered body in sport and physical culture. *Sociology of Sport Journal* 23, 162–88.

Brown, D.H.K. and Evans, J. (2004). Reproducing gender? Intergenerational links and the male PE teacher as a cultural conduit in teaching physical education. *Journal of Teaching Physical Education* 23, 48–70.

Brown, D.H.K. and Jennings, G. (in press). In search of the martial habitus: identifying core dispositional schemes. To be published in R. Sanchez and D. Spencer (eds), *Fighting Scholars: e.thnographies of habitus in martial arts and combat sports*. New York: Anthem Press

Brown, D.H.K. and Rich, E.J. (2002). Gender positioning as pedagogical practice in learning to teach Physical Education. In D. Penney (ed.), *Gender and Physical Education: contemporary issues and future directions*, pp. 80–100. London: Routledge.

Brubaker, R. (1993). Social theory as *habitus*. In C. Calhoun, E. Lipuna and M. Postone (eds), *Bourdieu: critical perspectives*, pp. 212–34. Cambridge: Polity Press.

Brubaker, R. (2004). Rethinking classical theory: the sociological vision of Pierre Bourdieu. In D.L. Swartz and V.L. Zolberg (eds), *After Bourdieu: influence, critique, elaboration*, pp. 25–64. The Netherlands: Kluwer Academic Publishers.

Burr, V. (1995). *An Introduction to Social Constructionism*. London: Routledge.

Butler, J. (1990). *Gender Trouble. Feminism and the subversion of identity*. London and New York: Routledge.

Butler, J. (2004). *The Judith Butler Reader* (edited Sara Salih, with Judith Butler). Malden, MA : Blackwell.

Cahn, S.K. (1994). *Coming on Strong: gender and sexuality in twentieth-century women's sport*. London: The Free Press.

Cammack, J.C. and Phillips, D.K. (2002). Discourses and subjectivities of the gendered teacher. *Gender and Education* 14(2), 123–33.

Change.org. (December 2011 to January 2012). Tell AIBA: play fair, don't ask female boxers to wear skirts. Retrieved 23 January, 2012, from www.change.org/petitions/tell-aiba-play-fair-dont-ask-female-boxers-to-wear-skirts

Change.org. (20 February 2012). Victory! Female boxers will not be forced to wear skirts in the ring Retrieved 23 May, 2012, from www.change.org/petitions/tell-aiba-play-fair-dont-ask-female-boxers-to-wear-skirts

Christensen, E. (2013). Micropolitical staffroom stories: beginning health and physical education teacher experiences of the staffroom. *Teaching and Teacher Education* 30, 74–83.

Clandinin, D.J. and Connelly, F.M. (2000). *Narrative Inquiry: experience and story in qualitative research*. San Francisco, CA: Jossey-Bass.

Clark, J. (2011). *Hawaiian Surfing: traditions from the pat*. Honolulu: University of Hawai'i Press.

Clough, P. and Nutbrown, C. (2007). *A Students Guide to Methodology* (2nd edn). London: Sage.

Collins, S. (2009). Gangster kids keep time for church. *The New Zealand Herald*, November 4. Retrieved from www.nzherald.co.nz

Comer, K. (2004). Wanting to be Lisa: generational rifts, girl power and the globalization of surf culture. In Neil Campbell (ed.), *American Youth Cultures*, pp. 237–65. Edinburgh: Edinburgh University Press.

Connell, R. (1983). *Which Way is Up? Essays on class, sex and culture*. Sydney: Allen and Unwin.

Connell, R. (1995). *Masculinities*. Oxford: Polity Press.

Creighton, J. (26 October 2011). Women's boxing split as governing body suggests skirts. Retrieved 23 March 2012 from www.bbc.co.uk/sport/0/boxing/15452596

Crotty, M. (1998). *The Foundations of Social Research: meaning and perspective in the research process*. St. Leonards: Allen and Unwin Pty Ltd.

Culver, D. and Trudel, P. (2006). Cultivating coaches' communities of practice: developing the potential for learning through interactions. In R.L. Jones (ed.), *The Sports Coach as Educator: re-conceptualising sports coaching*, pp. 97–112. London: Routledge,.

Curry, M., Jaxon, K., Russell, J.L., Callahan, M.A. and Bicais, J. (2008). Examining the practice of beginning teachers' micropolitical literacy within professional inquiry communities. *Teaching and Teacher Education* 24, 660–73.

Curtner-Smith, M., Todorovich, J.R., Lacon, S.A. and Kerr, I.G. (1999). Teachers' rules, routines, and expectations prior to and following the implementation of the National Curriculum for Physical Education. *European Journal of Physical Education* 4(1), 17–30.

Cushion, C.J. (2001). *The Coaching Process in Professional Youth Football: an ethnography of practice*. Uxbridge: Brunel University.

Cushion, C.J. (2007). Modelling the complexity of the coaching process. *International Journal of Sports Science and Coaching* 2, 395–401.

Cushion, C.J., Armour, K.M. and Jones, R.L. (2003). Coach education and continuing professional development: experience and learning to coach. *Quest* 55(3), 215–30.

Dagkas, S. and Quarmby, T. (2012). Children's embodiment of health and physical capital: the role of the 'pedagogised' family. *Sociology of Sport Journal* 29, 210–26.

Dagkas, S. and Stathi, A. (2007). Exploring social and environmental factors affecting adolescents' participation in physical activity. *European Physical Education Review* 13(3), 369–84.

Dagkas, S, Benn, T. and Knez, K. (2014). Religion, culture and sport in the lives of young Muslim women: international perspectives. In J. Hargreaves and E. Anderson (eds), *Routledge Handbook of Sport, Gender and Sexuality*, pp.198–205. Oxon: Routledge.

Dart, J. (2002). Surfing, subculture and performance capital. Unpublished dissertation for BSc in Media Studies, University of Plymouth.

de Garis, L. (2000). 'Be a buddy to your buddy': male identity, aggression, and intimacy in a boxing gym. In J. McKay, M. Messner and D. Sabo (eds), *Masculinities, Gender Relations, and Sport*, pp. 87–107. Thousand Oaks, CA: Sage Publications.

Deer, C. (2008). Reflexivity. In M. Grenfell (ed.), *Pierre Bourdieu: key concepts*, pp. 199–212. Stocksfield: Acumen Publishing.

Downey, G. (2010) 'Practice without theory': a neuroanthropological perspective on embodied learning. *Journal of the Royal Anthropological Institute* (16), Issue Supplement 1: S22–S40.

Edwards, C. and Imrie, R. (2003). Disability and bodies as bearers of value. *Sociology* 37(2), 239–56.

Elliott, A. (2009). *Contemporary Social Theory*. London: Routledge.

Ellis, C (2004). *The Ethnographic I: a methodological novel about autoethnography.* Walnut Creek: Alta Mira Press.

Ericsson, A., Prietula, M.J. and Cokely, E.T. (2007). The making of an expert. *Harvard Business Review.* (Available at: www.ncbi.nlm.nih.gov/pubmed/17642130)

Evans, J. (2004). Making a difference? Education and 'ability' in physical education. *European Physical Education Review* 10(1), 95–108.

Evans, J. and Davies, B. (1986). Sociology, schooling and physical education. In J. Evans (ed.), *Physical Education, Sport and Schooling: studies in the sociology of physical education.* London: Falmer Press.

Evans, J. and Davies, B. (2002). Theoretical background. In A. Laker (ed.), *The Sociology of Sport and Physical Education.* London: Routledge/Falmer.

Evans, J. and Davies, B. (2006). Social class and physical education. In D. Kirk, D. Macdonald and M. O'Sullivan (eds), *Handbook of Physical Education* , pp. 796–808. London: Sage.

Evans, J., Rich, E.J. and Holroyd, R. (2004). Disordered eating and disordered schooling: what schools do to middle class girls. *British Journal of Sociology of Education* 25(2), 123–42.

Evans, J.R. (2011). Elite rugby union coaches' interpretation and use of Game Sense in Australia and New Zealand: an examination of coaches' habitus, learning and development. Unpublished thesis, University of Sydney.

Evans, P. and Penney, D. (2008). Levels on the playing: the social construction of physical 'ability' in the physical education curriculum. *Physical Education and Sport Pedagogy* 13(1), 31–47.

Fagrell, B., Larsson, H. and Redelius, K. (2012). The game within the game: girls' underperforming position in Physical Education. *Gender and Education* 24(1), 101–19.

Featherstone, M. and Turner, B.S. (1995). Body and Society: an introduction. *Body and Society* 1(1), 1–12.

Fields, S.K. (2008). *Female Gladiators: gender, law, and contact sport in America.* Chicago: University of Illinois Press.

Fisette, J.L. (2011). Exploring how girls navigate their embodied identities in physical education. *Physical Education and Sport Pedagogy* 16(2), 179–96.

Fitzgerald, H. (2005). Still feeling like a spare piece of luggage? Embodied experiences of (dis)ability in physical education and school sport. *Physical Education and Sport Pedagogy* 10(1), 41–59.

Fitzgerald, H. and Kirk, D. (2009a). Physical education as a normalising practice: is there a space for disability sport? In H. Fitzgerald (ed.), *Disability and Youth Sport.* pp. 91–105. Routledge: London.

Fitzgerald, H. and Kirk, D. (2009b). Identity work: young disabled people, family and sport. *Leisure Studies*, 28(4), 469–88.

Fitzpatrick, K. (2013). *Critical pedagogy, physical education and urban schooling.* New York: Peter Lang.

Flanagan, E. (2012). Navigating staffroom stories: beginning health and physical education teachers' micropolitical experiences of the staffroom. Unpublished PhD dissertation, The University of Queensland, Brisbane.

Flintoff, A. (2008). Targeting Mr Average: participation, gender equity and school sport partnerships. *Sport, Education and Society* 13(4), 393–411.

Flintoff, A. and Scraton, S. (2001). Stepping into active leisure? Young women's perceptions of active lifestyles and their experiences of school physical education. *Sport, Education and Society* 6(1), 5–21.

Ford, N. and Brown, D. (2006). *Surfing and Social Theory.* London: Routledge.

Foucault, M. (1974). Prisons et asiles dans le mécanisme du pouvoir. Edition établie sous la direction de Daniel Defert et Francois Ewald avec la collaboration de Jacques Lagrange. *Dits et Ecrits, 1954–1988 / Michel Foucault t. II.* Paris: Gallimard.

Foucault, M. (1979). *Discipline and Punish.* New York, Vintage Books.

Franklin, R. (2013). Making waves: contesting the lifestyle marketing and sponsorship of female surfers. Unpublished PhD dissertation, Griffith University, Gold Coast.

Fusco, C. (2004). The space that (in)difference makes: (re)producing subjectivities in/ through abjection – a locker room theoretical case study. In P. Vertinsky and J. Bale (eds), *Sites of Sport: space, place, experience*, pp. 159–76. London and New York: Routledge.

Fusco, C. (2006). Inscribing healthification: governance, risk, surveillance and the subjects and spaces of fitness and health. *Health and Place* 12(1), 65.

Gabel, S.L. and Danforth, S. (2008). Disability and the international politics of education. In S.L. Gabel and S. Danforth (eds), *Disability and the Politics of Education. An International Reader*, pp. 1–13. Oxford: Peter Lang.

Gard, M. and Wright, J. (2005). *The Obesity Epidemic: science, morality and ideology.* London: Routledge

Garrett, R. (2004). Negotiating a physical identity: girls, bodies and physical education. *Sport, Education and Society* 9(3), 223–37.

Gerrans, P. (2005). Tacit knowledge, rule following and Pierre Bourdieu's philosophy of social science. *Anthropological Theory* 5(1), 53–74.

Gewirtz, S. (2002). *The Managerial School: post welfarism and social justice in education.* London: Routledge.

Giddens, A. (1979). *Central Problems in Social Theory: action, structure and contradiction in social analysis.* London: Macmillan.

Giddens, A. (1991). *Modernity and Self-Identity: self and society in the late modern age.* Cambridge: Polity Press.

Giroux, H. (1981). Hegemony, resistance, and the paradox of educational reform. *Interchange* 12(2–3), 3–26.

Goodger, J. (1982). Theories of change in sport: comments on some recent contributions. *International Review for the Sociology of Sport* 17(3), 99–109.

Goodley, D. (2011). *Disability Studies: an interdisciplinary introduction.* London: Sage.

Gorely, T., Holroyd, R. and Kirk, D. (2003). Muscularity, the habitus and the social construction of gender: towards a gender-relevant physical education. *British Journal of Sociology of Education* 24(4), 429–48.

Gorely, T., Sandford, R., Duncombe, R., Musson, H., Edwardson, C., Kay, T. and Jeanes, R. (2011). *Understanding Psycho-social Attitudes Towards Sport and Activity in Girls: final research report.* Loughborough University: Institute of Youth Sport.

Gramsci, A. (1971). *Selections from the Prison Notebooks.* London: Lawrence & Wishart.

Green, K. (2011). It hurts so it is real: sensing the seduction of mixed martial arts. *Social and Cultural Geography* 12(4), 377–96.

Greene, M. (1995). *Releasing the Imagination: essays on education, the arts, and social change.* San Francisco: Jossey-Bass.

Grenfell, M. (2008). Postscript: methodological principles. In M. Grenfell (ed.), *Pierre Bourdieu: Key Concepts,* pp. 219–28. Stocksfield: Acumen.

Grenfell, M (ed.) (2012). *Pierre Bourdieu: Key Concepts.* Stocksfield: Acumen.

Grenfell, M. and James, D. (1998). *Bourdieu and Education: acts of practical theory.* London: Falmer Press.

Griffin, P. (1992). Changing the game: homophobia, sexism and lesbians in sport. *Quest* 44(2), 251–65.

Gruneau, R. (1993). The critique of sport in modernity: theorising power, culture, and the politics of the body. In E. Dunning, J. Maguire and R. Pearton (eds), *The sports process: A comparative and developmental approach*, pp. 85–109. Champaign, IL: Human Kinetics.

Halbert, C. (1997). Tough enough and woman enough. *Journal of Sport and Social Issues* 21(1), 7–36.

Hall, A.M. (1993). Feminism, theory and the body: a response to Cole. *Journal of Sport and Social Issues* 17(2), 98–105.

Hanna, R. (2005). Kant and nonconceptual content. *European Journal of Philosophy* 13(2), 247–90.

Hardy, C. (2008). Hysteresis. In M. Grenfell (ed.), *Pierre Bourdieu: Key Concepts*, pp. 131–48. Stocksfield: Acumen.

Hardy, S. (1999). Where did you go, Jackie Robinson? Or, the end of history and the age of sport infrastructure. *Sporting Traditions* 16(1), 85–100.

Hargreaves, J. (ed.) (1982). *Sport, Culture, and Ideology.* London: Routledge and Kegan Paul.

Hargreaves, J. (1994). *Sporting Females: critical issues in the history and sociology of women's sports.* New York: Routledge.

Hargreaves, J. (1997). Women's boxing and related activities: introducing images and meanings. *Body and Society* 3(4), 33–49.

Hargreaves, J.E. (1987). The body, sport and power relations. In J. Home, D. Jary and A. Tomlinson (eds), *Sport, Leisure and Social Relations*, pp. 139–59. London: Routledge and Kegan Paul.

Harker, R., Mahar, C. and Wilkes, C. (eds) (1990). *An Introduction to the Work of Pierre Bourdieu: the practice of theory.* London: Macmillan.

Harris, A. (ed.) (2008). *Next Wave Cultures: feminism, subcultures, activism.* New York: Routledge.

Harrison, K. and Fredrickson, B. (2003). Women's sports media, self-objectification, and mental health in Black and White adolescent females. *The Journal of Communication* 53(2), 216–32.

Harvey, J. (1983). *Le corps programmé ou la rhétorique de Kino-Québec* [The programmed body or the rhetoric of Kino-Quebec]. Montreal: Albert Saint-Martin.

Harvey, J. and Sparkes, R. (1991). The politics of the body in the context of modernity. *Quest* 43, 164–89.

Harvey, S., Cushion, C. J. and Massa-Gonzalez, A.N. (2010). Learning a new method: Teaching Games for Understanding in the coaches' eyes. *Physical Education and Sport Pedagogy* 15(4), 361–82.

Hassanin, R. and Light, R. L. (2013) The use of *habitus* in research on experience and coach development. *Australian Association for Research in Education (AARE) Conference Proceedings.* Available at: www1.aare.edu.au/pages/static/conference.aspx?s=400andy=2012andso=

Hay, P.J. and lisahunter (2006). 'Please Mr Hay, what are my poss(abilities)?': legitimation of ability through physical education practices. *Sport, Education and Society* 11(3), 293–310.

Hay, P.J. and Macdonald, D. (2010). Evidence for the social construction of ability in physical education. *Sport, Education and Society* 15(1), 1–18.

Henderson, M. (2001). A shifting line up: men, women, and Tracks surfing magazine. *Continuum* 15(3), 319–32.

Heywood, L. (2008). Third-wave feminism, the global economy, and women's surfing: sport as stealth feminism in girls' surf culture. In A. Harris (ed.), *Next Wave Cultures: feminism, subcultures, activism*, pp. 63–82. New York: Routledge.

Holroyd, R. (2003). Fields of experience: young people's constructions of embodied identity. Unpublished Ph.D. thesis, Loughborough University

Huberman, M. (1989). The professional life cycles of teachers. *Teachers College Record* 91(1), 31–57.

Huddart, D. (2006). *Homi Bhabha: Routledge critical thinkers*. London: Routledge.

Humphreys, D. (1996). Snowboarders: bodies out of control and in conflict. *Sporting Traditions* 13(1), 3–23.

Hunter, L. (2002). Young people, physical education, and transition: understanding practices in the middle years of schooling. Unpublished PhD thesis, The University of Queensland, Brisbane.

Hunter, L. (2003). Doing a PhD, being a researcher, becoming an academic: learning through the thesis. In J. Wright (ed.), *Research in Sport, Health and Physical Education*, pp. 1–18. Wollongong: University of Wollongong.

Hunter, L. (2004). Bourdieu and the social space of the PE class: reproduction of doxa through practice. *Sport, Education and Society* 9(2), 175–92.

Illeris, K. (2011). *The Fundamentals of Workplace Learning*. London, Routledge.

Ingersoll, R. and Smith, T. (2004). Do teacher induction and mentoring matter? *National Association of Secondary School Principals Bulletin* 88(638), 28–40.

Iorfida, C. (20 January 2012). Big fight, big talk, plus boxing in skirts. Retrieved 23 March 2012 from www.cbc.ca/sports/blogs/chrisiorfida/2012/01/big-fight-big-talk-plus-boxing-in-skirts.html

Jackson, M. (1983). Knowledge of the body. *Man,* new series 18(2), 327–45.

Jacobs, I. (21 September 2009). Boxing: Cuban women too beautiful to box at 2012. Retrieved 23 March 2012 from www.sportsister.com/2009/08/21/boxing-cuban-women-too-beautiful-to-box-at-2012/

Jenkins, R. (2002). *Pierre Bourdieu.* London: Routledge

Johansson, T. and Miegel, F. (1996). Kultursociologi [Cultural sociology]. Lund: Studentlitteratur.

Jones, A. (1991). *At School I've Got a Chance*. Palmerston North: Dunmore Press.

Jones, R.L., Armour, K. and Potrac, P. (2004). *Sports Coaching Cultures*. London: Routledge.

Joyce, R. (2011). *Poverty Projections Between 2010–11 and 2013–14: a post-Budget 2011 update*. London: Institute for Fiscal Studies.

Kant, I. (1787/ 2003). *The Critique of Pure Reason*. Trans. J.M.D. Meiklejohn, 1830–1902. Project Gutenberg ebook, available at: www.gutenberg.org/ebooks/4280.

Kay, J. and Laberge, S. (2004). 'Mandatory equipment': women in adventure racing. In B. Wheaton (ed.), *Understanding Lifestyle Sports: consumption, identity and difference*, pp. 154–74. London: Routledge.

Keay, J. (2005). Developing the physical education profession: new teachers learning within a subject-based community. *Physical Education and Sport Pedagogy* 10(2), 139–57.

Keay, J. (2009). Being influenced or being an influence: new teachers' induction experiences. *European Physical Education Review* 15(2), 225–47.

Kelchtermans, G. and Ballet, K. (2002a). Micropolitical literacy: reconstructing a neglected dimension in teacher development. *International Journal of Educational Research* 37, 755–67.

Kelchtermans, G. and Ballet, K. (2002b). The micropolitics of teacher induction. A narrative-biographical study on teacher socialisation. *Teaching and Teacher Education* 18(1), 105–20.

Kidman, L. (ed.) (2001). *Developing Decision Makers: an empowerment approach to coaching*. Christchurch: Innovative Print Communications.

Kirk, D. (1998). Educational reform, physical culture and the crisis of legitimation in physical education. *Discourse: Studies in the Cultural Politics of Education* 19(1), 101–12.

Kirk, D. (1999a). Embodying the school/schooling bodies: physical education as disciplinary technology. In C.M. Symes and D. Meadmore (eds.), *The Extra-ordinary School: parergonality and pedagogy*, pp. 181–96. New York: Peter Lang.

Kirk, D. (1999b). Physical culture, physical education and relational analysis. *Sport, Education and Society* 4(1), 63–67.

Kontos, P. (2004). Ethnographic reflections on selfhood, embodiment and Alzheimer's disease. *Ageing and Society* **24**(6), 829–49.

Krippendorff, K. (2004). *Content Analysis: an introduction to its methodology.* Thousand Oaks, CA: Sage.

Kvale, S. (1996). *Interviews: an introduction to qualitative research interviewing.* London: Sage.

Laberge, S. (1995). Toward an integration of gender into Bourdieu's concept of cultural capital. *Sociology of Sport Journal* 12, 132–46.

Laberge, S. and Kay, J. (2002). Pierre Bourdieu's sociocultural theory and sport practice. In J. Maguire and K. Young (eds), *Theory, Sport and Society*, pp. 239–67. London: JAI Press.

Laberge, S. and Sankoff, D. (1988). Physical activities, body habitus and lifestyles. In J. Harvey and H. Cantelon (eds), *Not Just a Game: essays in Canadian sport sociology.* Ottawa: University of Ottawa Press.

Lacey, C. (1977). *The Socialisation of Teachers.* London: Methuen.

Lafferty, Y. and McKay, J. (2004). 'Suffragettes in satin shorts'? Gender and competitive boxing. *Qualitative Sociology* 27(3), 249–76.

Larsson, H. and Redelius, K. (2008). Swedish physical education research questioned – current situation and future directions. *Physical Education and Sport Pedagogy* 13(4), 381–98.

Larsson, H., Fagrell, B. and Redelius, K. (2011). Challenging gender: a queer lens on Physical Education teaching. *Swedish Journal of Sport Research*, 27–48.

Larsson, H., Redelius, K. and Fagrell, B. (2011). Moving (in) the heterosexual matrix. On heteronormativity in secondary school physical education. *Physical Education and Sport Pedagogy* 16(1), 67–81.

Lash, S. (1993). Pierre Bourdieu: cultural economy and social change. In C. Calhoun, E. Lipuna and M. Postone (eds), *Bourdieu: critical perspectives*, pp. 193–211. Cambridge: Polity Press.

Lau, R.W.K. (2004). *Habitus* and the practical logic of practice: an interpretation. *Sociology* 38(2), 369–87.

Lave, J. and Wenger, E. (1991). *Situated Learning: legitimate peripheral participation.* Cambridge: Cambridge University Press.

Le Breton, D. (2008). *Antropologie du corps et modernité.* Paris: Presses Universitaires de France.

Leane, E. and Buchanan, I. (2002). What's left of theory? *Continuum: Journal of Media and Cultural Studies* 16(3), 253–8.

Lee, J. and Macdonald, D. (2009). Rural young people and physical activity: understanding participation through social theory. *Sociology of Health and Illness* 31(3), 360–74.

Lepecki, A. (2004a). *Of the Presence of the Body: essays on dance and performance theory.* Middletown: Wesleyan University Press.

Lepecki, A. (2004b). Concept and presence: the contemporary European dance scene. In A. Carter (ed.), *Rethinking Dance History*, pp. 170–81. London: Routledge.

Light, R. (2004). Coaches' experience of *Game Sense*: opportunities and challenges. *Physical Education and Sport Pedagogy* 9(2), 115–32.

Light, R. (2008). 'Complex' learning theory in physical education: an examination of its epistemology and assumptions about how we learn. *Journal of Teaching in Physical Education* 27(1), 21–37.

Light, R. (2013). *Game Sense: pedagogy for performance, participation and enjoyment.* London and New York: Routledge.

Light, R. and Kirk, D. (2000). High School rugby, the body and the reproduction of hegemonic masculinity. *Sport, Education and Society* 5(2), 163–76.

Light, R.L. (2011) Opening up learning theory to social theory in research on physical education and sport. *Physical Education and Sport Pedagogy* 16(4), 369–82.

Light, R.L. and Evans, J.R. (2010). The impact of Game Sense pedagogy on elite level Australian rugby coaches' practice: a question of pedagogy. *Physical Education and Sport Pedagogy* 15(2), 103–15.

Light, R.L., Harvey, S. and Mouchet, A. (2014). Improving 'at-action' decision-making in team sports through a holistic coaching approach. *Sport, Education and Society* 19(3), 258–75.

lisahunter (2004). Bourdieu and the social space of the PE class: reproduction of doxa through practice. *Sport, Education and Society* 9(2), 175–92.

lisahunter (2006a, September). 'Girls get out there day' and 'Surf Jam': Reinscribing gender and consumer discourses or new spaces for participation? Invited speaker for the Active '06: Making a Difference Conference, Western Australian Department of Sport and Recreation, Perth.

lisahunter (2006b). Fueled by desire: token hotties, celebrities, girls who kick arse and hardcore candy as possible representations in board cultures. Paper presented at the 13th Commonwealth International Sport Conference, Melbourne.

lisahunter (2011a, 15 November). Surfing as public pedagogy: fleshing out symbolic violence, visual methods, practice and reflexivity. Paper presented at the Bourdieu Hui, University of Waikato.

lisahunter (2011b, 30 November). Caught in the act: symbolic violence in the intersections of public pedagogy, sex, surf, technology and research. Paper presented at the Australian Association for Research in Education, Hobart.

lisahunter (2013). What did I do-see-learn at the beach? Surfing festival as a cultural pedagogical sight/site. In Laura Azzarito and David Kirk (Eds.), *Physical culture, pedagogies and visual methods* (pp. 144–161). New York: Routledge.

lisahunter (in press). Seaspaces: Surfing the sea as pedagogy of self. In Barabara Humberstone and Michael Brown (Eds.), *Seascapes: Shaped by the sea.* Surrey: Ashgate.

lisahunter and Austin, H. (2008a, 21–24 January). Re-imag(in)ing surfers: learning to be female. Paper presented at the Association Internationale des Ecoles Superieures d'Education Physique (International Association for Physical Education in Higher Education), Sapporo, Japan.

lisahunter and Austin, H. (2008b, 28–31 May). Pedagogy of the surfing magazine: learning to be female. Paper presented at the Hawaii International Conference on Social Sciences, Waikiki, Hawaii.

lisahunter and emerald, e. (2013). A little-big event: the NZ Surf festival 2013. Kirikiriroa: The University of Waikato.

lisahunter, Rossi, T., Tinning, R., Flanagan, E. and Macdonald, D. (2011). Professional learning places and spaces: the staffroom as a site of beginning teacher induction and transition. *Asia-Pacific Journal of Teacher Education* 39(1), 33–46.

Lortie, D. (1975). *Schoolteacher: a sociological study.* Chicago: University of Chicago Press.

Loy, J. (1991). Missing in action – the case of the absent body. *Quest* 43, 119–22.

Lupton, D. (1995). *The Imperative of Health: public health and the regulated body.* London: Sage.

MacAloon, J.J. (1988). A prefatory note to Pierre Bourdieu's 'Program for a sociology of sport'. *Sociology of Sport Journal* 5, 150–52.

McCall, L. (1992). Does gender *fit*? Bourdieu, feminism, and conceptions of social order. *Theory and Society* 21, 837–67.

Macdonald, D. and Kirk, D. (1996). Private lives, public lives: surveillance, identity and the self in the work of beginning physical education teachers. *Sport Education and Society* 1(1), 59–75.

Macdonald, D. and McCuaig, L. (2012). Research principles and practices: paving the research journey. In K. Armour and D. Macdonald (eds), *Research Methods in Physical Education and Youth Sport*, pp. 16–28. London: Routledge.

Macdonald, D., Kirk, D., Metzler, M., Nilges, L., Schempp, P. and Wright, J. (2002). It's all very well, in theory: a review of theoretical perspectives and their applications in contemporary pedagogical research. *Quest* 54(2), 133–56.

McNay, L. (1999). Gender, habitus and the field: Pierre Bourdieu and the limits of reflexivity. *Theory, Culture and Society* 16(1), 95–117.

McNay, L. (2000). *Gender and Agency: reconfiguring the subject in feminist and social theory.* Cambridge: Polity.

Madison, D.S. (2005). *Critical Ethnography: method, ethics, and performance.* Thousand Oaks, CA: Sage.

Marcoulatos, I. (2001). Merleau-Ponty and Bourdieu on embodied significance, *Journal for the Theory of Social Behaviour* 31(1), 1–27.

Maton, K. (2008). Habitus. In M. Grenfell (ed.), *Pierre Bourdieu: Key Concepts*, pp. 49–68. Stocksfield: Acumen Publishing.

Mauss, M. (1973). The techniques of the body. *Economy and Society* 2(1), 70–88.

Mechikoff, R.A. and Estes, S.G. (eds) (2002). *A History and Philosophy of Sport and Physical Education. From ancient civilizations to the modern world.* Boston: McGraw Hill.

Mennesson, C. (2000). 'Hard' women and 'soft' women: the social construction of identities among female boxers. *International Review for the Sociology of Sport* 35(1), 21–33.

Mennesson, C. and Clément, J.P. (2009). Boxer comme un homme, être une femme. *Actes de la recherche en sciences sociales* 179, 76–91.

Messner, M.A. (1988). Sport and male domination: the female athlete as contested ideological terrain. *Sociology of Sports Journal* 5, 197–211.

Messner, M.A. (2011). Gender ideologies, youth sports, and the production of soft essentialism. *Sociology of Sport Journal* 28(2), 151–70.

Miles, M.B. and Huberman, A.M. (1994). *Qualitative Data Analysis: an expanded sourcebook of new methods* (2nd edn). Thousand Oaks, CA, London and New Delhi: Sage.

Moi, T. (1991). Appropriating Bourdieu: feminist theory and Pierre Bourdieu's sociology of culture. *New Literary History* 22(4), 1017–49.

Morrison, K. (2005). Structuration theory, habitus and complexity theory: elective affinities or old wine in new bottles. *British Journal of Sociology of Education* 26(3), 311–26.

Muller, T.K. (2007). The contested terrain of the Women's National Basketball Association Arena. In C. Carmichael Aitchison (ed.), *Sport and Gender Identities: masculinities, femininities, and sexualities*, pp. 37–52. New York: Routledge.

Mutch, A. (2003). Communities of practice and *habitus*: a critique. *Organization Studies* 24(3), 383–401.

Muzzey, J. (2003, April). Interview: Romain De Marchi. *Transworld Snowboarding*, 126–39.

Nash, C. and Collins, D. (2006). Tacit knowledge in expert coaching: science or art? *Quest* 58(4), 465–77.

Nealon, J. and Giroux, S. (2003). *The Theory Toolbox : critical concepts for the humanities, arts, and social sciences.* Lanham, MD: Rowman and Littlefield.

New Zealand Herald (2009a, August 27). Two teens arrested for serious assault. Retrieved from www.nzherald.co.nz

New Zealand Herald (2009b, August 31). Fifth man arrested in body-in-car case. Retrieved from www.nzherald.co.nz

Noble, G. and Watkins, M. (2003). So, how did Bourdieu learn to play tennis? *Habitus, consciouness and habituation. Cultural Studies* 17(3–4), 520–38.

O'Donovan, T.M. and Kirk, D. (2008) Managing classroom entry: an ecological analysis of ritual interaction and negotiation in the changing room. *Sport Education and Society* 12(4), 399–413.

Office for National Statistics (2004). *Living in Britain: Results from the 2002 general household survey.* London: Office for National Statistics.

O'Leary, T. (2002). *Foucault and the Art of Ethics.* New York: Continuum.

Olive, R. and Thorpe, H. (2011). Negotiating the 'f-word' in the field: doing feminist ethnography in action sport cultures. *Sociology of Sport Journal* 28, 421–40.

Olive, R, McCuaig, L and Phillips, M. (2013). Women's recreational surfing – a patronising experience. *Sport, Education and Society.* Published online 9 January 2013; DOI:10.1080/13573322.2012.754752

Oliver, K. and Lalik, R. (2000). *Bodily Knowledge: learning about equity and justice with adolescent girls.* New York: Peter Lang.

Paechter, C. (2003). Power, bodies and identity: how different forms of physical education construct varying masculinities and femininities in secondary schools, *Sex Education* 3(1), 47–59.

Pang, B., Macdonald, D. and Hay, P. (under review). 'Do I have a choice?' The influences of family values and investments on Chinese migrant young people's lifestyles and physical activity participation. *Sport, Education and Society.* Published online 5 September 2013; DOI: 10.1080/13573322.2013.833504

Paradis, E. (2010). Review of Sarah K. Fields *Female Gladiators: gender, law, and contact sport in America. Thirdspace: A Journal of Feminist Theory and Culture* 9, www.thirdspace.ca/.

Paradis, E. (2012). Boxers, briefs or bras? Bodies, gender and change in the boxing gym. *Body and Society* 18(2), 82–109.

Parviainen, J. (2002). Bodily knowledge: epistemological reflections on dance. *Dance Research Journal* 34(1), 11–26.

Penney, D. (ed.) (2002). *Gender and Physical Education. Contemporary issues and future directions.* London: Routledge.

Pillow, W. (2003). Confession, catharsis, or cure? Rethinking the uses of reflexivity as methodological power in qualitative research. *International Journal of Qualitative Studies in Education* 16(2), 175–96.

Plank, E. (22 January 2012). The Tweet That Changed Everything. Retrieved 23 January 2012 from http://weunite.dk/2012/01/the-tweet-that-changed-everything/

Polanyi, M. (1969). *Knowing and Being.* Chicago: University of Chicago Press.

Prosch, H. (1973). Polanyi's tacit knowing in the 'classic' philosophers. *Journal of the British Society of Phenomenology* 4(3), 201–16.

Pryor, J. and Rodgers, B. (2001). *Children in Changing Families: life after parental separation.* Oxford: Blackwell Publishing.

Quarmby, T. and Dagkas, S. (2010). Children's engagement in leisure time physical activity: exploring family structure as a determinant. *Leisure Studies* 29(1), 53–66.

Quennerstedt, M., Öhman, M. and Eriksson, C. (2008). Physical education in Sweden – a national evaluation. *Education-line*, 1–17.

Rawi, M. (17 January 2012). 'This is not about fabric, it's about athletes': British women boxers campaign against wearing 'elegant' skirts in the ring for 2012 Olympics. Retrieved 23 March 2012 from www.dailymail.co.uk/femail/article-2087459/This-fabric-athletes-British-women-boxers-campaign-wearing-elegant-skirts-ring-Olympics.html

Reay, D. (1995). 'They employ cleaners to do that': *habitus* in the primary classroom. *British Journal of Sociology in Education* 16, 353–71.

Reay, D. (2004). 'It's all becoming a habitus': beyond the habitual use of habitus in educational research. *British Journal of Sociology of Education* 25(4), 431–44.

Redelius, K. and Fagrell, B. and Larsson, H. (2009). Symbolic capital in physical education: To be, to do or to know? That is the gendered question. *Sport, Education and Society* 14(2), 245–60.

Rich, E. (2001) Gender positioning in teacher education in England: new rhetoric, old realities. *International Studies in the Sociology of Education* 11(2), 131–55.

Richards, T., with Blehm, E. (2003). *P3: Pipes, parks, and powder*. New York: Harper Collins.

Rivest, M. (18 September 2010). Disturbing news from the Women's World Championships: warriors, but still in skirts? Retrieved 23 January 2012 from http://blog.timesunion.com/boxing/disturbing-news-from-the-women-world-championships-women-athletes-in-skirts/4188/

Rønholt, H. (2002). 'It's only the sissies …': analysis of teaching and learning processes in physical education: a contribution to the hidden curriculum. *Sport, Education and Society* 7(1), 25–36.

Rosenberg, T. (2002). *Queerfeministisk agenda.* Stockholm: Atlas.

Rossi, A. and lisahunter. (2012). Professional spaces for pre-service teachers: sites of reality, imagination and resistance. *Educational Review* (January), 1–16.

Rossi, T. and Sirna, K. (2008). Creating physical education in remote Australian schools: overcoming the tyranny of distance through communities of practice. *Journal of Research in Rural Education* 23(5). Retrieved 7 September 2012 from http://jrre.psu.edu/articles/23–6.pdf

Rouhiainen, L. (2003). Living transformative lives. Finnish freelance dance artist brought into dialogue with Merleau-Ponty's phenomenology. Unpublished PhD thesis, Helsinki, Finland: Acta Scenica, Theatre Academy.

Sandford, R.A. and Rich, E.J. (2006). Learners and popular culture. In D. Kirk, M. O'Sullivan and D. Macdonald (eds), *Handbook of Research in Physical Education*. London: Sage.

Save the Children (2011a). *Severe Child Poverty: nationally and locally.* London: Save the Children.

Save the Children (2011b). *The UK Poverty Rip-off: the poverty premium 2010.* London: Save the Children.

Schempp, P., Sparkes, A. and Templin, T. (1993). The micropolitics of teacher induction. *American Educational Research Journal* 30(3), 447–72.

Schwandt, T. (2001). *Dictionary of Qualitative Inquiry.* London: Sage.

Scott goggle tan contest (no date). *Snowboarder Magazine.* Retrieved 5 February 2010 from www.snowboardermag.com/features/online-exclusives/scottgog/

Seidman, Steven. (2008). *Contested Knowledge: social theory today* (4th edn). Malden, MA : Blackwell.

Shilling,C. (1991). Educating the body: physical capital and the production of social inequalities. *Sociology* 25(4), 653–72.

Shilling, C. (1993). *The Body and Social Theory.* 2nd revised edn 2003. London: Sage.

Shilling, C. (2004). Physical capital and situated action: a new direction for corporeal sociology. *British Journal of Sociology of Education* 25(4), 473–87.

Shilling, C. (2005). The rise of the body and the development of sociology, *Sociology* 39(4), 761–7.

Shirato, T. and Webb, J. (2003). Bourdieu's concept of reflexivity as metaliteracy. *Cultural Studies* 17(3–4), 539–52.

Silk, M. and Andrews, D. (2011). Physical cultural studies: engendering a productive dialogue. *Sociology of Sport Journal* 28(1), 1–3.

Silva, E. and Warde, A. (2010). Epilogue: Bourdieu's legacy? In E. Silva and A. Warde (eds), *Cultural Analysis and Bourdieu's Legacy: settling accounts and developing alternatives*, pp. 157–60. New York: Routledge/Taylor and Francis.

Sirna, K., Tinning, R. and Rossi, T. (2008). The social tasks of learning to become a physical education teacher: considering the HPE subject department as a community of practice. *Sport, Education and Society* 13(3), 285–300.

Sirna, K., Tinning, R. and Rossi, T. (2010). Social processes of health and physical education teachers' identity formation: reproducing and changing culture. *British Journal of Sociology of Education* 31(1), 71–84.

Sparkes. R. (1990). Social practice, the bodily professions and the state. *Sociology of Sport Journal* 7, 72–82.

Stedman, L. (1997). From Gidget to Gonad Man: surfers, feminists and postmodernisation. *Journal of Sociology* 33(1), 75–90.

Steinberg, S. (2010). In praise of urban educators and urban kids. In S. Steinberg (ed.), *19 Urban Questions*, pp. xi–xii. New York: Peter Lang.

Stephenson, B. and Jowett, S. (2009). Factors influencing the development of English youth soccer coaches. *International Journal of Coaching Science* 3(1), 3–16.

Stewart, M-L. (2001). *For Health and Beauty: physical culture for Frenchwomen, 1880s–1930s*. Baltimore, MD: Johns Hopkins University Press.

Surfer Magazine (2010). The greenest board: is Tom Wegener's Alaia the kindest of them all? *Surfer Magazine* website www.surfermag.com/features/tom-wegener-alaia-green-board/ Accessed 1 January 2014.

Swartz, D. (1997). *Culture and Power: the sociology of Pierre Bourdieu*. Chicago: University of Chicago Press.

Sweetman, P. (2003). Twenty-first century dis-ease? Habitual reflexivity or the reflexive habitus. *The Sociological Review* 51(4), 528–48.

Taylor, B. and Garratt, D. (2010). The professionalisation of sports coaching: relations of power, resistance and compliance. *Sport, Education and Society* 15(1), 121–39.

The Canadian Press (11 April 2011). Olympic boxing authority to discuss women wearing skirts. Retrieved 23 March 2012.

Thomas, J. (1993). *Doing Critical Ethnography*. Newbury Park: Sage.

Thompson, P. (2008). Field. In M. Grenfell (ed.), *Pierre Bourdieu: Key Concepts*, pp. 67–81. Stocksfield: Acumen.

Thorpe, H. (2004). Embodied boarders: snowboarding, status and style, *Waikato Journal of Education* 10, 181–201.

Thorpe, H. (2009). Bourdieu, feminism and female physical culture: gender reflexivity and the habitus-field complex. *Sociology of Sport Journal* 26, 491–516.

Thorpe, H. (2010). Bourdieu, gender reflexivity and physical culture: a case of masculinities in the snowboarding field. *Journal of Sport and Social Issues* 34(2), 176–214.

Thorpe, H. (2011). *Snowboarding Bodies in Theory and Practice*. Basingstoke: Palgrave Macmillan.

Thorpe, H. (2012a). Sex, drugs and snowboarding: (il)legitimate definitions of taste and lifestyle in a physical youth culture. *Leisure Studies* 31(1), 35–51.

Thorpe, H. (2012b). Transnational mobilities in snowboarding culture: travel, tourism and lifestyle sport migration. *Mobilities* 7(2), 317–45.

Thorpe, H., Barbour, K. and Bruce, T. (2011). 'Wandering and wondering': theory and representation in feminist physical cultural studies. *Sociology of Sport Journal* 28, 106–34.

Tinning, R. and Fitzpatrick, K. (2012). Thinking about research frameworks. In K. Armour and D. Macdonald (eds), *Research Methods in Physical Education and Youth Sport*, pp. 53–65. London: Routledge.

Tonkiss, F. (1998). Continuity/ change. In C. Jenks (ed.), *Core Sociological Dichotomies*, pp. 34–48. London: Sage

Turner, B. (1984). *The Body and Society: explorations in social theory*. Reprinted 1996. Oxford: Basil Blackwell.

Turner, B.S. (1988). *Status*. Milton Keynes: Open University Press.

Turner, V.W. (1967). *The Forest of Symbols: aspects of Ndembu ritual*. Ithaca, NY: Cornell University Press.

UNICEF (2007). *Child Poverty in Perspective: an overview of child well-being in rich countries*. Innocenti Report Card 7. Florence: UNICEF Innocenti Research Centre.

van Gennep, A. (1908). *The Rites of Passage*. Chicago: University of Chicago Press

Veenman, S. (1984). Perceived problems of beginning teachers. *Review of Educational Research* 54(2), 143–78.

Visweswaran, K. (1994). *Fictions of Feminist Ethnography*. Minneapolis, MN: University of Minnesota Press.

Wacquant, L. (2002). The sociological life of Pierre Bourdieu. *International Sociology*, 17, 549–56.

Wacquant, L.J.D. (1989). Towards a reflexive sociology: a workshop with Pierre Bourdieu. *Sociological Theory* 7(1), 26–63.

Wacquant, L.J.D. (1992). Toward a social praxeology: The structure and logic of Bourdieu's sociology. In P. Bourdieu and L. Wacquant, *An invitation to reflexive sociology* (pp. 1–59). Oxford: Blackwell.

Wacquant, L.J.D. (1995a). Pugs at work: bodily capital and bodily labour among professional boxers. *Body and Society* 1(1), 65–93.

Wacquant, L.J.D. (1995b). The pugilistic point of view: how boxers think and feel about their trade. *Theory and Society* 24(4), 489–535.

Wacquant, L.J.D. (1998). Pierre Bourdieu. In R. Stones (ed.) *Key Sociological Thinkers*, pp. 215–29. London: Macmillan.

Wacquant, L.J.D. (1998). The prizefighter's three bodies. *Ethnos* 63(3), 325–52.

Wacquant, L.J.D. (2004). *Body and Soul: notebooks of an apprentice boxer*. New York: Oxford University Press.

Wacquant, L.J.D. (2011). Habitus as topic and tool: reflections on becoming a prizefighter. *Qualitative Research in Psychology* 8, 81–92.

Wainwright, S.P. and Turner, B.S. (2003). Reflections on embodiment and vulnerability. *Journal of Medical Ethics: Medical Humanities* 29, 4–7.

Webb, J., Schirato, T. and Danaher, G. (2002). *Understanding Bourdieu*. Crows Nest, NSW: Allen and Unwin.

Wenger, E. (1998), *Communities of Practice: learning, meaning and identity*. Cambridge: Cambridge University Press.

Wilcox, E. (2005). Dance as l'interventrion: health and aesthetics of experience in French contemporary dance. *Body and Society* 11(4), 109–39.

Willis, P. (1977). *Learning to Labor: how working class kids get working class jobs*. New York: Colombia University Press

Woodward, K. (2006). *Boxing, Masculinity and Identity. The 'I' of the tiger.* New York: Routledge.

Woodward, K. (2008). Hanging out and hanging about: insider/outsider research in the sport of boxing. *Ethnography* 9, 536–61.

Wright, H.K. (2001). 'What's going on?' Larry Grossberg on the status quo of cultural studies; an interview. *Cultural Values* 50(2), 133–62.

Wright, J. and Macdonald, D. (eds) (2010). *Young People, Physical Activity and the Everyday.* London: Routledge.

Wright, J., Macdonald, D. and Groom, L. (2003). Physical activity and young people: beyond participation. *Sport Education and Society* 8(1), 17–34.

Young, I.M. (1980). Throwing like a girl: a phenomenology of feminine body comportment, motility and spatiality. *Human Studies* 3, 137–56.

Zeng, Z. (2009). *The Body View.* Beijing: The Press of Encyclopedia of China.

Zhenhua, Y. (2008). Embodiment in Polanyi's theory of tacit knowing. *Philosophy Today* (Summer), 126–35.

Index